Witnesses to the Unsolved

Prominent Psychic Detectives and Mediums
Explore Our Most Haunting Mysteries

Edward Olshaker

ANOMALIST BOOKS
San Antonio * Charlottesville

Table of Contents

PREFACE TO THE NEW EDITION

While many among us view the field of parapsychology with suspicion, the truth is that more than one-third of major police departments across the United States, and many more throughout the world, use psychic detectives to help solve their most difficult cases. And they're by no means alone. In late 2001, a team of psychic "remote viewers" was hired by the U.S. government to aid in the fight against terrorism, following a high-level directive to "think outside the box."

In the same open-minded investigative spirit, I set out to obtain the insights of renowned police psychics and mediums and interweave their impressions with the public record in a quest to assemble the pieces of some of our most perplexing mysteries.

Some of their revelations surprised me—and continued to yield new surprises long after the first edition of *Witnesses to the Unsolved* appeared in 2005.

Without giving away too much, allow me to share how the readings of a medium and a psychic detective on the circumstances of the murder of Martin Luther King, Jr. both eerily foreshadowed the revelation of a startling fact by a close associate of Dr. King more than three years later.

In a chapter about the assassination in the 2008 book *What Would Martin Say?*, King's attorney and advisor Clarence B. Jones revealed that he learned from FBI documents that there had been "traitors" in King's inner circle—"one black and one white." Jones said he was "as surprised and hurt as Martin would've been to learn that not only was his own government out to destroy him, but it was being aided and abetted by people on the inside whom he'd trusted."

Jones' disclosure sounded chillingly similar to psychic detective

Robert Cracknell's reading, in which he said he strongly sensed treachery "from within the camp of Martin Luther King, and that there must have been some collusion" with powerful enemies of King. Medium Janet Cyford also seemed to foretell Jones' bombshell revelation, sounding surprised at the unexpected information that came through when she said, "There's this awful sadness that comes over [King]…This sounds very ridiculous, but it's almost like—he's likening it to Judas…"

In my extensive research, I had found nothing in the historical record—or even in the realm of "conspiracy theory"—indicating that an aspect of the King case involved one or more traitors from within who conspired with his enemies to destroy him. Therefore, Cyford's troubling assertion during her reading that there was a "Judas," and Cracknell's similar finding of treachery from within, sounded like unlikely stories. They sound a lot less unlikely after Clarence Jones' similar revelation, which adds a troubling new dimension to a complex murder mystery that many consider far from solved.

This surprising new development naturally leads one to wonder how much of our history, even its most publicized episodes, in fact remains concealed from us. It is these hidden areas that prominent psychic sleuths and mediums play a unique role in illuminating, while also expanding our horizons by demonstrating the extraordinary forms of perception that are possible.

FOREWORD
BY COLIN WILSON

It is a pleasure to introduce this remarkable piece of investigative journalism, for it is about a subject that has absorbed me for years. It was in 1984 that I wrote a book called *The Psychic Detectives*, and became fascinated by that strange ability possessed by many psychics to "read" the history of a crime, and often to pinpoint the criminal.

It started in the early '80s, when I was browsing through a massive *Encyclopedia of the Occult and Supernatural*, and came upon the article called "Psychometry." This, I learned, was the ability that some people have of holding an object in their hands, and suddenly becoming aware of its history.

Such people are not necessarily psychics or mediums. It happened in 1921 to a highly skeptical Frenchman named Pascal Forthuny, who was invited to witness a demonstration by a clairvoyant in Paris. As one member of the audience passed a letter to her, Forthuny snatched it, and said: "It must be easy enough to invent some nonsense." He clapped the letter to his forehead, assumed a solemn expression, and said: "Ah, this letter is from a murderer ..." And the person to whom it belonged said: "As a matter of fact, it's from the Bluebeard Landru, who is now on trial for eleven murders." Forthuny naturally thought this was an absurd coincidence and was urged to try again. Someone handed him a fan. Forthuny ran his fingers over it, gazed into space, and said: "I have a feeling of being suffocated, and I seem to hear someone calling 'Elisa.'" He was staggered when he was told that the fan belonged to an old lady who had died seven years ago gasping for breath, and that her companion was called Elisa.

Forthuny went on to develop this strange faculty, which he had not even suspected he possessed, and soon became a well-known clairvoyant.

The encyclopedia article on psychometry revealed some astonishing facts. This curious faculty had been "discovered" by an American professor of medicine named Joseph Rodes Buchanan who taught at a medical school in Kentucky. One day he happened to be talking to a bishop named Leonidas Polk, who told him that he could distinguish brass in the dark because when he touched it, it produced a "brassy" sensation on his tongue.

Buchanan decided to try it out with his students. He would wrap various metals in brown paper, then ask the student to guess what metal it was by holding it in his hand. He was delighted when some of the students—about half, in fact—were able to guess right every time. Not only could they detect iron, lead, copper and brass, but substances like salt, sugar, pepper and vinegar.

The explanation, Buchanan thought, lay in an electrical current that flows through our nerves, and which he called "nerve aura"—in other words, the same ability that enables us to distinguish salt from sugar with the tip of the tongue. Buchanan's experiments seemed to demonstrate that we have the same "sensitiveness" in our fingers, and he found that, as you might expect, it works better when the hands are damp with perspiration.

Understandably, Buchanan's discoveries caused tremendous excitement. They particularly impressed a professor of geology named William Denton, who taught at Boston University, because Buchanan had used a phrase about "the past being entombed in the present." Would it, Denton wondered, work with rocks and fossils as well as with metals like brass and lead?

He started by wrapping a piece of volcanic lava in thick brown paper, and handed it to his sister Anne. She immediately seemed to see a bay with ships, and an "ocean of fire," hissing as it poured into the sea—it seemed so real that she had to stop. Denton was delighted, since he knew that the lava was from an active volcano, Kilauea, in Hawaii, and that the American fleet had been in the bay at the time it erupted.

Next he tried handing his wife, Elizabeth, a fragment of bone chipped out of Jurassic limestone. She immediately had a vision of a beach, with huge animals with long necks and heads that looked rather like a sheep. These were probably plesiosaurs, the species the Loch Ness monster is supposed to belong to.

Denton then tried her with a fragment of mastodon tooth. His wife said she felt as if she had turned into a huge creature with unwieldy legs and large, flapping ears, going down to a stream to drink. Another ancient bone fragment brought a picture of bird-like creatures with membranous wings fishing in shallow water—we know that pterodactyls feed on fish.

What bothered Denton was the possibility that his wife was simply reading his mind. So he tried wrapping dozens of specimens in parcels, then mixing them all up together so even he no longer knew which was which. And still the results were incredibly accurate. A fragment of meteor brought a vision of empty space, with the stars looking huge and bright. A piece of chamois horn brought a fine description of the Alps. A pebble from a glacier produced an impression of being frozen in a great depth of ice. A piece of rock from the Niagara river brought a vision of looking down a deep hole with something like steam boiling up from its depths, and a continuous roar. A stone from the Mount of Olives near Jerusalem brought a description of a brown desert landscape, and a walled city. Denton had no doubt that if he could have got hold of a piece of wood from the Cross, his wife would have been able to describe what Jesus looked like.

One of the most impressive proofs that this was not mere imagination came when he used a piece of mosaic pavement from the villa of the Roman orator Cicero. His wife saw a Roman building with pillars, rows of helmeted soldiers, and a blue-eyed fleshy man wearing a toga. The only problem was that Cicero was tall and thin. But after Denton had published this story in a book, he learned that the villa had previously belonged to the Roman emperor Sulla, who was fleshy and blue-eyed.

A fragment of mosaic from Pompeii brought Denton an interesting piece of information. His wife observed that Vesuvius was vomiting water, not lava. A check with a history book revealed that Pompeii had indeed been drowned in a sea of boiling mud.

We can see why Buchanan and Denton were so excited. The implications were staggering. They had proved that human beings have a natural faculty, like our sense of taste or smell, that can enable us to look back into history. Denton called it "a telescope into the past."

At this point, it suddenly became clear that things were not as simple as that. One of Buchanan's best "sensitives" was a man named Charles Inman, and when Buchanan handed him sealed letters, he was able to describe the character of the writers, and even what they looked like. Buchanan tried to explain this by suggesting that the "nerve aura" of the writer had left traces on the letter, which the sensitive had managed to sniff out, like a kind of psychic bloodhound.

Inman was just as successful with photographs in sealed envelopes, which Buchanan again explained by pointing out that the photograph had been handled by the sitter. But when Inman was just as successful with photographs that had been cut out of that morning's newspaper, Buchanan realized he had a problem. Since newspaper photographs had obviously not been in contact with the sitter, there was plainly something wrong with the bloodhound theory. And while he was still searching for a new explanation, everything suddenly went disastrously wrong.

What happened was that a family named Fox, who lived in upper New York state, realized they had a ghost. For more than a year, the Foxes had been disturbed by rapping and banging noises, whose cause they were unable to trace. And one night in March 1848, 12-year-old Kate Fox asked the mysterious knocker to repeat noises she made by snapping her fingers, and was startled when it obliged.

Since it was April Fool's day the next day, Mrs. Fox suspected a hoax, and asked the knocker to give the ages of her children. It did so promptly and accurately, even adding the age of a child who had died. Mrs. Fox said: "If you are a spirit, give two knocks," and there were two resounding raps. "Are you an injured spirit?" asked Mr.

Fox, and there were two more raps.

A succession of simple questions brought the information that it was a man, aged 31, who had been murdered in the house.

Mrs. Fox asked if she could call the neighbors in, and again there were two raps. The room was soon crowded with people asking questions, and one of them, Mr. Duesler, soon took the lead and devised a simple code, with which the spirit conveyed that it was a peddler who had been murdered five years earlier for his money, and buried in the cellar.

In fact, a skeleton and a peddler's box were found many years later, buried in the basement. But, as the spirit prophesied, the murderer was never brought to justice.

The case caused a sensation. Within weeks, "spirit-rapping" had caught on. All over America, people discovered that if they held hands around a table in the dark, "spirits" would make rapping noises, and even lift the table. The new craze quickly crossed the Atlantic, and soon Queen Victoria and Prince Albert were trying it at Osborne, and the Tsar of Russia in St. Petersburg. And back in New York State, a new religion called Spiritualism was launched in 1851, and quickly spread all over the world.

Understandably, the scientists were horrified. They denounced Spiritualism as a revival of medieval superstition. And suddenly, Buchanan and Denton found themselves out in the cold. It was no use explaining that what they were doing was science, not witchcraft. No one was listening. And "psychometry" was so completely forgotten that you will not even find the names of Buchanan and Denton in most modern histories of paranormal research.

This sounds disgraceful, but perhaps it is not as unfair as it seems, as I soon realized as I read the books of Buchanan and Denton. For what Buchanan had discovered could *not* be explained scientifically. If Charles Inman could get as much information from a newspaper photograph as from a picture on film, then he was not simply using his ordinary five senses. And "normal" explanations about "psychic bloodhounds" ceased to explain anything.

This came as a disappointment to me. In 1970 I had written a book called *The Occult*, which had been commissioned by an

American publisher, and as I began to research it, I was delighted to learn that I was not expected to believe a dozen unbelievable things before breakfast. For I had been trained as a scientist, and was slightly ashamed to be spending my days writing about the "supernatural." (Unfortunately I needed the money.) Yet as I began to study the immense annals of psychical research, I soon came to realize that there is as much evidence for telepathy, "second sight," and glimpses of the future as there is for atoms and electrons. I even dreamed of creating a philosophy of "the occult" that was as down-to-earth and practical as physics or biology. And Buchanan's theories seemed to be the key to such a science. Then I read about Inman's ability to describe the personality of subjects in *newspaper* photographs, and suddenly found myself out on a limb, a hundred feet in the air.

What was I to do? Retrace my steps and admit that it had all been a mistake? Or shrug, and say that if psychometry could not be reduced to a strictly materialistic explanation, that was just too bad?

I was already aware that some things defy "scientific" explanation. For example, here in Cornwall, where I live, every countryman accepts the reality of a strange faculty called dowsing. When I found a pool of water at the bottom of our field, I guessed it came from the farmer's old water pipes, and my wife rang the local dowser. Within a quarter of an hour, he had located the pipe, and the plumber dug where he said, and found the leak. It is no use telling a Cornishman that dowsing is unscientific, and therefore cannot exist—he knows better.

But could not dowsing be compared to picking up some "radio signal" from running water?

Not quite, for a good dowser seems to be able to find practically anything. I once hid a number of coins under our carpet—pennies, shillings, and half crowns—and watched a dowser find every one of them with his pendulum. What is more, he announced what each one was, and got it right each time.

This taught me something that is known to every dowser—that dowsing uses a sixth sense that is just as "normal" as our other five.

And it can be used in crime detection. A famous west country writer, the Rev. Baring Gould, tells how a wine merchant and his wife were found murdered and robbed in the cellar of their house in Lyon. A local water diviner named Jacques Aymar was called in, and went to look at the bodies in the cellar. Then his dowsing rod seemed to pick up the scent like a bloodhound, and he announced that there had been three culprits. He walked through the town following their trail with his dowsing rod held out in front of him, until he came to the bank of the river Rhone. A journey downstream took them to the place where the murderers had gone ashore. The police finally caught up with one of them, a hunchback, in the local jail, where he was being held for robbery, and he quickly confessed. His accomplices had escaped over the frontier into Switzerland. And Baring Gould goes on to quote at length the Lyon court records that describe how the hunchback was found guilty and executed.

I can vouch that rivers constitute no obstacle to a good dowser from a case I investigated and presented on BBC television.

It concerned a woman named Mina Bravand who had vanished from her home near Basel, Switzerland. She had been depressed, and her sister Johanna thought she might have committed suicide by throwing herself in the river Rhine, which ran past her flat. Johanna decided to approach a dowser who was famous for tracing missing persons—his name was Edgar Devaux, and he had a figure like a barrel.

Devaux asked to see a photograph of the missing woman, and held his pendulum above it. He shook his head. "She is dead, and her body is in the river."

Now Devaux did something that staggered me. He held his pendulum above a map of the Basel area, traced the course of the Rhine, then, as the pendulum began to swing, made a cross with a pencil. "She is there."

Johanna went to the local diving club and asked them to help. Devaux stood by and directed the frogmen where to plunge into the turbid, fast-flowing river. Suddenly, one of them staggered out of the water, looking sick and shocked. He had touched a body, but it had eluded him and floated away in the current.

Devaux shrugged. "Don't worry." He began to hurry along the

riverbank, the pendulum in front of him. A few miles further on, there was a barrage across the river, where the current is used to drive turbines. "Her body is trapped there," said Devaux. And he proved to be correct. A few days later, the decomposed body was found trapped in the barrage.

What took my breath away was that Devaux was just as happy using a map of the Rhine as walking alongside the river. That could only mean one thing. It was not his pendulum that detected the body, or some "signal" that he picked up like a radio set. It was his mind itself. Devaux explained what he wanted—using the dead woman's photograph as a clue—and his mind went off and found the body. And it then showed Devaux where to find the body on a map of the Rhine.

That meant that Devaux was really two people—one who knew where to find the body and one who didn't.

And that seems to apply to "psychics" in general. Their abilities simply defy common sense. Robert Cracknell, who figures largely in this book, developed his abilities during a traumatic childhood during the Second World War, when he was sent away from home as an "evacuee" and felt lost and miserable. This, he tells me, is true of many psychics. I think that such insecurities prevent potential psychics from closing their minds in the way that more fortunate people are able to. They are like someone with a toothache, who hears every sound in the middle of the night when the rest of us are asleep.

He had demonstrated his credentials to the Oxford Society for Psychical Research by repeating one of the most difficult psychic feats ever devised: the apparently impossible "empty chair test," suggested by the great psychical investigator Eugene Osty. In a demonstration strictly controlled by the research organization, Cracknell was asked to concentrate on a particular chair an hour before a meeting, and gave a careful description of the person he felt would occupy it, a young man, and even some details of his personal life. One hour later, the audience filed in and chose seats at random. The man who sat in the chair not only corresponded to Cracknell's description, but verified that all the details of his personal life were correct.

It should be totally impossible to describe something that has not yet happened. But, Cracknell insists, some unknown part of the mind already knows the future, and it will suddenly allow psychics to catch a glimpse of it. There is no way he can make this happen, except by keeping his mind receptive.

A few months after I met him in 1976, Bob had one of his most remarkable "glimpses."

A journalist who had been interviewing him asked: "Do you have any impressions about the Janie Shepherd mystery?" Cracknell admitted he had never heard of it.

It seemed that on February 4, 1977, a pretty Australian blonde named Janie Shepherd vanished in the Queensway area of London. Four days later, her blue Mini, with a "For Sale" notice on the windscreen, was found in Notting Hill Gate. But there was no sign of Janie.

As soon as the journalist mentioned her name, Cracknell had a flood of impressions—of a blue Mini, of a contraceptive device lying on the back seat, and of a girl who had been raped and then strangled. The killer had dumped the body in a place called Nomansland Common, north of London.

The reporter checked with Scotland Yard, and rang Cracknell to say that no contraceptive device had been found. Bob did not believe it—his vision had been too clear.

The next day, when he came home from work, he received a visit from two detectives, and it was immediately clear that they thought he was the killer. The contraceptive device had been found, but the police had kept this information secret. Since Cracknell knew it, it followed he must be Janie Shepherd's killer. He tried to explain that he was a psychic, and that he often found himself in this position of suddenly "knowing" things.

"Look, I'll give an example. The man you want has a scar on his cheek. He's a Jamaican, or something like that. And he's in prison at the moment on another sex charge."

As the detectives exchanged glances, Cracknell knew he was correct. As they left it was obvious that they no longer suspected Bob.

It was two months later before Janie Shepherd's badly decomposed body was found on Nomansland Common, in Hertfordshire, and identified through dental records.

The "Jamaican" who was in custody was actually Barbados-born David Lashley, and he had already served twelve years for rape. Soon after his release on parole in 1976, another young woman had been raped in her car, half a mile from where Janie's Mini had been found. Her attacker had left her for dead, but she managed to drive to a hospital, and later gave a description of a man with a scarred cheek who said he hated white women. Yet Lashley was not interviewed because the police description of him failed to mention the scar on his cheek.

But as a convicted rapist, he was interviewed soon after Janie's disappearance, and the police noted the scar on his cheek. The young woman he had almost killed identified him, and he was sentenced to another twelve years.

It was shortly before he was due for release in 1989 that he got into conversation with another convicted rapist, Daniel Reece—the two had become close friends because they were both obsessed with keep-fit exercises. And as they were discussing another case of a man who had just received a long sentence for rape, Lashley remarked: "He should have killed her. If I'd killed that one who put me in here, like I did Janie Shepherd, I'd still be a free man." And he went on to describe how he had abducted Janie with a butcher's knife, raped her in a dark mews, then strangled her. He then strapped the body upright in the passenger seat and drove it to Nomansland Common.

When he went on to tell Reece that he looked forward to getting his revenge on women when he left prison, Reece decided that he had to tell someone. On February 17, 1989, Lashley was re-arrested as soon as he was released. And in March 1990, he went back to prison, this time for life.

I saw one more remarkable example of Cracknell's powers in operation. In 1980, his autobiography *Clues to the Unknown* was accepted by Hamlyn Publishers. Since I had written the Introduction, I was invited along to lunch, together with Bob Cracknell.

At that time, in November 1980, the killer known as the

Yorkshire Ripper had been murdering and mutilating women since July 1975. A year earlier, in November 1979, he had almost been caught when he had attacked a 16-year-old girl in Huddersfield, but her boyfriend heard her screams and the attacker fled. For a whole year, the Yorkshire Ripper had been lying low.

At the lunch, I mentioned that Yorkshire Television had asked me to appear on a program about the Ripper, but had refused because it might provoke him to kill again. At that point, Bob said that he had an intuition that the Ripper would commit one more murder, within the next two weeks. The Hamlyn's publisher and sales director heard this prophecy, and I advised Bob to place it on record with the Oxford Society for Psychical Research.

A few days later, on November 17, Jacqueline Hill, a Leeds University student, was murdered and mutilated on her way home. Over the telephone, Bob told me he believed this would be the last Yorkshire Ripper murder. And that weekend, in a newspaper interview, he stated that he believed the killer lived in Bradford.

On January 4, 1981, Bob Cracknell had just arrived at our house in Cornwall to stay overnight when the phone rang. It was his wife Jennie, ringing to tell us to switch on the television. And there we saw a police spokesman being interviewed, stating that a Bradford man had just been arrested in the red light area of Sheffield, and that charges would be proffered against him. The man was Peter Sutcliffe, who had just picked up a prostitute when the police checked his identity; by the following day, Sutcliffe had admitted that he was the Yorkshire Ripper.

In spite of all this, Cracknell is a skeptic about spiritualism and life after death. He believes that his strange powers have nothing to do with "spirits," but are as natural as a man with acute sense of smell or perfect pitch. I am by no means so certain. And one reason concerns the case of a friend of mine who was murdered in his home in the San Fernando Valley of California in August 1977.

His name was Douglas Scott Rogo, and he was one of the most brilliant psychic investigators of the 20th century. Only a few weeks before his death I had telephoned him to ask him if he meant to join me at a conference in San Francisco, but he said he was unable to get away. The next time I saw his name was when a newspaper announced that he had been stabbed to death in an exceptionally brutal manner.

A neighbor had observed that the sprinklers in Scott's backyard had been on for two days. A policeman who was called to the scene found the side door open, and Scott's body lying on the study floor, with multiple stab wounds.

The pathologist stated that half an hour before his murder, Rogo had eaten french fries, and taken the plate to the kitchen. A wineglass on the kitchen table contained a fingerprint that was definitely not Rogo's. Unfortunately, the police lab said the print was too smudged to be of any use.

American police are quite open about their use of psychics — unlike the British police, who often make use of them, but prefer not to admit it. Detective Tim Moss, of the LAPD, turned to half a dozen psychics he often used and asked for their impressions. Most of them had a clear mental picture of the killer, and one of them described him so accurately that a police artist was able to make a sketch. He had a moustache and long dark hair, and the psychic was even able to add that he had a Hispanic name, and wore a black leather jacket.

The investigators went painstakingly through the names in Scott Rogo's address book, and interviewed each person in turn. And one morning, Detective Moss walked into the interview room, and was thunderstruck to find himself confronting the man of the drawing. He had long, dark hair and a moustache. His name was John Anthony Battista, and in his car there was a black leather jacket.

But since there was no evidence against Battista, Moss was forced to let him go. And for eight months, the investigation stalled.

Then another psychic contacted the police, telling them that he had a clear impression that the killer had left his fingerprint behind on a glass. Moss went back to the fingerprint lab and begged them to have another try at the wineglass. This time, better forensic techniques enabled them to make a good photograph of the print. It proved to be that of John Battista.

Faced with this evidence, Battista shrugged and said that he had already admitted being in Rogo's house two months earlier. They had met when Battista was hitchhiking, and become friends. Battista insisted that Rogo must have simply overlooked the glass hanging around his study. But Moss knew that was absurd—Scott Rogo was known for his obsessive tidiness, and glasses were washed as soon as guests left the house. Battista must have been in Rogo's study the evening he died.

A jury agreed with Moss, and Battista was sentenced to fifteen years. Moss is fairly certain that the motive was money—that Battista had gone to Rogo's home to demand cash, and killed him when he refused.

What kind of powers could enable a psychic to "see" a murder scene so accurately that he can provide a police artist with a picture of the killer? Joseph Rodes Buchanan, who coined the word "psychometry," would have said that we all possess these powers, but that psychics possess them to a far greater degree than the rest of us, just as bloodhounds possess a keener sense of smell than human beings. But Buchanan's "sensitives" had to hold an object in their hands to read its history. The psychic who told Detective Moss about the fingerprint on the glass had never been near the scene of the crime.

I believe Buchanan was right, and that we all possess these powers, although in most of us they are undeveloped. For example, how many of us find ourselves thinking about Aunt Doris just before the postman delivers a letter from her? How many of us, like my wife, often know who is on the other end of the telephone before we pick it up? It may not happen often, but it happens often enough to demonstrate that psychic powers really exist. But most of us are too busy, too concerned with practical things, to pay attention to these odd glimpses.

Scott Rogo himself would have added another important possibility. When he was a teenager, he woke up one night and found himself floating near the ceiling of his bedroom, while his body lay below him on the bed. For a horrible moment, he thought that he had died. Then, to his relief, he found he could re-enter his body. It was this "out-of-the-body experience" that led to his interest in psychical research. Having experienced it, he had no doubt that the "soul" (or whatever it is) can exist outside the body.

Scott was fascinated by the experience of a young American soldier called George Ritchie, who was pronounced clinically dead in 1943 after succumbing to a severe infection. He was later brought back to life with an adrenalin injection in the heart, and it was then that he described how, after his "death," he found himself standing beside his own body, and tried to attract the attention of a nursing orderly in the room. The orderly strode straight through him. And Ritchie walked out of the hospital, invisible to everybody, and saw that there were dozens of "dead" people like himself, wandering around in a bewildered state. Ritchie also noticed that some of these wandering spirits tried hard to influence the living, and sometimes succeeded.

Is it possible, then, that psychics receive some of their information direct from the dead? Could it be that the psychic who told Detective Moss about the glass with a fingerprint on it received his information from Scott himself?

Now, as paradoxical as this sounds, Scott himself was not wholly convinced of life after death. He regarded himself as a scientist, and he would not accept anything without proof. He pointed out that most "spirit mediums," who claim to be able to communicate with the dead, are also telepathic. So when someone goes to see them to ask about a dead relative, the medium may be simply picking up information from the mind of the other person.

This may seem to be setting absurdly high standards of proof, but Scott Rogo could have argued that, in a matter as important as life after death we need to be one hundred percent certain.

I have come across only one murder case that seems to pass these tests, and to prove that the dead can communicate with the living.

A young ex-army officer named Eric Tombe vanished in April 1922. He had been the business partner of a man of dubious reputation named Ernest Dyer, with whom he ran a stud farm at Kenley, in Surrey. The business was unsuccessful, and when the stable burned down, an insurance investigator had found empty petrol cans in the ruins, and Dyer dropped his claim.

Dyer had been borrowing money from Eric Tombe, and the two men had quarreled. After Tombe's disappearance, Dyer also vanished, saying only that he was "going north."

At about the time of Eric Tombe's disappearance, his mother had a dream that he was dead, and was lying at the bottom of a well, which was covered by a stone slab.

Her husband, the Rev. Gordon Tombe, was the vicar of a village in Oxfordshire, Little Tew. And as the dreams about the well continued, he decided to give up his living, so he could devote his life to searching for his son. He went to the stud farm, where Dyer's wife was still living, but she said she had no idea what had happened to Eric, or to her husband. As far as the vicar could see, there was no well on the farm.

Next the vicar went to Scotland Yard, and told his story to a detective superintendent named Carlin. The policeman was skeptical about Mrs. Tombe's dreams of a corpse down a well. But when he checked with Eric Tombe's bank, he realized that a crime had been committed. Tombe's account had been overdrawn, and most of the money had been withdrawn after Eric Tombe's disappearance.

Carlin put out a general enquiry to police stations in the north of England. And from Scarborough, he learned of the fatal shooting of an unknown man a few months earlier. A chief inspector named Abbott had paid a visit to a man who called himself Fitzsimmmons, to questions him about passing dud checks. Fitzsimmons had produced a revolver, and in the ensuing struggle, shot himself. In the dead man's room, Inspector Abbott found Eric Tombe's checkbook, full of forged signatures. Carlin had located the missing Ernest Dyer. But there was still no clue to the whereabouts of Eric Tombe.

The Rev. Gordon Tombe finally persuaded Carlin to go and investigate the stud farm at Kenley, which was by now derelict. The search team could find no well. But on the edge of the paddock there were four cesspits, each covered with a heavy stone slab. The first three proved to be empty, but the fourth was full of rubble. When this was removed, it revealed an arched recess. In this they found the corpse of Eric Tombe, who had been shot. An inquest returned a verdict of murder by his business partner Ernest Dyer.

So Mrs. Tombe's dreams had been accurate. How had she known that her son was in a kind of well covered with a slab? A skeptical psychical researcher would suggest that as he was about to be shot, Eric Tombe might have sent out a frantic telepathic message, which had been received by his mother's unconscious mind. Her unconscious had then sent her the dream about her son's death.

But this explanation has a fatal flaw. Eric Tombe had been shot from behind with a shotgun, which had blown off the back of his head. Death occurred so suddenly that there would be no time for a telepathic message. And since Mrs. Tombe also dreamed about the well covered with a stone slab, there can be only one explanation that covers all the facts: that Eric Tombe somehow survived his death, and was able to communicate with his mother in a dream.

In which case, we might suggest, there seems a reasonable chance that Scott Rogo also survived his death, and may have been responsible for the capture of his murderer.

But that leads us to the most interesting question of all. If we all possess latent psychic powers, why can we not call upon them when we need them—for example, to locate missing car keys or a mislaid mobile?

Any good psychic could provide one interesting answer. Psychic powers may be more trouble than they are worth.

In July 1941, a Dutch house painter named Pieter van der Hurk fell off a ladder and smashed his skull. When he woke up in hospital, he realized he could read the minds of his fellow patients. He told the man in the next bed: "Your father gave you a gold watch when he died, but you have already sold it." The man admitted shamefacedly it was true. Van der Hurk could also see into the future—when a fellow patient left hospital, he told a nurse: "He is a British agent, and he will be killed." Again, he was right—the man was murdered two days later.

But when he left hospital, van der Hurk was unable to go back to work. He was simply incapable of concentration. His mind was like a radio that picks up half a dozen stations at the same time. In fact, his psychic powers were a nuisance. They told him more about the people around him than he wanted or needed to know, and he spent much of his life in a state of confusion due to information-overload.

He might well have ended as a down-and-out if a friend had not taken him to the theatre to see a well-known mind reader. And van der Hurk suddenly realized that he could also make a living on the stage. He proved to be so good at it that he quickly became famous under his stage name—Peter Hurkos. Members of the audience would give him notes in sealed envelopes, and Hurkos would read them without opening them. They would hand him personal items such as watches or rings, and Hurkos was unfailingly accurate in describing their history. He became, in fact, one of the world's greatest psychometrists.

He also became one of the world's best known "psychic detectives." One day, the Limburg police approached him for help in the case of a young coal miner who had died of a gunshot wound. Hurkos asked for some item of clothing that had belonged to the dead man, and the police brought him a coat. As soon as he held it, Hurkos was able to tell them that the coal miner had been killed by his stepfather, who was in love with his wife. The gun, said Hurkos, was in a gutter of the roof of the dead man's house.

The police found the gun where Hurkos said it would be, and fingerprints on it tied it to the dead man's stepfather, who was convicted of the murder.

This was the first of many criminal cases that were solved by Hurkos. After the Second World War he went to America, and frequently helped the police.

He was also studied by the eminent paranormal researcher Andrija Puharich. And it was Puharich who told me a typical study of Hurkos. As they were looking at a sunset, Hurkos suddenly burst out excitedly: "I see a hand with a cut wrist, and blood running from it." Questioned by Puharich, Hurkos said he thought it had to do with Puharich's friend Jim Middleton, and with Middleton's brother Art. Puharich immediately rang Middleton, and asked about his brother. Middleton was astonished, because he had just received a phone call from Art's psychiatrist, warning him that Art was deeply depressed. Middleton immediately hurried to see his brother, who admitted that he had been contemplating suicide by slashing his wrists. Jim Middleton's visit made him change his mind.

We can see why psychic powers can be inconvenient. Who would want to receive messages about slashed wrists while enjoying a sunset?

But this is carrying the argument to an extreme. Although Hurkos became a psychic by falling off a ladder, there are less drastic ways of achieving the same result. According to Buchanan, all you have to do is to hold an object in your hands and then relax deeply as you try to "read" its history. With enough practice, Buchanan found, you can begin to pick up increasingly clear impressions. Buchanan's friend William Denton was astonished by how many of his students could hold a geological specimen in their hands, and experience visions of remote ages. Both had no doubt that we can develop this "telescope into the past" through practice, and that it can introduce us to a whole new world of experience. But Buchanan's crucial point was this: that the most important step towards developing these powers is to know that they exist.

According to Andrija Puharich, thousands of children are now being born who already possess psychic powers. In one primary school in Beijing, a class of 60 children all demonstrated the ability to read pages that have been torn out of books and sealed in tin cans—sometimes pages that had been screwed into a ball.

Puharich was convinced that, within the next 50 years, human beings will take psychic powers as much for granted as we take sight and hearing, and will be able to use psychometry to travel back in time as easily as we now take a bus to work.

The number of psychics who produced accurate information about Scott Rogo's murder convinces me he could be right.

All this will at least prepare you for some of the surprises you will find in the following pages.

Ed Olshaker is a longtime freelance journalist who also spent 20 years working as a publications editor for the Army and the Department of Health and Human Services. An intense curiosity about the metaphysical led him to explore ancient and modern spiritual teachings, meditation, and psychic phenomena. But a strong down-to-earth streak—evident in the writing he has done over the years on a wide range of subjects—caused him to focus on psychic detection as mediating the paranormal and the practical.

But one of his happiest ideas was to combine his many interests in researching the hidden history of our own time—with a view to learning what light "psychic detection" can throw on such mysteries as the death of Martin Luther King, Vincent Foster (the longtime close associate of Bill and Hillary Clinton), the rock idol Kurt Cobain, Secretary of Commerce Ron Brown (whose plane crashed en route to Croatia), and even of William Colby, the enigmatic former head of the CIA. This book will establish Ed Olshaker's reputation as America's leading historian of the unsolved.

Prologue

Our society is truly of two minds when it comes to psychic phenomena. The dominant view, reflected in most media coverage of the paranormal, is usually characterized by cynicism and mockery, yet a remarkably different attitude can be found in countless police departments' use of psychics in the investigation of mysterious deaths and disappearances.

Ironically, confirmation of the prominent role of psychic detectives comes to us from the most unlikely, and most hostile, of sources—*Skeptical Inquirer*, the journal of the Committee for the Scientific Investigation of Claims of the Paranormal (CSICOP). The abstract of a research article in the Winter 1993 issue concludes: "The popular media give the impression that police departments in the United States use 'psychics' for assistance in solving difficult cases. But do they? ... A survey was administered to the police departments of the 50 largest cities in America. The results revealed that 65 percent of these cities do not use and have never used psychics."

An impressive statistic. The revelation that approximately 35 percent of major police departments in major cities have worked with psychics underscores dramatically the degree to which this intuitive form of investigation is accepted and valued even in a solidly conservative American institution, placing crime-fighting psychics squarely in the establishment rather than on the fringe. And the true figure could well be higher than the 35 percent who admit to their use. For understandable public relations reasons, many police departments maintain deniability by having no official policy on psychics, allowing individual detectives the freedom to use whatever works for them, but with an implicit understanding that their use of psychics is to be kept low-profile and sometimes off-the-books. And being polled for a CSICOP article on the use of psychics is akin to publicly answering a Christian Coalition questionnaire on whether one has committed adultery (only the survey on psychics is potentially more humiliating in our society). So 35 percent might be a low estimate. No one, least of all a police official, wants to be ridiculed as a paranormal kook.

Police detectives' rationale for sometimes keeping their employment of psychics a secret is vividly illustrated by the experience of Nancy Myer, one of the psychic detectives featured in this book. In one of the more memorable paragraphs of her autobiography *Silent Witness*, Myer recalls that police detectives with whom she worked "were constantly serenaded with the theme to the *Twilight Zone* or the song 'Can You Read My Mind?' from the movie *Superman*. Others were subject to such pranks as finding crystal balls or dead bats left on their desks. It wasn't an easy time. When not subject to outright ridicule, they were constantly hounded to have me pick the next winner at the track or reveal who was having an affair with whom, and a whole host of juvenile stunts."

How many of us would appreciate working under such demeaning circumstances?

Even worse is the experience of "getting the third degree," as one psychic complained in a radio interview, explaining why she quit trying to help police. From the police department's point of view, it is understandable that they might ask—especially when it's the psychic approaching them, and not vice versa—"Just how do you happen to know so many details?" Psychic detective Robert Cracknell, who provides his insights on the cases in this book, once nearly had his helpfulness rewarded with arrest for murder after he supplied authorities (who did not know he was a psychic) with a detail that only the killer would have known.

Another difficult aspect of working as a psychic detective work is that, in investigating cases of murder and other violent crime, many of them tune in and experience the agony of the victims. Perhaps even more harrowing, some of them place themselves in the minds of the killers. One leading psychic I contacted in 1997, Greta

Alexander, had spent nearly four decades "experiencing" violent death in this way; such trauma is bound to take a toll, and perhaps contributed to the poor health she was suffering at that time. There are surely more pleasant ways of making a living, and for Alexander, who rarely accepted compensation for her emotionally draining crime-fighting work, it wasn't even a living. (She passed away on July 17, 1998, and is remembered not only for her tireless work as one of America's most gifted psychics, but also for charity work in her hometown of Delavan and nearby Peoria, Illinois, where she founded the House of Hope, providing inexpensive lodging for families of cancer patients.)

Consider, as well, that police departments tend to consult psychics on the toughest, most intractable cases, in the same way that gravely ill people often turn to alternative medicine only after all else has failed—yet another reason their work can be unusually challenging.

The use of metaphysical means to investigate crimes goes back a long way. Judy Guggenheim, co-author of *Hello from Heaven*, pointed out during a radio interview, "Clearly these experiences have been with us forever. Cicero, in 60-something BC, refers to having solved the murder mystery of a friend by this friend coming to him in a dream and describing in great detail exactly what happened, who had been the perpetrator, and how to intercept the perpetrator before he left town." In a similar story told in the Bible, Joseph analyzed images in dreams to save Egypt from famine.

Intriguingly, Cicero's intuitive approach to crime-solving is shared by at least one prominent homicide detective who says he has made use of information that came to him while asleep. *Mindhunter* author John Douglas—former head of the FBI's serial crime unit and the model for FBI profiler Jack Crawford in *The Silence of the Lambs*—recalled that when he was overwhelmed with a heavy caseload of gruesome serial murders, he received answers from a seemingly unlikely source: "I had so many cases, I'd go to bed, having read one, and force myself to dream about it. I used to come up with ideas in the middle of the night—I'd get up and write [them] down." Where were the answers coming from when

Douglas was asleep? Is this information-gathering technique really any different in nature from that of the "sleeping prophet" Edgar Cayce, who accessed valuable information from the astral realm while in an unconscious state? Similarly, some of history's most brilliant scientists—Isaac Newton, Albert Einstein, and George Washington Carver come to mind—humbly acknowledged the Higher Power that was working through them.

Psychic detective work is in fact no stranger than what the majority of us believe in and practice every day of their lives. According to a poll by the Pew Research Center for Politics and the Press, three-quarters of Americans believe in God and 53 percent say prayer is "an important part" of their daily lives. In other words, most of us—perhaps including numerous practitioners of the sciences— routinely use mental telepathy to contact our invisible Creator. Sooner or later, we will integrate these transcendent experiences into our everyday lives, rather than go on leading incompatible double lives—our church/synagogue/mosque life in which we commune with the realm that is unseen (yet absolutely real, as the sages and saints of all religions assure us), and our secular life in which so many of us mock psychic phenomena.

Seen from this perspective, the so-called paranormal is just a natural part of life. So why do so many people tend to giggle about the metaphysical? Why does the media in particular wear a smirk? It all seems to come down to ignorance and fear of the unknown. Joseph McMoneagle, reportedly the most talented of the US government's remote viewers (scientifically trained clairvoyants), has summed it up well: We don't make fun of the basic five senses, so why do people ridicule the sixth sense?

The work done by McMoneagle and his colleagues in the Defense Intelligence Agency's Stargate program shows that it is not only local law enforcement that has found psychics useful. During Stargate's 1978-1995 run, its remote viewers' achievements included locating American hostages, finding and describing secret Soviet military installations, and pinpointing North Korean biological and nuclear weapons.

And the remote viewing does not appear to have stopped with

the official closing of the program. In late 2001, some former Stargate psychics were rehired by federal agencies to aid in the fight against terrorism. As with police psychics, their employment is kept low-key, yet is hardly a secret. The *London Sunday Times* reported on November 11, 2001, that "Prudence Calabrese, whose Transdimensional Systems employs 14 remote viewers, confirmed that the FBI had asked the company to predict likely targets of future terrorist attacks …" In the January 21, 2002, *New York* magazine, reporter Geoff Gray quotes a former Justice Department attorney on the department's past and current use of remote viewers: "The FBI does not use psychics as official sources, the lawyer says; it happens 'under the table.' After September 11, 'the attorney general told us to think outside the box,' says this person, who still works closely with federal law-enforcement officials. 'This is definitely thinking outside the box.'"

Former President Jimmy Carter, speaking to a college audience, described how the government brought in an outside psychic when spy satellites failed to locate a secret government plane that disappeared over Zaire. According to Carter, the head of the CIA turned to a California woman said to have psychic ability. "She went into a trance," Carter recalled. "And while she was in the trance, she gave some latitude and longitude figures. We focused our satellite cameras on that point and the plane was found."

Nevertheless, for many of us this entire subject carries an aura of disrepute, often for good reason. After all, aren't psychic predictions almost always wrong? Even the psychic giant Edgar Cayce made mistakes in his forecasts. This should not come as a surprise, for there are endless variables to take into account when looking into the future, especially the immeasurably dynamic factor of free will.

Yet it is also true that psychic detectives featured in this book have publicly predicted crimes that later occurred. While assisting police investigating the Yorkshire Ripper serial murders, Robert Cracknell had an insight that the murderer would kill one more time and then be arrested—not by the criminal investigators but by traffic cops stopping him for a minor infraction, as indeed happened. More recently, in answer to an email inquiry during the serial sniper spree of 2002, Cracknell wrote on October 23 that "the perpetrator is not acting alone and is not an American citizen of long standing" and "an arrest is imminent." The following day, police arrested the Jamaican-born immigrant John Lee Malvo and his partner-in-crime John Muhammed, who both would be found guilty of murder. Psychic detective Bertie Catchings also shared a memorable intuitive insight in late 2002—that kidnap victim Elizabeth Smart was still alive, and that no further harm would come to her—an insight that proved accurate when the Utah teenager was found, safe and healthy, in 2003.

Similarly, when Nancy Myer was asked by an FBI official at a public event in 1977 what his next major case would be, she shared a horrible vision of mass murder that came to her at that moment; although the scene she described for him in front of several witnesses struck her as impossible—hundreds of killings caused by one madman—it proved to be a prediction of the Jonestown, Guyana People's Temple slaughter, a case the FBI official would be indeed assigned to a year later. This ability to operate as true-life versions of the "Pre-Cogs" of Steven Spielberg's *Minority Report*, the movie based on Philip K. Dick's short story about psychic crime-predictors, only seems to surface occasionally, though, in unexpected psychic flashes. This book, however, does not concern forecasting the future, but rather deals with tuning in to events that have already manifested.

Another reason for skepticism is that there are indeed cheaters and frauds in this field, which is especially tragic because people seeking their assistance are often particularly vulnerable. Technology, the great magnifier of all things good and bad, has made possible the unfortunate proliferation of 900-number dial-a-psychic lines that tend to tarnish the entire field, genuine practitioners along with the impostors. Dishonest individuals can be found in all fields—medicine, politics, law, home and car repair, corporate management, the clergy, and even scientific investigation of the paranormal—yet the psychic field is uniquely prone to abuse because this type of work, by its very nature, is difficult to measure or regulate as a consumer service. But honest investigation reveals plenty of psychics and mediums who are dedicated, honest, and blessed with genuine ability, as numerous police and federal-agency officials have confirmed. As the great yogi Paramahansa Yogananda once noted, "The existence of imitation gold does not decrease the value of pure gold."

And the existence of genuine gold was dramatically demonstrated in a recent study of some of the USA's best mediums conducted at the University of Arizona by a team of researchers led by Dr. Gary Schwartz, a professor of psychology, medicine, and neurology. In an abstract for the *Journal of the Society for Psychical Research* posted on the internet in 2001, Schwartz and three colleagues summed up the study and its striking results:

> When multiple mediums attempt to receive After-Death Communications (ADC's) from a single individual (the sitter/subject) who has experienced multiple losses, will accurate and replicable ADC information be obtained? Five highly skilled mediums were flown to the Human Energy Systems Laboratory for research on ADC. An Arizona woman, unknown to all of the mediums, who had experienced six significant losses over the past ten years, served as the primary subject. She filled out detailed pre-experimental questionnaires about her losses. Each medium met individually with the sitter. There was no communication between the mediums about the sessions. Two chairs were place side by side, a few feet apart, separated by a screen that eliminated visual cues. Except for an initial greeting, the only communications allowed from the sitter were simple yes or no responses to possible questions from the mediums ... A second sitter was tested with two of the mediums. The mediums' average accuracy was 83% for sitter one and 77% for sitter two. The average accuracy for 68 control subjects was 36%. In a replication and extension experiment, mediums' average accuracy in an initial ten minute period that did not allow yes-no questioning was 77%. The data suggest that highly skilled mediums are able to obtain accurate (p less than one in ten million) and replicable information. Since factors of fraud, error and statistical coincidence cannot explain the present

findings, other possible mechanisms should be considered in future research. These include telepathy, super psi, and survival of consciousness after death.

A more recent study of mediums conducted by the Scottish Society for Psychical Research (SSPR) yielded similar results. "The rules of chance would suggest an accuracy rating of 30%, but the mediums' average was 70%, with some hitting 80% on some of the participants," reported Jenifer Johnston in the March 28, 2004 issue of Scotland's *Sunday Herald*. According to Gordon Smith, one of the 13 mediums tested, "The conditions were very strict—I had to arrive an hour before the participants and never got to see them." The findings of this carefully controlled study have fascinating implications. Tricia Robertson, vice-president of the SSPR, sees the results as compelling evidence "that mediumship can honestly gain information that ordinary people can't."

Coincidentally, when Robert Cracknell's psychic talent was tested at Oxford University, he scored an 80-percent accuracy rate—virtually identical to that achieved by the mediums tested in the University of Arizona study—and leading psychic detectives such as Nancy Myer and Bertie Catchings have built their reputations on similar displays of genuine ability. Although the word "psychic" is generally used to refer to both psychics and mediums, they work in different ways: Psychics tune in to specific events, using a non-physical "sixth sense," while mediums such as Janet Cyford, Betty Muench, and Philip Solomon receive messages from spirit guides and departed individuals who now live in a higher dimension.

I asked these highly regarded psychics and mediums for their insights into some of our most intriguing mysteries, then followed the leads they provided, examining their impressions in relation to the known facts. These talented individuals are presented here not as judges or jurors announcing final rulings, but as witnesses presenting evidence. Is it possible that they have provided the missing pieces to some of the most puzzling cases of recent history? Let's explore and find out.

Featured Psychic Detectives and Mediums

Bertie Marie Catchings—assisted police investigations of mysterious deaths and disappearances in Texas, Oklahoma, and Louisiana. Over her four-decade career, Catchings has achieved recognition as one of the USA's top psychic detectives, and was named the best psychic in Texas in *The Book of Texas Bests*. Psychic ability appears to run in her family, from her great-grandmother who, as a little girl during the 1840s, is said to have shared an upsetting vision of her hometown of Vicksburg, Mississippi being destroyed in a war; to her late son John Catchings, a psychic detective who helped law enforcement on hundreds of cases.

Robert Cracknell—supplied accurate information to criminal investigators in cases including the Yorkshire Ripper serial murders, the kidnapping of heiress Gaby Mearth, and other high-profile crimes. He first received international notice when he achieved an 80-percent accuracy rating when tested at the Society of Psychic Research, Oxford University. Described as "one of the most remarkable psychics of the twentieth century" by author Colin Wilson, and "Britain's number 1 psychic detective" by Fleet Street tabloids that reported on his crime-fighting work, Cracknell went on to establish his own detective agency. He is the author of *The Lonely Sense* and *The Psychic Reality*, and was recently shown solving a fraud case on the internationally broadcast television series "Psychic Investigators."

Janet Cyford—has provided countless individuals with evidence of the survival of the soul through private readings and mediumship development groups. The author of *The Ring of Chairs: A Medium's Story*, Cyford grew up in a family of mediums and became active organizing seminars and workshops presenting the mechanics of mediumship before the public in Great Britain during her early twenties. Alarmed by what she regards as a reckless and potentially dangerous approach to spirit contact in the "channeling" phenomenon that first became popular in the 1980s, she emphasizes the importance of practicing mediumship according to a safe, methodical, time-tested process.

Betty Muench—a medium who received information through "automatic writing" done on her typewriter, she completed over 1,000 readings, often working with detectives hired by families of crime victims. Muench, who was featured in *The 100 Top Psychics in America*, explained, "Most of what I receive in the readings are insights around the case, sometimes through the victim and sometimes with images/visions created by the involvement of everyone, victim, victim's family members, suspects, and investigators." According to novelist Lois Duncan, whose daughter was murdered, Muench's readings on the case contained "valid information that could have come only from [daughter] Kait... [Muench] freely admits that she doesn't have the slightest idea what the information is supposed to mean. She just takes it down as if it were dictation." Betty Muench passed away on April 10, 2010.

Nancy E. Myer—has investigated close to 500 homicides, working with police departments throughout the United States and in Europe, Japan, Mexico, Canada, and Australia. She has appeared on television's *Unsolved Mysteries, Paranormal Borderline, Sightings, National Geographic's Mysteries of the Unexplained, 48 Hours, Geraldo,* and Court TV's "Psychic Detectives," among others; and in publications including the Time Life Series *Mysteries of the Unknown* volume *The Psychics.* Myer's initially reluctant journey from housewife to crime-solver is recounted in her autobiography

Silent Witness: The True Story of a Psychic Detective. She also teaches seminars in meditation and developing psychic ability.

Philip Solomon—a trance medium, reports his spirit communications with Kurt Cobain and Martin Luther King, Jr. He is a co-author of the 1999 book *Beyond Death: Conditions in the Afterlife*, written with paranormal researcher Hans Holzer, Ph.D., who has tested many prominent mediums over the years and ranks Solomon as the world's best. Solomon also writes a column for *Psychic News* and was featured for many years on BBC Radio in Birmingham, England.

Chapter 1:
Vincent Foster and the Shadow-Government Corruption Trail

"... Behind the ostensible government sits enthroned an invisible government, owing no allegiance and acknowledging no responsibility to the people. To destroy this invisible government, to dissolve the unholy alliance between corrupt business and corrupt politics is the first task of the statesmanship of the day ..." —Declaration of Principles of Theodore Roosevelt's Progressive Party, 1912

If a movie is ever made about the mysterious death of Vincent Foster, it might open with a view of a framed photograph he reportedly kept in his office, showing kindergarten buddies Mack McLarty and Bill Clinton along with the year-older Foster in Hope, Arkansas, where the Fosters' backyard once adjoined the Clintons'. The president recalled at Foster's memorial service that they used to play a game called mumblypeg, throwing penknives into the ground and trying to make them stick. "The penknives didn't stick, but the friendships did," said Clinton. All the way to the White House, where Foster served as Deputy Counsel.

Leaving behind a prosperous and fulfilling life in Little Rock, Foster found himself immediately swamped with a variety of demanding tasks, which fell into three categories: official White House business, which soon came to include the Whitewater controversy and Travel Office firings; personal business of the Clintons, which sometimes overlapped with the first category; and leftover business from the Rose law firm. Unusual pressures in one

1

of these three categories brought about his violent, untimely end, according to the picture assembled here.

Foster's death was ruled a suicide by former Independent Counsel Robert Fiske and then Kenneth Starr. Although the media treats these findings as the final verdict, a Zogby opinion poll taken in January 2000 found that 75 percent of Americans surveyed did not believe the official story that Foster drove to Fort Marcy Park in northern Virginia and shot himself in the mouth. Questions persist regarding conflicting accounts of whether a gun was found on the scene, and if so, what position it was in; why the gun was not one of the two guns he owned; whether he was shot in the mouth or in the neck, and why pictures showing the latter were suppressed; why witnesses were badgered to change their accounts, and, even when they stood firm, later saw their testimony changed in the official account; the curious lack of blood; the unusual position of the body, laid out perfectly straight, hands at his sides, as if ready for burial; and much more, justifying the reluctance of many Americans to believe the conclusion announced by the federal government they seem to have stopped trusting several decades ago.

Doubters of the suicide story have included Webb Hubbell, Associate Attorney General at the time of Foster's death, who reportedly said of his one-time Rose law firm partner, "Don't believe a word you hear. It was not suicide. It couldn't have been," before later changing his view and accepting the official story. Hillary Clinton insisted, "Of a thousand people, of those who *might* commit suicide, I would never pick Vince." Phillip Carroll, Foster's mentor at the firm, later recalled his similar reaction: "I kept saying no! That wasn't Vincent Foster. He was my favorite. He was so competent. He was a very strong individual. I keep coming back to foul play. There had to be foul play involved." Foster's children have reportedly expressed the same view.

During the Clinton administration's rocky beginning, Foster did take the setbacks and press criticism of him to heart. He exhibited symptoms of depression and got a prescription for the antidepressant Desyrel. Perhaps this was not terribly unusual, yet there was something uniquely foreboding about Foster's final days, which he spent in an agitated state that went beyond mere depression. According to his wife Lisa, he could not sleep, his heart raced, and he rubbed his hands together compulsively. He installed a security system for his townhouse and feared his White House phone was tapped. He voiced regret over having gotten into such a terrible mess, but would not reveal what the mess was. What was tormenting him, and what really happened on July 20, 1993?

Not a Suicide

"The whole thing smells of political intrigue and shady dealings," psychic detective Robert Cracknell noted. "Did he get himself into a situation which was far too deep to escape from with his own integrity intact? One feels that he was possibly threatening to release information, which would destroy a prominent figure."

"My impression is that of a contract killing," he concluded. "This is not a man who would commit suicide. He would cling on to every possible outside chance of being able to use his influence and find a solution."

"Sadly, this case could well end up amongst many others as 'unsolved,' due to the feeling I have of it being a contract killing— one or two men brought in to do the deed, and then disappear. I am sure many of his ex-associates may well have the same feeling, but without evidence, who would point a finger?"

Cracknell also hinted that a personal matter might have been used as leverage to intimidate Foster (an aspect of this mystery that another psychic also picked up on, as we will see). "His life was full of intrigue. Certainly he had a very secret and private life (or was the secret known to others?)"

Similarly, longtime psychic sleuth Bertie Catchings concluded that Foster was being threatened by powerful people who in turn felt threatened by his refusal to cooperate and by the possibility that he might tell all. After examining the basic case materials I showed her at her home—photographs of Foster and Fort Marcy Park, and the alleged suicide note—she noted, "His life had been threatened a bunch of times. Where are you going to hide when you're a visible person? He could speak and tell and show evidence if the right kind of pressure was on him, and he just knew a little too much."

A Mideast Connection?

Catchings, who said she had not followed the case in the news, said Foster found himself in danger when he realized too late that criminality was involved in something he was working on at the time. She sensed that the explosive matter centered on business dealings that involved a Mideastern influence: "I think he was assassinated to do a big coverup job. Most of the people who were involved in this scam were people who had some powerful spot where they could be used, but there was a power greater than the President of the United States pulling all the strings—professional criminals, I believe, from a foreign country—foreign powers, foreign connections ... figuring out ways to get involved in some business propositions that may have looked legitimate on the surface to people that are fairly intelligent."

"He thought it was a good thing, and then he began to find out that it was a foreign power that was trying to capitalize and use people—they always work on greed, and everyone's a little greedy."

Foster was eliminated, she concluded, "because he did know a few names of some people, and some were from foreign countries, and one of them was in the Mideast."

I showed Catchings the alleged Foster suicide note, along with a sample of Foster's known writing. The controversy over the authorship of the note is somewhat puzzling, because even if Foster can be definitely shown to have written it, it does not appear to be a suicide note. Lacking the usual elements—such as farewells to his loved ones, intention to kill himself, and explanation for the act—the note reads more like a therapeutic venting of his professional concerns, and partly like a legal defense relating to the relatively minor White House Travel Office scandal. Yet I included the note with the other case materials because it is generally considered an important piece of evidence in the case.

Catchings went over it with a magnifying glass. "This suicide note—all the "i's" and all the "t's" are *printed*, and in no instance in his writing [the comparison sample] did he do that ... I'll guarantee you he didn't have anything to do with this."

But if Foster did not write the note, why would others go to the trouble to fake a suicide note, only to make it so lackluster, non-committal, and arguably non-suicidal in tone?

On the other hand, the torn-up note was found with no fingerprints on it; and three handwriting experts hired by Jim Davidson, the publisher of *Strategic Investment* who is deeply suspicious about Foster's death, found the note to be a forgery. Former New York police detective Vincent Scalice, Reginald E. Alton of Oxford University, and Ronald Rice, an investigator and documents examiner from Boston, said they found significant differences between the writing in torn-up note and known samples of Foster's handwriting. If it is a fake, the most logical reason for the forgery might have been to mislead investigators down the Travel Office scandal trail, in order to detract attention from the actual scandal, whatever it might be.

In addition, Catchings' psychic hunch of a Mideast link appears to be supported by the experience of Patrick Knowlton, a witness in Fort Marcy Park in northern Virginia shortly before Foster's body was discovered there. Knowlton had described a "Hispanic-looking" man guarding a Honda with Arkansas license plates; reporters who walked the streets with Knowlton confirmed that dozens of men followed this key witness, and the license plate of one surveilling car was traced by reporter Ambrose Evans-Pritchard to Jordanians living in Vienna, Virginia. More on the Mideast connection later ...

Arkansas and Beyond

A strange thing happened, said Catchings, when she tried to make out one of the words on the Foster note. "The name Steven, Steven, Steven was what was pulling at me," she said, though the word looked nothing like Steven. "Right now I say that this Steven ... you're hitting pay dirt there. I know that that name 'Steven' had something to do with all this stuff."

"I believe in that little bit of light that I got at that moment, when I was reading this letter [Foster note], that my son John

Catchings, who—the picture right there—is trying to help me help you." I turned around to see, on the wall behind me, the framed photograph of John, a renowned psychic detective who died of complications from diabetes in 1992. Bertie Catchings says she maintains contact with him telepathically and in dreams.

"Or somebody, somebody is trying to send me at least one word. John used to say, in working on cases, that you just need a little ravel to undo a whole sweater, just a little tiny ravel."

As an attorney with the Rose law firm, Foster had done work for Stephens, Inc., the Little Rock corporation that is the largest non-Wall Street investment firm in the world. Could this be the crucial "Steven" sound that came through psychically? Using it as a starting point, as we shall see, it appears to tie together disparate elements of different psychic readings as interlocking pieces of a jigsaw puzzle.

But assembling the puzzle is not so simple. According to medium Betty Muench's reading, the Foster mystery is *"so convoluted that there is no one person who can clarify this, not even Foster."* The continuing speculation into this case here on Earth appeared to be temporarily holding Foster back from advancing in the afterlife. *"It is as if the inquiries into his death and into his life will be seemingly keeping him confused and wanting to move forward as if to get away from it but that he must face things at this time before he can move forward."*

"Faceless" Influences

Medium Janet Cyford, who, like Muench, receives information from "the other side," also found that this case is a mystery even to Foster. "It's almost like he can't put this together himself," she noted.

Foster's message brought through by Cyford is that "I should have been able to stand up for myself, protect myself. I thought I was pretty fit, but this came at me from nowhere."

Seeing through Foster's eyes, so to speak, she said that he has no memory of having been moved after being shot to death. "If the body was moved, I don't feel that he's aware of that." (The question naturally arises as to what, and how much, a person "sees" immediately after a sudden death. All indications are that as the real or "astral" self departs at the moment of death, he or she no longer has a great interest in the body left behind—the body is no longer perceived as "me," and the newly freed consciousness is now focused primarily on other things.)

"The next thing I want to tell you is that it was somebody else that fired the gun ... He didn't take his own life. There was a slim, slightly built individual ..."

"Now I'm asking him how he saw this man, because often once they're dead they see something that goes on ... Do you remember the film *Ghost*? ... I think [the hero in *Ghost*] was stabbed—he'd run after the assailant, but it was really the spirit self that was running after the assailant. When he walks back to where he sees the body lying down there ... it's a separation of the consciousness from the physical self. [Foster] was aware of a slimly built man, younger than himself, who had fired the gun."

"He was shot at quite close range as well ..." Cyford noted. "I don't see anybody else around, but—when I say 'I,' he's saying he didn't see anybody else around, but there were people back, possibly toward the parking lot." (This conclusion that Foster was killed in Fort Marcy Park, rather than murdered elsewhere and then dumped in the park, is Cyford's only key difference with other psychics and mediums on this case, and seems to be largely based on Foster's spirit having no memory of being moved.)

The shooter was sent only to intimidate Foster, at the very worst to wound him, according to this reading, but ended up killing him. "It was like a contract thing. I don't think the man that shot him knew who he was doing it for, or why. He was just told to do this."

This finding that lethal force was not intended—that the killing was in a sense accidental—is somewhat remarkable and unexpected. Yet, as we will see, one of the USA's leading psychic detectives reached a virtually identical conclusion.

Regarding witness Patrick Knowlton's concern about the suspicious-looking behavior of a man seemingly guarding a car in the park's parking lot, Cyford says "this gentleman [Foster] is saying they had nothing to do with it. That was something else altogether. The witness is—it's like after the fact, of seeing something, thinking, 'well, that was suspicious.' The car and the men around it had nothing to do with him being shot." The witness, however well-intentioned, "put two and two together and made eight."

Foster was targeted because "he'd made a stand about something some weeks before," and that "as he puts it together in his mind, he feels that the stand he made about how he was doing something, how he was keeping the information … he was standing by his own principles, the way he was trained, what his job was, and he was not prepared to back down. He had a strong feeling that he was shot because of this, but I've never known a spirit to come and point a finger at anybody."

The crisis that led to his death "happened very quickly," she pointed out, with Foster "suddenly being aware that he could be called or subpoenaed … there was the possibility that they'd come to him for the information that he had." A friend "had warned him to be more diligent about how he kept the information," and Foster defiantly maintained, "they've no right to bring this stuff out, to ask for this stuff."

Under pressure to produce information, he refused to cooperate. Cyford emphasized that "he wants you to know that the people that were putting pressure on him to come up with that information were faceless, almost."

"This House that Sinks"
This picture of anonymous influences deep within government also came up in medium Betty Muench's reading. The spirit group she channels noted that "… *there is this which will suggest that he will be looking down at something that he is still very much concerned about. It will be a square building within walls that will seem to fit closely around the building and there is a sense of this building sinking down behind the walls. This would suggest that then Vincent would be concerned that there is this which would be all walls then and not the building or functional aspect of the building still intact. It is as if it disappears before his view.*"

The reading further explained: *"This house that sinks is not the White House but another aspect of government which will be a bureaucratic facility, and it will be that which will seem to do those investigations and which should be investigated itself."*

Investigators of this mystery have noticed a peculiar pattern of behavior on the part of the Federal Bureau of Investigation. First, the agency declined to do an investigation, leaving it to the Park Police, an organization with little experience handling violent crimes. But why would the FBI stay out of such an important case? When ice-skater Nancy Kerrigan was hit on the leg with a stick, the FBI quickly jumped in and solved the mystery; yet in a case involving the most prominent White House official to die violently since President John Kennedy, the FBI chose to stand aside.

And when FBI agents finally did assume a role in the case—when assigned to the investigation conducted by Special Prosecutor Robert Fiske, who expanded his Whitewater business-deal inquiry to look into Foster's death—they are alleged to have actively sabotaged the inquiry.

For solid information on FBI agents' behavior, on forensic and witness evidence, and other aspects of the Foster case, we are indebted to a handful of investigative reporters—especially Christopher Ruddy of the *Pittsburgh Tribune-Review* and Ambrose Evans-Pritchard of the *London Sunday Telegraph*—who took on this giant story while the media at large ignored it. But first, a caveat: Ruddy's reporting was financed by anti-Clinton billionaire Richard Mellon Scaife, an heir to the Mellon fortune who decided at the outset that the president "has people bumped off at will." The fiercely anti-Clinton Evans-Pritchard holds similar views.

This being stipulated, it is important to acknowledge that Ruddy, despite his ideology and the agenda of his sponsor, has bravely uncovered significant facts that can serve as a useful base for future researchers.

Former FBI Director William S. Sessions, curiously fired the day before Foster's death, told Ruddy that the FBI was kept out of the investigation because of a "power struggle within the FBI and the Department of Justice" that began before Clinton took office.

The effort to remove Sessions began near the end of the Bush Administration, with trivial charges that included his having taken his wife on a government airplane. Clinton finished what Bush started with the historically unprecedented firing of the FBI chief on July 19, 1993, before even nominating a successor, and denying Sessions a chance to defend himself.

It appears that both administrations targeted Sessions for removal because they feared investigation of their own wrongdoing by a tough, independent FBI chief. A *Wall Street Journal* editorial entitled "What's the Rush?," which appeared the same day Sessions was fired, questioned Clinton's haste, implying that the president feared an investigation of his travel office scandal by Sessions. The *Journal* also pointed out, "The original Bush administration investigation [of Sessions], it should be carefully noted, was announced immediately after it became public that the FBI had launched an investigation into the controversial prosecution of the head of the Atlanta branch of the Banca Nazionale del Lavaro over illicit loans to Iraq. [Bush Attorney General] Barr's own investigator, a prominent former judge, exonerated the Justice Department handling of the BNL case ... Strange things are going on in law enforcement, as the BNL and BCCI cases show ..." The Justice Department's attempted concealment of evidence clearing Atlanta bank official Christopher Drogoul of wrongdoing was an effort to make a minor player the fall guy for the huge "Iraqgate" scandal. Sessions announced he would get to the bottom of this apparent high-level criminality, and thus became a marked man himself.

The timing of Foster's death—one day after the firing—coupled with the heavy-handed commandeering of Foster's office by White House counsel Bernard Nussbaum and others, focused suspicion on the Clinton Administration in the minds of many of the president's detractors. Furthermore, ironically for Clinton, his ruthless dismissal of Sessions removed his best bet for a legitimate investigation of the suspicious death of his friend Vincent.

Ruddy reports that agents of the FBI have intimidated witnesses, such as the man referred to as the confidential witness, noting, "The confidential witness—also the man alleged to have first found

10

Foster's body—charged that FBI agents had badgered him, and that his testimony, such as not seeing a gun in Foster's hand, had been misrepresented in the Fiske report."

In addition, according to a Ruddy source, the Fiske investigation's lead prosecutor Miquel Rodriguez "developed grave doubts about the FBI's ability to properly investigate the case. For example, important photographic evidence, said to be unusable by certain FBI experts, was turned over by Rodriguez to an outside agency that produced remarkable results." In addition, "Evidence uncovered during the Starr probe showed that FBI investigators had used distorted copies of original photos for analysis."

Fiske's replacement by Kenneth Starr, who kept the same FBI personnel on the case, seems to have made no difference in the handling of the Foster investigation. "When Rodriguez insisted on conducting a painstaking review of the case, he met with stiff opposition from FBI agents assigned to Starr's probe," writes Ruddy (describing the same kind of puzzling bureaucratic obstruction that would be criticized years later in a memo by FBI whistleblower Colleen Rowley, who complained that the Washington office "continued to, almost inexplicably, throw up roadblocks" blocking investigation of valuable leads that might have prevented the September 11 terrorist attacks). Rodriguez resigned in frustration.

Witness Patrick Knowlton makes similarly remarkable allegations. "Knowlton has maintained that FBI agents lied in their report of what Knowlton told them about events in Fort Marcy Park July 20, 1993, shortly before Foster's body was found there," Ruddy notes. "Further, Knowlton claims that immediately after his comments became public, and he was subpoenaed by Starr to testify before a grand jury, he was subjected to harrowing intimidation and harassment by federal agents."

Why would an alleged rogue element of the FBI want to hide the truth about Foster's death? It might help to take a broader view, seeing the *"sinking building"* in Muench's reading not only as the FBI, but as the Department of Justice in general, with some agents of its sub-agency the FBI acting as the enforcement arm for some of their superiors—an alarming possibility that has precedents going as far back as the Warren Harding Administration, when FBI agents burglarized the offices of congressmen investigating the Justice Department's participation in the Teapot Dome scandal. (Beyond the symbolism of the Muench reading's *"square building within walls that will seem to fit closely around the building and ... a sense of this building sinking down behind the walls,"* the Justice Department headquarters appears to fit this description literally, with its four sides encompassing an inner courtyard—a square within a square, as seen from above.) What is Foster's connection? And how does this tie in with the Mideast and Stephens, Inc.?

Far-reaching Tentacles

When Foster was still in Arkansas, the Rose law firm assigned him to do work for the information technology corporation Systematics (later taken over by Alltell), owned by billionaire Jackson Stephens and brother Witt Stephens, who died in 1992. Systematics was one of several front corporations for the worldwide dissemination of Prosecutor's Management Information System (PROMIS) software, a powerful tracking system allegedly stolen from the Inslaw Corporation by the Department of Justice during the 1980s. This would seem to connect Catchings' "Steven" clue with Muench's channeled description of some bureaucratic government agency. The Inslaw scandal has links to others, and to a trail of violent deaths that continued into the 1990s. Was Foster another victim of this web of high-level corruption? To find out, it is crucial to first get a better grasp of the role of the Justice Department, a story that is complex and far-reaching.

Inslaw, owned by William and Nancy Hamilton, made a deal with the US Justice Department in 1982 to install their powerful criminal-tracking software in the offices of 42 US Attorneys. Amazingly, the Justice Department then refused to pay the $10 million they had promised, forcing the Hamiltons into bankruptcy.

Unfortunately for the Hamiltons, Earl Brian, a close friend of Attorney General Ed Meese, had a controlling interest in the competing company Hadron, Inc. William Hamilton says he saw the handwriting on the wall when he received a call in 1983 from

Dominic Laiti, chairman of Hadron, Inc. Laiti allegedly said Hadron wanted to buy Inslaw, and emphasized that Hadron "has very good political contacts in the current administration." Hamilton refused to sell Inslaw, and says Laiti replied, "We have ways of making you sell."

Unable to get control of Inslaw or its software legally, the Justice Department simply took PROMIS. The Hamiltons filed a civil suit against the Justice Department, and in September 1987, U.S. Bankruptcy Judge George Bason ruled in William and Nancy's favor, finding that Justice Department officials "took, converted, and stole" PROMIS through "trickery, fraud and deceit," and awarded the Hamiltons $6.8 million. Judge Bason likened the behavior of the nation's top law-enforcement agency to a car-shopper who goes for a test drive and steals the car.

Shortly after Bason's ruling, his reappointment to the court was denied, and, incredibly, he was replaced by S. Martin Teel, one of the Justice Department attorneys he had ruled against. "Even jaded, case-hardened Washington attorneys called the action 'shocking' and 'eerie,'" wrote Maggie Mahar in *Barron's National Business and Financial Weekly*.

Investigative reporter Joseph Daniel "Danny" Casolaro spent over a year looking into the Inslaw case, and theorized that it was one arm of a massive tangle of corruption that included the Bank of Credit and Commerce International (BCCI) scandal, government drug trafficking, Iran-Contra, the alleged "October Surprise" deal to delay the release of U.S. hostages in Iran until the Carter Administration ended, and much more—various tentacles of what Casolaro came to call "the Octopus." The PROMIS system, Casolaro claimed, appeared to have been stolen by Justice and given to Earl Brian to reward him for his help in the secret 1980 deal with the Iranians.

One of Casolaro's sources, scientist Michael Riconosciuto, claimed he had worked on modifying PROMIS software for Earl Brian. Riconosciuto clearly had knowledge that was considered a threat to powerful people; in a sworn affidavit in 1991, he alleged that Peter Videnieks of the Justice Department called him and "attempted during this telephone conversation to persuade me not to cooperate with an independent investigation of the government's piracy of Inslaw's proprietary PROMIS software being conducted by the Committee on the Judiciary of the U.S. House of Representatives … Videnieks also outlined specific punishments that I could expect to receive from the U.S. Department of Justice if I cooperate with the House Judiciary Committee's investigation."

Riconosciuto went ahead and testified anyway, and retribution was carried out just as he had predicted in his affidavit. He was falsely charged with manufacturing amphetamines and jailed, and in a legal case that he says Videnieks also used as leverage, his wife Bobbi lost a child-custody dispute with her ex-husband and was jailed. Also, a number of individuals connected with Riconosciuto died suddenly during a short time period.

Despite death threats, Danny Casolaro persisted in his research, believing that a source he was to meet in Martinsburg, West Virginia held the final piece of the puzzle. He did, however, tell his brother, Dr. Anthony Casolaro, "I have been getting some very threatening phone calls. If anything happens to me, don't believe it was accidental."

Casolaro was found dead in the bathroom of his room at the Martinsburg Sheraton Hotel on August 11, 1991. Both wrists were slit repeatedly and deeply. His notes were missing, and a brief "suicide note" was found. After destroying evidence by cleaning up the crime scene, and embalming the body without authorization, West Virginia authorities ruled the death a suicide. But few people believe this conclusion.

Betty Muench's reading addressed the rumor that a high-ranking Justice Department official was present at the murder, stating that it is indeed true. Casolaro's mistake was in trusting this man who is *"someone used to misguide others … who will speak softly and who will seem to be in charge but indeed is a puppet used to misguide others … not only will have misguided but will have been a part of the killing itself. This was to make sure that it was reported back at a certain time and confirming then that this was complete."*

This reading added that Casolaro *"was at the point in his*

investigation that he was stepping on toes everywhere … not only in past administrations but in this one as well [the first Bush Administration, in power at the time of his death]."

Congressional attempts to investigate the Inslaw scandal and the death of Casolaro were thwarted by the Justice Department. As detailed by reporter Karen Bixman, writing in *In These Times:*

> The House Judiciary Committee received the same stonewall treatment from the Justice Department as had the earlier Senate committee. Attorney General Dick Thornburgh refused to appear before the committee and refused to let Congress review Justice Department files ...
>
> The final House report, released September 10, 1992, accused Justice Department officials of criminal misconduct and recommended the appointment of a special prosecutor. Attorney General William Barr refused to appoint a special prosecutor, but appointed Chicago attorneys Nicholas Bua, Charles Knight, and five Justice Department prosecutors to investigate the Justice Department's misconduct.
>
> He then impaneled a federal grand jury to conduct an investigation. After listening to a considerable amount of evidence, Bua dismissed the grand jury and quickly impaneled another one. A group named Citizens Committee to Clean Up the Courts charged that Bua and Knight were impeding the investigation and covering for the Justice Department.
>
> In June 1993, Nicholas Bua sent the report of his investigation to the Justice Department, exonerating Justice Department officials [and] stating that there was no truth to the charges regarding the Inslaw case. The Bua report stated facts absolutely contrary to the findings of the U.S. Bankruptcy Court Judge, the U.S. District Court Judge, and the Congressional investigation.

Inslaw's attorney Elliot Richardson, best-known for his honorable service as US Attorney-General during the Nixon Administration, reacted with outrage—"What I have seen of [the report] is remarkable both for its credulity in accepting at face value denials of complicity in wrongdoing against Inslaw, and for its failure to pursue leads making those denials implausible"—a polite, lawyerlike way of saying that the highest levels of the US government, including the judiciary, were rife with corruption (not even counting the mysterious deaths connected to the Inslaw scandal).

An Old Scandal Invades a New Administration

Note the timing of the submission of the Bua report—June 1993. Inslaw submitted its rebuttal to the judicial ruling to Associate Attorney-General Webster Hubbell on July 12. Could this potentially have shined a spotlight on various aspects of the software scandal, including matters of which Foster had direct knowledge?

The date of July 12 is a vital key to this mystery, if we focus on Foster's condition before and after. His discouragement and unhappiness before that date appear to have been a manageable type of frustration not unusual in Washington, especially for a newcomer like himself. In his final week, however, it suddenly escalated into an emergency. Although Foster's wife Lisa testified that Foster "appeared awful ... worried and stressed" when she came to join him in Washington on June 5, his behavior in his final week indicated some new, sudden pressure in addition to the accumulation of frustrations and bad publicity that had already put a strain on him. On July 13, Vince told Lisa he was thinking about resigning. Foster's executive assistant Deborah Gorham recalls receiving concerned calls from Foster's wife Lisa and their eldest son during his final days, asking about his mood. Lisa remembers Vince mentioning his depression to her for the first time around July 16—a "depression" that included handwringing, insomnia, fear that his phone was bugged, and a sudden need to install a home-alarm system. On that day he felt his heart pounding so hard that he had the White House infirmary check his blood pressure twice, although they found nothing wrong physically.

His phone records for Friday, July 16 show two calls of a minute or less to a psychiatrist's office, indicating he got an answering machine and left no message. His sister Sheila also called a psychiatrist that same day, expressing grave concern for him. According to the FBI report, the psychiatrist, Dr. Robert Hedaya, told them that Sheila said Vince "was dealing on a daily basis with Top Secret matters and that his depression was directly related to highly sensitive and confidential matters" and as a result "was in a bind, needed desperately to talk to someone ..."

This characterization of the work that suddenly made Foster agitated, sleepless, and desperate does not appear to describe the Clintons' Whitewater land deal, the Travel Office firings, or the failed nominations of the administration's first two Attorney-General nominees; but it certainly does appear to describe the leftover work for Systematics that Foster took with him to the White House, especially when viewed in conjunction with the timing of Foster's horrible personal emergency.

In his February 20, 1995, *New York Post* column, conservative pundit John Crudele asked whether the Inslaw rebuttal of July 12, 1993 might have triggered the depression and agitation suffered by Foster during his final week of life, pointing out that one of the companies selling the software was in Arkansas, and that "Foster and Hubbell not only owned a small amount of stock in that company but might also have done lots of lawyering for that firm and its sister concerns."

"Could Foster have figured out what was about to transpire?" Crudele asked. "Might he have worried that Inslaw's secret witnesses were going to bring him down? Or could this all be just a preposterous coincidence of the calendar?" Though he raises the possibility of an Inslaw connection, Crudele agrees with the finding of suicide.

This appears, however, to be a mild interpretation of events, not taking into account the apparent surveillance and intimidation of Foster that prompted him to install a security system during his fearful final days. This campaign of harassment would suggest that, beyond being a mere Systematics stockowner and employee fearing unfavorable publicity from the testimony of witnesses, he himself might have faced being called as a witness to share potentially explosive information.

Could the pressure on Foster that week also have been, at least in part, a way of sending a warning to Hubbell, his longtime buddy and Rose law firm colleague? Vince and his wife Lisa spent the weekend of July 17-18 on the eastern shore of Maryland, where, coincidentally or not, he met with Hubbell at the estate of Michael Cardozo, who headed Clinton's legal defense team. On Monday the 19th, a deeply worried and upset Foster called his Arkansas physician, who had a Washington pharmacy deliver 30 tablets of Desyrel to Foster's home that afternoon. That evening he declined an invitation to join President Clinton and a few other friends at the White House to see *In the Line of Fire*, Clint Eastwood's thriller about a plot on the president's life. The next day, eight days after the Inslaw corporation's rebuttal to the Bua report was delivered to Hubbell, Foster was found shot to death in the park. Hubbell would eventually uphold the Bua ruling.

Deep Intrigue

According to this scenario, the Inslaw scandal of the two previous administrations played a key role in this mystery. The people who took over the Justice Department during the Reagan-Bush years appear to have retained a substantial portion of their power after Clinton's election to the presidency, resulting in a behind-the-scenes power struggle between President Clinton and Bush's holdovers in the "sinking house" that might be at the heart of the Foster story. The key, veteran White House reporter Sarah McClendon asserted when I spoke with her by phone, is that before leaving office, "Bush made political appointees into career employees," packing the department with moles who would continue to serve him and his cronies. (McClendon, who covered the White House beginning with the Franklin Roosevelt Administration, died in 2003 at the age of 92.)

"Bush has been manipulating the Clinton Administration ever since they got in there," McClendon told an interviewer at the time, alleging that Clinton's predecessor "has been causing to happen, or pulling strings to happen, tragic things ... 30 percent of the policymakers in the Justice Department are his people!" (Yet, as we will see, she also emphasized that the Foster story ultimately goes back as far as the Carter Administration when one follows the shadowy big-money trail.) McClendon's observation is corroborated by retired US Navy Lt. Commander Al Martin, a former Iran-contra operative turned whistleblower, who noted, "That was one of the distinctions of the Clinton Regime. There was a record number, over 1,700 Bush holdovers in senior positions in various federal agencies."

Maggie Mahar, reporting for *Barron's* back in 1988, revealed that the planting of moles began even earlier than Bush, toward the end of the Reagan Administration, when the outcome of the 1988 election was considered uncertain: "'I know of at least 50 or 60 career government employees who have been reassigned or forced out,' says one department insider. Another charges the department with using FBI background checks in order to manufacture reasons for forcing employees to leave. 'They're trying to find— or force—openings for political appointees that they want to bury as what we call 'moles' in the department,' explains a longtime Justice Department hand. 'They bury the moles so that the next administration can't find them.'"

"The moles, he goes on, are political appointees who are moved into GS (government service) jobs normally held by career government employees. 'It could take the next administration two years to figure out who are the career employees and who are the political appointees dropped into their slots,' he says."

McClendon saw Foster's death as tied to the Justice Department-Systematics-Stephens connection. And she was affected personally through her friendship with attorney Paul Wilcher, a lawyer for Riconosciuto who tried to continue investigating where Danny Casolaro left off. Early in the Clinton Administration, Wilcher wrote Attorney-General Janet Reno a 105-page letter—a poignant mixture of legal brief and impassioned plea to save the current administration and the nation itself—describing the workings of a "shadow government" infesting the Justice Department as well as other agencies. He warned Reno that "although you may not realize it, you are still surrounded in the Justice Department, the FBI, the

BATF, and elsewhere throughout the government by Reagan-Bush holdovers many of whom are determined that you will *never* learn about the core issues and ugly truths which I have laid out for you here in some detail."

In the letter he begged the Attorney-General to "*never* permit the Bush-Reagan holdovers who surround you to use the Department as their protector for the CIA and 'Shadow Government' who are still pursuing the hidden agenda of the two prior Presidents."

Wilcher urged Reno, "Be sure to take the counsel of *the career people within the Justice Department.* Many are immensely talented and have taken these jobs because they have a passion for justice. They are the conscience of the Department, and will serve you well."

So it appears that despite the ascendancy of a new administration in 1993, the Department of Justice remained largely in the hands of the Reagan-Bush loyalists who had ruled for the preceding 12 years. In June 1993, one month before Vincent Foster's death, Paul Wilcher failed to show up as usual at a weekly study meeting conducted by Sarah McClendon. After she and other friends of Wilcher tried in vain to contact him, McClendon notified the District of Columbia police, who, after her repeated demands, forced their way into Wilcher's apartment, where they found his dead body.

The reading by Betty Muench reveals that, as one might suspect, Wilcher's letter to Attorney-General Reno came into the hands of one of the holdovers— "*someone who will have waylaid this information and who will have usurped the power of Reno and who will have acted in her stead.*"

"*She will not have much knowledge of this situation, which is the intention of this so-called shadow government group,*" the reading noted, adding that this group "*will keep her so uninformed that she will seem ignorant. While Reno will have certain authority, it is small in view of the powers that are set up around her to keep her in the dark.*" This reading referred to actions by the shadow government "*which will upset the government as it now stands and thus threatens this nation and the world.*"

Forgotten victims would also include whistleblowers who tried to expose the federal bankruptcy system, which, in the Inslaw case and others, is alleged to have functioned as yet another arm of the Justice Department plunder machine, illegally seizing the assets of ordinary citizens and rewarding the cronies of high Reagan-Bush officials. Attorney Dexter Jacobson was murdered on August 14, 1990, just before he was to present evidence of Chapter 11 corruption. Another attorney, Gary Ray Pinnell, was set to come forward on the same issue when he was killed on February 11, 1991.

And there's a good chance that Vincent Foster belongs on the list as well. A brilliant attorney who graduated first in his class at the University of Arkansas and achieved the top bar exam score, Foster was admired for his competence, integrity, and decency. Yet his work for Stephens' Systematics entangled him with shadow-government entities involved in the worldwide dissemination of the Justice Department's stolen PROMIS software, a system that not only was employed to track US criminal cases but also was being sold at considerable profit to banks overseas and to foreign intelligence agencies including those in Israel and Jordan. (Ironically, this software that was so valuable in tracking terrorists also ended up in the hands of Osama bin Laden, who obtained it from Russian organized crime figures, who had received it from FBI traitor Robert Hanssen, according to a barely remembered June 15, 2001, *Washington Times* report; the PROMIS software provided bin Laden "the ability to monitor US efforts to track him down, federal law enforcement officials say," according to Jerry Seper, the story's author.)

Foster's work for Systematics paralleled media mogul Robert Maxwell's role selling PROMIS software internationally through Degem Computers, both men acting as conduits between the business world and the intelligence community, both men dying mysteriously. A hazy picture begins to develop of Foster, in this nest of vipers, being pressured to do or say something that violated his conscience, and seeing no way out.

BCCI—The Little Rock-Mideast-Justice Department Connection

Also integral to the Stephens-Justice Department connection pointed to by the combined readings of the psychic detectives is BCCI, the international bank which Jackson Stephens brought into the United States in 1978, first achieving notoriety with the Bert Lance credit scandal during the administration of President Jimmy Carter, Stephens' Naval Academy friend. Was BCCI—which reportedly laundered money for Manuel Noriega, various drug lords, terrorist Abu Nidal, Ferdinand Marcos, rogue elements of the CIA and Mossad, and others—doing the same for the criminal profiteers who took over the Justice Department in the 1980s and made a killing selling the stolen PROMIS software system worldwide? Were Justice Department officials, as BCCI-scandal sources have claimed, bribed into protecting the giant bank?

Consider that when extensive evidence of BCCI's bank fraud came to light, the Department of Justice failed to act, and even obstructed justice. It took New York District Attorney Robert Morganthau and his team, and similar prosecutors in England, to finally break the back of BCCI. "We have no cooperation from the Justice Department," Morganthau said as he tried to take on the colossal bank. "In fact, they are impeding our investigation, and Justice Department representatives are asking witnesses not to cooperate with us."

In *The Outlaw Bank*, authors Jonathan Beaty and S.C. Gwynne note, "Perhaps the most disturbing aspect of the BCCI affair in the United States was the failure of the U.S. government and federal law enforcement to move aggressively against the outlaw bank. Instead of swift retribution, what took place over more than a decade was a cover-up of major, alarming proportions, often orchestrated from the very highest levels of government."

The Morganthau investigation and similar prosecutions overseas eventually brought down BCCI in 1992, the year before Foster died; but by the same principle that energy cannot be destroyed, all that money and power carried on in other forms, predictably recycled back into the hands of the same rich and powerful. (For instance,

Stephens, Inc. purchased the bankrupt BCCI's Hong Kong branch from the receivers.) The international bank still appears to be a vital piece of the Foster puzzle, not only connecting to Stephens and the Justice Department, but also to the Mideast. Playing a prominent role in Jordan and other Mideast nations, BCCI was widely known as an "Arab bank"—although it grew to become much more than that.

And Foster's work for Stephens, Inc. appears to have involved a substantial amount of business with the Mideast, a key aspect of the Foster mystery cited in two of the psychics' readings. Writing in *The Guardian*, reporter Martin Walker describes Foster's link to "the Arabian connection, the role of the shadowy Abdullah Taba Bakhsh, with his 10 percent slice of Little Rock's Worthen Bank, the one that lent Clinton $3.5 million in February [1992] for the presidential campaign."

"Foster knew David Edwards, an old friend of Clinton who had briefly shared his Oxford apartment. Foster knew that Edwards was the frontman for Bakhsh, as for so many Arabs from his days with the Stephens Brothers investment firm in Little Rock."

"Stephens Brothers owned Worthen Bank, and while in their employ Edwards helped broker the BCCI bank's bid to buy First American Bank in Washington, DC. The legal work was handled by the Rose law firm," Walker notes.

Young attorney Hillary Rodham Clinton, Foster's protégé at Rose, played a role at that time; Peter Truell and Larry Gurwin, writing in *False Profits*, state that "in 1978, she did legal work for Systematics, Inc., when it was sued for its role in [BCCI founder Agha Hasan] Abed's scheme to collect stock in First American."

In 1991, as the bank's scandal was unfolding, *Time* reported on its use of "the black network," which "functions as a global intelligence operation and a Mafia-like enforcement squad. Operating primarily out of the bank's offices in Karachi, Pakistan, the 1,500-employee black network has used sophisticated spy equipment and techniques, along with bribery, extortion, kidnapping and even, by some accounts, murder." They quote an Arab operative of the gang: "I was recruited by the black network in the early 1980s. They came to me while I was in school in the U.S …" BCCI's team of gangsters are suspected in the murder of journalist Anson Ng, who was found dead while gathering information on the bank's corruption. They also may be connected to the death of Casolaro, as BCCI was one tentacle of the "Octopus" that he was planning to warn the world about.

In describing BCCI's influence, Truell and Gurwin also corroborate the Muench reading's emphasis on a behind-the-scenes battle between Clinton and the alleged Bush holdovers in the "sinking square house" who allegedly sought to undermine him. "Clinton's ties to Stephens and the BCCI network attracted some media interest during the [1992] campaign. What reporters didn't discover, however, was that Clinton's association with Stephens was the subject of an FBI investigation in 1992, according to government sources. The purpose of the probe was, in part, to determine if Clinton was connected with BCCI. One investigator said he believed that the probe might be politically motivated, instigated by Republicans who wanted to undermine the Arkansas governor." And yet, as the authors note, "If Bush's supporters were, in fact, behind the investigation, it would be extremely ironic, in view of [Bush's] own ties to Stephens and other BCCI associates."

So while the two major parties fight it out bitterly, the fact remains that they largely serve the same masters. Robert Fiske, the first Whitewater independent counsel, and Clinton lawyer Robert Bennett, once worked together defending BCCI figures Robert Altman and Clark Clifford. Numerous congressmen of both parties, heavily funded by the powerful bank, naturally came to its defense when it was accused of crimes, as did former President Jimmy Carter, who repeatedly downplayed BCCI's wrongdoing. But the story of "the Arab bank" of course goes far beyond these US political connections, and the Foster case similarly follows an international trail.

The spirit group channeled by Betty Muench corroborated Bertie Catchings' insight regarding a Middle East connection. According to this reading, the nation of Jordan figured prominently in business dealings by certain powerful figures. "*This will have been*

24

a group which will have feared that the way in which this information will have been possibly divulged by Foster would bring down certain others who will have been beneficial to their own cause. This is where the Jordanian influence begins. There will be this which will have had someone within the so-called scandal, who will have made promises on the behalf of Jordan and that then there will have been this which would have been put in jeopardy. To seek to know what that might have been, then it would be imperative to know what actions were being considered around Jordan in that time frame."

The next sentence, however, is not encouraging: *"This is all so entangled that there is no way in this time for any one person to be able to untangle this and thus it was with Foster himself."* The reading adds, *"There is within the Jordanian government information which will shed light on this matter and that there will be this which will have some close ties to the embassy."* Referring to the Jordanians whom reporter Ambrose Evans-Pritchard tracked down by their license plate after they followed Fort Marcy Park witness Patrick Knowlton, the channeling noted, *"The men will have been on hire from this source."*

Significantly, though, this reading noted that the two Jordanians were sent as *"a diversion."* Perhaps they did so as a favor to their American partners in the business dealings. This appears to make logical sense, for Foster's death apparently resulted from his conflict with people on the US government end of the alleged business partnership, not Jordanians or other Arabs. These two Jordanians themselves had no issue with Knowlton, and possibly were used not only to intimidate Knowlton, Evans-Pritchard, and other challengers of the official Foster verdict, but also to confuse and mislead them down a foreign-conspiracy trail—a perfect red herring to keep investigative reporters far off track.

Muench's reading also depicted Foster temporarily halted in his soul's progress by his country's ongoing focus on the puzzle of his death. *"There is this image of a face which will be that of Vince, this looking up at the heavens as if praying, as if seeking guidance. There is this within now which does not move for Vince. It is as if the inquiries into his death and into his life will be seemingly keeping him confused and wanting to move forward as if to get away from it but that he must face things before he can move forward. There will be this which he will seem to be considering and that he will seem to consider that he would convey his truth as he will have known it, but he is confused about just what he did know."*

Dissemination of a False Story

Where did Foster actually die? The reporting of Ruddy and Evans-Pritchard makes a powerful forensic case that Foster did not die in the park, but was moved there after his death. The Muench reading stated that, *"it was thought that it would be more conducive to a story of scandal to put this body in a place that would be near to another facility and that this will have been done, not by the ones who were seeking to gain access to information from him."* This echoes Bertie Catchings' assertion that the men who moved the body were not the ones who had caused his death, but were other individuals who had been hired to simply, so to speak, "throw out the trash," as she described it.

Psychic detective Nancy Myer concurred that Foster was never in the park alive, but was carried there after dying elsewhere. "I do get the impression of three men—one driver, and two who carry the body. They move swiftly and are quite physically fit. Their easy movements carrying his weight indicate good strength. They're all dressed in business suits, shirts, and ties."

The Muench reading's statement—*"it was thought that it would be more conducive to a story of scandal to put this body in a place that would be near to another facility"*—puzzled me, for I was not aware of Fort Marcy Park being near any kind of important facility. I consulted a Northern Virginia map, and checked the list of parks in the index—no mention of the tiny Civil War fort named after General George McClellan's chief of staff. I scanned the map until I found it, and sure enough, practically adjoining the park, we find the Central Intelligence Agency, the FBI's longtime bureaucratic rival.

The Muench reading further noted, *"There will have been this supposed false story which will have been planted in another group entity and that group will have acted on some kind of assumption."* If Foster's body was indeed disposed of in such a way as to focus attention on the CIA, this might shine some light on the sensational stories that were circulated alleging that Foster and Hillary Clinton were under CIA investigation for spying. The outrageous espionage story—which matches the Muench reading's highlighting of *"a group who would find some power in creating intrigue where there is none"*—gained publicity when the respected James R. Norman, a senior editor for *Forbes* magazine, was convinced by certain shadowy sources that Foster, along with the First Lady, had been under CIA surveillance for selling U.S. nuclear secrets to Israel in exchange for millions of dollars he hid in a Swiss bank. After *Forbes* refused to run Norman's "Fostergate" article, it ran instead in the right-wing *Media Bypass.*

In a storyline that takes the PROMIS software connection to a credibility-straining extreme, Norman alleges that a rogue group of CIA hackers obtained the incriminating evidence of espionage and managed to remove Foster's millions of dollars, all through electronic snooping made possible by the secret back-door feature added to PROMIS software before it was sold and installed in banks worldwide.

To accept this scenario, one must believe that Foster, the top scorer on the Arkansas Bar Exam, stupidly got caught by the banking-transaction spying feature built into the software, and also believe, contrary to a lifetime of evidence, that he—as well as the First Lady—would be spectacularly reckless, disloyal, and criminal. We are further meant to accept that the Israelis—reportedly partners with the United States in the dissemination of the bugged system—would leave information on the identities and activities of their spies on computers that are vulnerable to invasion via the secret electronic window. Not only Foster, but hundreds of well-known leaders, both Democratic and Republican, are said to have had their accounts electronically emptied and the billions placed in a secret Treasury escrow account, according to this story.

Yet the fabricated tale gets even more far-fetched. Once Foster's and Hillary Clinton's alleged spying roles were found out, Norman tells us, Foster was killed by his spy-masters to ensure his silence. "There was apparently a three-person Mossad-contracted team that went into the apartment that Foster had gone to that afternoon where he was apparently lured by a female person from the White House staff who I think still works in the White House," Norman told a radio audience.

Why they came up with a story that blames Jews is a mystery; perhaps it was simply a lack of originality in their choice of scapegoat. There are grains of truth in all this disinformation, making it appear credible to some people. Foster took several mysterious one-day trips to Switzerland, starting before Clinton took office as president, according to research into travel records by Ambrose Evans-Pritchard. And there was allegedly an element of espionage involved in Foster's work with the dissemination of PROMIS to intelligence agencies and banks overseas, involving coordination between Systematics and the top-secret National Security Agency. There may even be a secret rogue group of CIA computer hackers called "the Fifth Column," as Norman claims. But in examining a story that has Foster and the First Lady selling nuclear secrets, and a female White House employee luring Foster to his death on behalf of the Mossad, the question naturally arises as to why the sources of this disinformation campaign did not come up with a story of greater subtlety and believability.

An insightful observation by James Dale Davidson of *Strategic Investment Newsletter* may point to the answer. Imagining himself in the shoes of the spreaders of disinformation, he notes, "It might even be worth hiring some goofballs to spread preposterous theories about nonexistent conspiracies in order to discredit persons who might stumble upon evidence of the real thing." Thus, even the most responsible researchers get tarred with the same dreaded epithet—"conspiracy theorist"—as the disseminators of the Vince-and-Hillary atomic spy tale.

Further Alleged Connections

In this convoluted story that takes us from Arkansas to Washington and overseas, does former President Clinton appear anywhere in the picture?

"Bill Clinton had nothing to do with this," Janet Cyford noted emphatically during her reading, although I had not asked about or suggested involvement by Clinton, and she was not the only psychic to stress that point without the subject even being raised. Understandably, the mere choice of this subject raises suspicions about one's motivations.

Bob Cracknell, however, maintained that we should be examining the early part of the Clinton Administration, observing that "the whole period of that administration will come under intense public scrutiny. I will not commit myself to a definite time frame. But as they say, 'hold the front page.' I feel quite sure that the media will continue to investigate this whole period."

Cracknell's psychic vision of this case, however, does not go into the same degree of detail as his insights into many other cases in this book. If there is indeed a Clinton Administration connection, what scandal might it have involved? Christopher Ruddy, proud of his label as that administration's number-one media enemy, notes in *The Strange Death of Vincent Foster* that "Foster was involved in the Clinton administration's most controversial actions, such as the failed nominations of Zoe Baird and Kimba Wood for attorney general, the Waco standoff, the health care proposal, and the travel office affair. At the same time, Foster was also serving as the personal attorney for Bill and Hillary Rodham Clinton ..."

Yet no one has yet supplied compelling evidence as to how or why any of these issues—almost all of them minor—could have resulted in the suicide or murder of Foster. Years of investigation of Whitewater, Travelgate, and Foster's death by independent counsels and anti-Clinton journalists turned up no convincing connection of a Clinton scandal to Foster's murder. Foster served only briefly, for exactly one-sixteenth of the administration, dying six months to the day after Inauguration Day. In those early days, the only major scandal of which we have knowledge was the government's handling of the Waco siege, and no one has even begun to demonstrate how that tragedy or any other Clinton controversy might connect to the sudden death of Foster three months later.

Combining the available evidence with the insights of the psychic detectives, it appears that the most likely way Clinton might fit into the picture, if at all, is as an asset controlled by the behind-the-scenes big-money interests—international powers greater than the president. Is it possible that Foster's potential testimony threatened to set in motion a domino effect that might have caused a number of connected scandals to come to light? The possible repercussions might easily have cut across party lines, as political figures closely tied to international power brokers such as BCCI have included the Clintons, the Bushes, and countless members of Congress—leaders possessing considerable power, yet arguably less power than the mega-corporations and banking conglomerates pulling their strings. Therefore, if Foster's death prevented a far-reaching bipartisan array of shady BCCI-related dealings from coming to light, then it conceivably might have benefited Clinton along with many others. But this is a far cry from suggesting that the president would have caused or desired the violent death of his longtime friend.

The picture that takes shape appears to provide the clearest answers to the questions posed by the harshest and most persistent of the Clintons' critics, such as Barbara Olson. In Olson's *The Final Days*, which reached the top of the best-seller list shortly after she perished in the hijacked plane that struck the Pentagon on September 11, 2001, she listed crucial questions that she believed Hillary Clinton ought to answer about Foster in order to truly earn the $8 million advance she received for her autobiography. "Those who had previously occupied Foster's position did not have access to National Security Agency files," Olson pointed out. "What was Vincent Foster doing with NSA material?" One answer is that, according to many reports, the software-related business Foster was still working on for Stephens, Inc. involved dealings with the top-secret intelligence agency.

Why did members of Hillary's staff "hold the Justice Department investigators at bay?" Olson inquired, asking Hillary to "please explain why they didn't want a Justice Department investigation, and to whom they were reporting." The answer can most likely be found in the record of Justice Department malfeasance described earlier in this chapter, behind-the-scenes manipulation that allegedly threatened the Clinton Administration, corruption reported to be more far-reaching and deadly than that found in the Whitewater land deal or Travel Office firings. There were compelling reasons not to trust the Justice Department to investigate Foster's death. At the same time, of course, it would not be terribly surprising if Foster's professional and personal papers contained information that in some instances reflected poorly on the Clintons, but rushing in to remove such documents hardly makes Hillary's staff murderers or accomplices to murder.

Betty Muench's reading touched on the question of whether the president and former First Lady know or suspect anything about Vincent's death. "*There is within the president and the First Lady ... this which will know that this man's death was unnecessary. They do not have hidden agendas insofar as this man is involved. There will be this which is in them now anger and that they will have vowed to make this right in due time. There will be information which will seem to cause guilt in certain people over the driving of this man to his demise. There will be in them this anger ... no fear for their own safety but simply anger ...*"

The reading continues with an unusual passage, apparently looking down the road to the afterlife: "*... and there will be this which will allow them then to reconnect with Vincent when there will come the possibility ... when he will be able to open up again and impress on them. He will be able to make impression on them both and there will be this which will permit then that there will be a simple explanation of the seemingly hidden actions of Vincent insofar as protecting the presidency. There is a simple explanation which will have been drawn all out of proportion and he will in that then be a victim of this system.*"

Moment of Death

Foster's last known words were spoken to White House employee Linda Tripp; after finishing lunch, around 1 P.M., he told her there were some leftover M&Ms in his office, said "I'll be back," and then departed. At approximately 6 P.M. his body was found in the park. What happened during the missing five hours? Psychic detective Nancy Myer described what she saw when she tuned in to this case:

> The last live thought patterns I can detect from Mr. Foster occur in a business office that appears to be underground. "The office is cluttered, but not in a messy way. There are a lot of piles of papers on the desk he is standing near.
>
> He's in a business shirt and tie. The tie is loosened slightly. He's angry, arguing with an older man who intimidates him.
>
> Mr. Foster is being asked to do something that he considers illegal. He is not going to do it.
>
> The man points out that he has done illegal things before.
>
> This time Foster has had enough. He threatens to resign and expose the whole bunch of them. He insists he will not cooperate and that is that.
>
> The older man warns him that he is messing with the wrong people. Asks one more time.
>
> Foster insists he's done with the whole mess. Leaving the White House for good.
>
> The older man leaves Foster alone in the room.
>
> Foster paces, he's frightened and unsure what to do. He is considering contacting the FBI ... He hurries out of the room and down the hall. He enters an office where the older man is with three young men who look like security people.
>
> A heated argument ensues ending with Mr. Foster nearly hysterical, making wild accusations, and refusing to cooperate. He has been pushed too far.
>
> Foster, still yelling at the old man, is escorted out of the office by the security types. He has completely lost it. A struggle starts; they're trying to subdue him. They back him into a small room.
>
> As the altercation becomes more violent, one man draws a firearm. Unfortunately it goes off accidentally.
>
> Mr. Foster is mortally wounded.
>
> A cleanup and cover-up follow this terrible accident.
>
> In my personal opinion, Vince Foster's death is

accidental ... It is definitely not suicide, nor is it part of some vast conspiracy.

The bizarre uniqueness of this chilling scenario, movie-like in its level of detail, gives it a peculiar ring of truth. After years of argument over suicide versus murder, here we're told it was an accident! But considering the level of force being used against Foster, the killing described here arguably fits the description of homicide of a lesser degree, perhaps involuntary manslaughter. The pressure on Foster, including this alleged direct physical intimidation at gunpoint, seems to have foreshadowed his eventual destruction one way or another.

"I was surprised by what I found," Myer later noted.

Myer's picture of Foster under pressure, one individual against a nameless, faceless power entity, matches that of all the other psychics and mediums.

Summing up this case from Foster's own point of view, in a passage that echoes Robert Cracknell's vision of Foster possibly in "a situation which was far too deep to escape from with his own integrity intact," Betty Muench's reading points to *"this giant involvement by Foster"* in a complex, far-reaching, and ultimately corrupt web of business dealings, *"and that there will be this which Foster now can look back upon and ask himself why he would even seek to control or work with such great and large energy. There will be this which will suggest that he could not have been in control and that he was heavily influenced by others. There will be this then which makes him simply a 'pawn.' Now he will see that he had no real influence in any of it and he was indeed no more than a messenger in all this."*

"There will be this then which he can forgive himself for and he will know that he would have [been] asked more questions had he continued to live. He would have been also [been] asked many questions which he could indeed not answer. There will be this then which will say that out of all these involvements there could have stepped out anyone from any part of the entire spectrum and caused this death of Foster."

This last sentence suggests that the killing, far from being skillfully orchestrated from above, was more likely an unpredictable and unplanned result of pressure exerted on Foster by thuggish elements further down the chain of command. The two psychic readings that go as far as to describe the shooting both depict enforcers who did not intend to use lethal force on that day. We find confusion, surprises, stupidity, and impromptu scrambling to cover up, rather than an ingenious, intricate conspiracy. It's not like in the movies.

Summing up the tragedy, Muench's spirit guides point out that in this complex tangle of corruption, *"there will have been only two real connecting forces and that this will have had to do with the Justice Department and with the software involvement. There will be in all this then the knowing that Foster will have been allowed to think that he was in control and given much rope. When he will have come to this realization that he was being manipulated then there will have been this which he will have expressed as a desire to get out of it all. However this did not mean that he would take his own death as the measure of escape."*

Personal Blackmail?

And the reading proceeded to add a shocking twist to the story: *"He will have been threatened with certain 'other' exposure which he did not want revealed; something personal, and that will be information which will have been held over his head unless he would cooperate with certain groups who will have wanted to get answers in any way they could ... he will have tried to answer to them but they would not allow him to complete and end this. There will be this which he did know about ... certain things occurring in the White House and yet he will not have felt that this was important enough to sacrifice himself. There will have been other demands on him to acknowledge other things which he did not believe to be true but still the oppression continues. The fear of exposure of something personal would have been more important to him. He will have been soft as a person and this was weighted when all this pressure on him began. The oppressors will have used all manner of psychological dealings, accusations which he did not believe true and could not be a part of digging this out."*

Bob Cracknell's psychic reading similarly pointed to vulnerability on a personal matter. The Muench reading also noted that *"he did not want to be seen as a betrayer,"* and *"was not one of the ability to play these deadly games."* In this respect, the gentlemanly Foster seems to have differed sharply from President Clinton, if one recalls how the sex scandals of Clinton's enemies seemed to become public with perfect timing when Clinton's own personal life was under investigation.

The phrase *"did not want to be seen as a betrayer"* is significant, signaling that perhaps the personal matter involved another person's scandal, and that he himself would feel responsible if the secret were to come out. *"He did manage to call a halt to speculations which will have gone off in all the wrong directions. He was protecting his employers but not for any reasons that are known today,"* the reading added.

Yet while the personal issue allegedly being used as leverage by his tormentors was of concern to him, it is said to be only a minor piece of the total picture. *"Compared to the magnitude of the involvement with all the hidden and covert activity he was involved in, he did not fear the personal matter as much as others thought. He was trying to protect someone but that this someone did not realize the pressure that was being put on Foster. He was loyal and he did not convey the degree of pressure on him. He tried to hold it to himself and this was too much for one person. Those in the Justice Department had only speculation which they could not prove and used this covert way to try to break out some confirmation from Foster."*

After this reading, Muench observed, "This was so complicated that he could not control it, and when he realized he never was supposed to be in control he gave up. Foster was a good man with integrity, and dealing with all these others must have been an eye opener as to what government was all about. With so many forces at work it is not unreasonable to think that somewhere there will be a miscommunication that would take an action such as murdering Foster … He was loyal and I think especially to Hillary and he may have wanted to protect her from certain knowledge he had acquired."

Foster had been a loyal friend to and admirer of Hillary, going all the way back to her creation of Arkansas' first legal aid clinic. As he watched her describe the ambitious plans for the incoming Clinton Administration, he was visibly moved. "Foster was tremendously idealistic about the move to Washington," recalled Alan Leveritt of the *Arkansas Times*. "When Hillary made her farewell speech to the Rose law firm and told how they were to make a better life for America, Vincent was the only one in the room crying ..."

A principled idealist and gentleman, unaware of the extent of evil in Washington, moved to tears by the thought of making a difference. It almost seemed destined to end in tears, too.

The Big Picture

Assembling the pieces of the puzzle provided by psychic detectives and mediums, a picture takes shape that does not match the two main schools of thought on the Foster mystery. Fiske, Starr, the Washington establishment, and the big media declared the official depression-suicide conclusion to be the final word. The main challengers of this view cite numerous flaws in the investigations and point to evidence of a heavy-handed government cover-up including intimidation of witnesses, while never actually breaking through the high-level obfuscation to establish what happened; they make a compelling forensic case that Foster was murdered, but do not establish who did it and why.

An intriguing third possibility takes shape when we combine this chapter's psychic-detective readings with the known facts. It takes us back to Arkansas and the Rose law firm and Foster's work for Systematics, a front corporation for the dissemination of the US Justice Department's illegally obtained software system to banks and intelligence agencies overseas, including those of Middle East nations. The trail appears to go beyond Little Rock, beyond Washington, with connections to the corrupt bank BCCI, earlier administrations, other scandals, international intrigue, and a number of additional deaths.

When he brought this leftover Rose law firm business to

Washington during the Clinton Administration's early days, perhaps his new position at the heart of national power made him the object of even greater pressures. Longtime friend and colleague Webb Hubbell recalls Foster saying of his newly acquired White House pass, "This is gold, Hubb." But it might have proven to be double-edged gold, so to speak. It appears that Foster might have been called to share information that others wanted to suppress, or that he himself wanted to keep confidential—or perhaps a combination of the two. Under sudden pressure from "faceless" influences, he might not have fully understood who was coercing him or why; apparently little has changed since Francis Bacon spoke of perceiving "all governments as obscure and invisible."

If the combined insights of the psychic detectives are on the right track, then so are the accounts offered by two prominent journalists—one liberal, one conservative—who independently offered a similar scenario, only to be regarded as pariahs for not following the conventional wisdom.

White House reporter Sarah McClendon saw Foster's death as part of a far-reaching story that encompasses previous administrations, BCCI, and the Inslaw scandal, recalling that "Hillary and Foster were assigned by the Rose law firm to be the lawyers for Systematics ... And when they came to the White House, Foster was doing political work for Hillary and Clinton. But he was also still working on this Systematics."

Echoing the Muench reading's point about Foster ultimately discovering he was being used as a pawn, McClendon said, "I think that Foster was a tool and he was used. And Foster had found out some very bad things that are goin' on in the government." She also insisted, during the Clinton Administration, that the full story went back four administrations, to when BCCI was brought into the United States by President Jimmy Carter's Naval Academy classmate Jackson Stephens. In an ironic footnote, young attorneys Foster and Hillary Clinton reportedly performed legal paperwork that helped the giant bank penetrate the U.S. market in those early days.

Interviewed on Diane Rehm's National Public Radio show,

McClendon shocked her host, declaring, "I'm quite positive Foster was murdered." She claimed to have received her information from a source within the government.

Rehm later noted, "I was so taken aback that all I could do was gasp, 'That's really quite a charge, Sarah.' In retrospect, I should have asked whether she had proof to back up her accusations, rather than let the statement go unchallenged."

McClendon was not alone in following the shadow-government trail. John Crudele, columnist for the *New York Post*, also posed the question of whether Foster's death might be connected to his involvement in the long, deadly saga that began with the Justice Department's theft of Inslaw's PROMIS software, with Inslaw's July 1993 submission of its rebuttal to the Bua report as the triggering event. In *A Washington Tragedy: How the Death of Vincent Foster Ignited a Political Firestorm*, author Dan Moldea derides Crudele's analysis as one of the "wild conspiracy theories on the internet and the tabloid press," inexplicably condemning it as worse than author Michael Kellett's baseless accusation that Bill and Hillary Clinton killed Foster. The harsh attacks endured by McClendon and Crudele seem to be the inevitable price journalists pay for not following the herd, but the public, by an overwhelming majority, continues to share their deep skepticism about the official conclusion. This mystery will not be laid to rest anytime soon.

And yet, while we explore and debate this personal and national tragedy, the spirit of Vincent Foster is said to be paying attention to other things. Medium Janet Cyford found him focused on his family, especially on recent milestones in the lives of his children. She said he wishes he could be with them in earthly form, but even though he cannot, he is very much with them in spirit. And his main message for those who care about him, Cyford noted, is "just that he's not really gone."

Chapter 2:
The Ron Brown Mystery—
An Unreported Assassination?

"Brown had a .45-inch inwardly beveling circular hole in the top of his head, which is essentially the description of a .45-caliber gunshot wound."—Lt. Col. Steve Cogswell, a deputy medical examiner, Armed Forces Institute of Pathology

"I opened my big mouth in the morgue and said, 'Wow, look at the big hole in Ron Brown's head; it looks like a bullet hole.' I said that, and my life has never been the same."—Chief Petty Officer Kathleen Janoski, Chief of Forensic Photography, Armed Forces Institute of Pathology

In the spring of 1996, Secretary of Commerce Ron Brown approached his upcoming trade mission to Croatia with uncharacteristic apprehension.

"I think Dad had a premonition about his trip to Croatia," his daughter Tracy L. Brown wrote in her 1998 account *The Life and Times of Ron Brown*, recalling that "some of his behavior at home before he left, and also in Paris before he flew to Croatia, was out of character."

Though his wife was bedridden with the flu, too sick even to eat or drink, he urged her to go with him to the bank to refinance the house, Tracy Brown tells us. "Let's wait until you get back," Mrs. Brown pleaded. "No, we're going to do it. We really need to do it," he insisted, until she relented and went with him to the bank.

39

Ron Brown's daughter also wonders why her non-religious father went out of his way to find a chapel in Paris to pick up religious medals for his family: "After the plane crash, we found the medals as well as the text of a prayer inside Dad's briefing book."

A year before Tracy Brown revealed these details to the world, a reading by medium Betty Muench had said essentially the same thing, describing the Commerce Secretary's inner concerns: *There is within this, and not on the surface, a factor which will have been known to Ron, and he will have been someone who feared that this would be his fate. He will have been afraid of this kind of demise ... there will be this which did not want to go on this journey, and especially at this time in Bosnia, and at this time of year. There will have been this in Ron which has a sense of fear of this trip. He will have tried to change this but that it was seemingly required of him. This was not his idea and yet it will seem to be on record as such. Having a sense of danger, not just from a possible air crash, but from other repercussions at what was happening at home, will have made Ron very skittish. This was a trip which was not necessary but that it was made to seem so and in that then he was set up.*"

"A Fluke of Luck"

Did some powerful entity that was out to silence Ron Brown cause his plane to go down? Was there sabotage of the Air Force Boeing 737 carrying Brown and 34 others that crashed into a mountainside in Croatia? Did a false beacon guide the plane off-course, as some observers have alleged? Or might the crash have been nothing more than a horrible accident?

The first psychic to do a reading on this case said the plane crash was purely an accident, which Brown survived, and that hired killers who were tracking Brown seized this opportunity to finish him off—a scenario that came as something of a surprise. Yet the second psychic to analyze this case independently came up with the same basic answer, and remarkably, a third and fourth psychic did the same.

"My belief is that it had been arranged by certain people ... that he was not to come back from Bosnia," Bertie Catchings emphasized. "And the plane crash, I believe, was just a fluke of luck."

"I think there were several plans made for the murder of these people," she noted. Her use of the plural brings to mind other possible targets, such as the Commerce Department's Assistant Secretary Charles Meissner, who may have been silenced for the same reasons Brown was eliminated, which we will explore shortly. Other logical targets would include any crash survivors who possibly witnessed Brown's assassination, such as Sgt. Shelly Kelly, a flight steward who reportedly survived the crash with only minor injuries yet died before getting to the hospital.

"[They] had people on the ground that actually had been assigned to murder Ron Brown and also to murder Sgt. Shelly Kelly," Catchings continued. "When the assassins—there were three assassins—came upon this deal, they found that Ron Brown was still alive, and he was shot, because that's what they were paid to do ... And they had some fatigue camouflage clothing on and had planned to have it passed off as though they were some of the enemy soldiers fighting, in the crossfire, that had done it; blame it on one side or the other [in the Yugoslavian civil war]."

"But they wanted Ron Brown dead because he had been offered a deal to be involved in some corruption in which they wanted him to make a deal ... with some foreign sources. I'm not sure which particular countries were supposed to benefit from the deal that was to be cut. But my feelings are it was more than one country and more than one deal and that foreign sources had offered a large amount of money for certain favors, to get the U.S. Commerce Department to do things the way they wanted it done, to benefit these various countries."

Catchings then drew a chilling connection between governments and terrorism, noting as part of her reading that foreign governments use hired killers to silence potential whistleblowers or witnesses; in the process, they hide behind the terrorists in their employ, who would take the blame should they get caught. When these kinds of atrocities are in the news, sometimes it is terrorists acting on their own, "but sometimes the political people inside these countries are actually paying for the terrorists to make things happen so they will prosper from deals, and that certain people who are not cooperating with this profit or corruption will be eliminated." Brown survived the plane crash, Catchings said, so he was shot at the accident scene by hired assassins who capitalized on the opportunity.

Betty Muench's spirit guides found that *"There is a sense of anger and rage and that there will be this which is like a half-kick or half-stomp at the ground with his right foot. There will be this which will show Ron Brown in a state of mind in which he is trying to control himself … to control his rage; and that he will be someone who will be most angry over the speculations about him and his death. There will be this which he will not have wanted and that is to leave so many loose ends in his life. He wanted order … There will be in this then for him this which is the knowing that he must change his rage into something else in order that he too will be able to understand and accept the circumstances of his life and his death. There will be in this then the knowing in him that there will have been many, many situations which will have been the source of some embarrassment to himself and then also to his workplace, the administration. There will have been this which will have been demonstrated as a close relationship between himself and the president, but that no such friendship was real. There will have been this in Ron which was like a loose cannon and that then this is the way in which such problems are resolved by this administration."*

What is this last sentence really saying? I pursued it further in a follow-up question, which will be explored later.

Brown *"will have been afraid of this kind of demise,"* the original channeling pointed out. Brown's spirit is found to be angry not only because of the circumstances of his death but also because of leaving so many loose ends. *"There will be in this then the idea that he is disturbed at this time and does not seek other avenues just yet and appreciates the opportunity to vent some of his anger."*

This reading eerily echoes Bertie Catchings' assertion that Brown's death was caused not by the crash but by assassins who swooped in afterwards like vultures for the kill: *"As this turns out there will have been the danger but that the accident itself was not the danger. There will have been those on the periphery of his life who always seemed to wait for him to be in a position that he could be dismissed in some way. He was aware of this and yet he did not change his own way of doing things. Those who waited are like predators and they will have pounced on this accident. They will have used this then to finish other work that they wanted done. The accident which was indeed an act of stupidity on the part of the people in charge of the flight … it was something that seemingly fell into the hands of his enemies. There is in this then the cause for his anger."*

Robert Cracknell also perceived an accident, noting, "I do not believe that the plane was sabotaged but that it should not have taken off due to adverse weather conditions …" In researching this case, one finds in most reports that visibility was poor. Cracknell saw a covert influence in the sending of "agents, not necessarily of American nationality," to recover documentation in Brown's possession. "I have a definite vision of a briefcase containing computer CDs. This briefcase would have been carried by Ron Brown."

After sharing this psychic vision, Cracknell asked, "Was Brown, after the plane crashed, alive and did he attempt to hang on to this briefcase but was subsequently shot in the head, to make him release it?" But this, as Cracknell makes clear, is a hypothesis posed by his logical mind examining his psychic vision of the computer CDs in light of the known facts.

"Brown's death was an extremely fortuitous event and prevented a great deal of embarrassment, should he have cut a deal with prosecutors," Cracknell pointed out, describing the Commerce Secretary's controversies during the Clinton Administration.

Cracknell's first psychic impression was of intrigue that involved powerful influences attempting to pressure Brown regarding his personal life, just as was possibly done in the Foster case. "Two things emerge here, very strongly," he observed. "One is blackmail, but more important—an overall impression of drug involvement. Not that Brown was necessarily a willing partner in any form of drug running. I have an impression of a man who enjoyed the liberties and 'jollies' that one might receive whilst on official business, and he took advantage of the freebies, which were readily available. Forgive me here, but I feel he was a bit of a libertine and found himself caught up in some kind of compromising situation …"

After reviewing photographs of the crash scene, Nancy Myer shared a psychic vision similar to that of Catchings, Cracknell, and Muench. She perceived an accident, not sabotage of the flight, yet also saw more to the story:

> I get the impression of a serious mechanical problem combined with a navigational error on the part of the air traffic controller. The pilots, unfamiliar with the area, did not realize the controller had made a mistake until it was too late.
>
> By that time they were grappling with an engine that was cutting on and off. The combination was lethal.
>
> As the plane was descending they were fired on by ground troops who thought the plane was attacking their position. It is quite possible that this ground fire may have hit Brown.
>
> He was unconscious as the plane crashed, dead on impact. He did not suffer for any length of time. He knew he was going to die, and had time to make peace with that and God. His last thoughts were of the sorrow he was causing his family.

It is intriguing to note how psychic detectives, like the rest of us, can witness the same event, yet interpret it differently. Remarkably, Myer and Catchings tuned in to this tragic scene and saw a very similar vision—(1) an accident rather than sabotage, and (2) gunfire from ground troops—or what appear to be ground troops—causing the apparent bullet wound found in Brown's head. Yet Myer described the shooters as combatants in the Yugoslavian civil war, while Catchings described them as hired terrorists disguised as troops to blend into the environment and mislead any witnesses.

According to Janet Cyford's spirit guides, it was still too soon to explore this story in the kind of detail that direct communication through a medium can bring forth. Yet sometimes a non-answer can speak volumes, in this case leaving one wondering what horrible event, apart from the crash itself, might have happened on that plane.

The Flight Attendant

If Brown indeed survived the crash, the odds are high that there were other survivors among the 35 passengers. Judicial Watch, a legal advocacy organization that challenged the Clinton Administration (and later the Bush Administration) on numerous fronts, claimed to have obtained confidential Commerce Department documents in 1999 revealing that at least two of the plane's passengers survived. Shortly after the tragedy, reports circulated that Sgt. Shelly Kelly, the Air Force steward mentioned earlier, survived the crash with minor injuries, yet died en route to a Dubrovnik hospital several hours later.

We find a difference of opinion regarding Kelly's death, with Robert Cracknell stating, "My impression is that she died as a result of the crash and that there were no mysterious circumstances surrounding it." According to Bertie Catchings, however, Sgt. Kelly "was witness to [the shooting of Brown] … this particular young lady was alive and so the way that she was killed—of course if a person had done an examination of her body, he would have known—but my feelings are that her neck was broken and she had several other injuries to her back … it seems like something like a pipe was used, but also hands were used to kill Sgt. Kelly."

The possibility that "hands were used" to murder a helpless plane-crash survivor is horrible to contemplate and a rare, virtually unheard-of occurrence. Yet this description of Kelly's death matches what came through in Betty Muench's channeled reading. When the plane crashed, "*she will have been seemingly thrust forward with her face pushed into something. She will have had head injuries which were not attended to and that she will have been treated as if she had no injuries. There will have been this which was conscious within her and that she will have been untreated for so long will have made her fear for her life. There will have been this conscious fear in her but that this is now subsided into deep thought, inner thought, on how this could have occurred.*"

"*She will know that there will have been others who will have been aboard who will have been alive after the crash. She and they will have marveled that anyone could have survived on the site. There will have been a male dressed in an unusual uniform who will have been injured and he too will have been ignored. There will be this which did not in her opinion have to do with any incompetence on the part of the medical people.*"

"*There is this which will seem to come down over her face and it is being presented to her as oxygen. She resists at first but then begins to float out of her own being. Something over the face as if for an emergency with her. Her own condition was used to dispose of her ... smothered.*" It is saddening and infuriating to contemplate that the deaths of Kelly, Brown, and other passengers might have been terrorist murders that might go unrecorded in history.

This reading also hints at intrigue in two possible areas: (1) "*there is this which suggests to her that much of this trip was monitored as if by unseen forces. Opportunities were seized ...*" and (2) her personal eyewitness knowledge of the plane's sudden final movements, described below, may have caused culpable aviation personnel to feel threatened by her potential testimony pointing to criminal negligence. While eliminating plane-crash survivors for this reason sounds excessive, it would match what the reading calls "*overkill for the condition.*" It is one more possibility, although eliminating survivors because they witnessed one or more assassinations seems more likely here.

Though Sgt. Kelly is now safe in the spirit world, the plane's final sharp turn was deeply engraved in her consciousness, as we see at the beginning of Muench's reading: "*There is an image which will be seen as something which will be on a dial and it will move back and forth and that it will have been from the pivot point and then straight downward and then suddenly it is moved to the right. There will be this which will seem to be lighted from behind and it is like a radar of sorts; in which there is this dial which moves. There will be this which is something in the eye of Shelly [something she saw in her mind] — there is this which she will know now was moved at the very last minute and that there will have been this which will*

46

not have been on the plane itself. There will be this which comes from the ground control. There will be this which will have been suddenly moved as if on a command. There will be this which will suggest then that there will be this which affected the flight of this airplane."

"While Shelly is not versed in all the aspects of ground control, she will have seen within this sudden movement and she will have known that this was something that was wrong. There will be this then which will have occurred before the plane crashed."

The conclusion of this reading seems to raise more questions than it answers: "There will be this which was found and that it would reveal this change in the charting. There will be this which will show this dial, this radar or this instrument was changed. Suddenly, much in all this seemed to Shelly to happen suddenly ... opportunities were seized and there will be in that then much intrigue; and in this instance there would be seen then this which is overkill for the condition. Too many have been taken out because of the lack of control in certain levels of government."

To my question on the conflicting reports of whether a black box was found, the reading noted, "the so-called black box will hold this change of pattern and when this instrument will have indicated that this should be so. The record of maneuvers exists and will show that the sudden turn was for no real reason."

Gunshot Wound Allegations

It is intriguing to note that it was June 1997 when Betty Muench channeled the message "that the accident itself was not the danger ... those who waited are like predators and they will have pounced on this accident," for five months later the world would first learn of the apparent bullet hole in the Commerce Secretary's head. And we are still waiting in vain for an answer to the simple, logical question posed by Robert Cracknell: "Surely, in an attempt to try to solve the mystery, the body could still be exhumed and an autopsy carried out. Why is this not being done?"

A story broken by the *Pittsburgh Tribune-Review's* Christopher Ruddy, who had earlier covered Vincent Foster's death for the same newspaper, revealed that Air Force Lt. Col. Steve Cogswell, a deputy medical examiner at the Armed Forces Institute of Pathology (AFIP), "believes the head wound could have been caused by a bullet from a .45-caliber gun."

Although Cogswell did not personally examine Brown's body, Ruddy noted, "he believed the wound was suspicious based on photographs and X-rays of the remains and conversations with those who examined the corpse."

Chief Petty Officer Kathleen Janoski, chief of forensic photography at the AFIP, came forward a month later, in January 1998, to back up Cogswell. Both have been punished for their honesty.

"I opened my big mouth in the morgue and said, 'Wow, look at the big hole in Ron Brown's head; it looks like a bullet hole,'" Janoski recalled. "I said that, and my life has never been the same."

In one of the few television news investigations of this explosive turn of events, the Christian Broadcasting Network's Dale Hurd reported that after Lt. Col. Cogswell spoke out about the need for an autopsy, he "was transferred to dental forensics at another site: in effect, a demotion. Had he ever had a problem like this before?"

"'Oh, no,' he says. 'I was the golden boy. The evaluations previously said, 'He's the man we'd pick for the toughest missions.' I was the team leader of choice to investigate any sort of airplane crash or death, no matter how complicated, and no matter how politically sensitive."

Similarly, Hurd noted, CPO Janoski "was given 32 hours to clear out her office, had her staff taken away from her, and is now an assistant to an audio-visual manager at another location." And, after receiving threats, she began taking precautions concerning her own safety.

"Cogswell's career has been ruined and his record tarnished. His performance evaluations before the Ron Brown cover-up described him as 'extremely capable' and 'the number one forensic pathologist in the Department of Defense.' His latest evaluation describes him as 'disruptive,' 'immature,' with behavior that results in 'conflicts with superiors,' and says he needs 'counseling.'"

That last word is perhaps the most ominous. The CBN report

quotes Tom Devine of the whistleblower-protecting Government Accountability Project: "Numerous whistleblowers have ended up in psychiatric institutions without any due process or even the right to find out what was the matter with them. The tactics are very, very ugly."

In spite of the retribution suffered by Cogswell and Janoski, two more officials—Lt. Col. David Hause and Air Force Major Thomas Parsons—also came forward to assert that Brown appeared to have a gunshot wound and that an autopsy should be done.

Janoski described the retaliation she and her three colleagues suffered for their candor: "We were all supposed to go to the American Academy of Forensic Sciences meeting in February. We had our tickets, we had our reservations, we'd paid our registration fees. And right before we were supposed to leave, the director of AFIP canceled our orders immediately. Also, Dr. Cogswell was forbidden to lecture, forbidden to go on trips. Cogswell, Hause, and Parsons were no longer permitted to do any autopsies."

How far does this troubling cover-up extend? According to attorney Larry Klayman of Judicial Watch, "We know that Colonel William Gormley [the AFIP pathologist who examined Brown's body] himself admitted on Black Entertainment Television that it was the White House, Joint Chiefs of Staff, Commerce, and Transportation Departments which called the AFIP off from conducting an autopsy."

After Ruddy first reported on the discovery of the apparent bullet hole, the story received a brief flurry of attention in the broader media, including the Associated Press and some television news programs. Yet, for the most part, the media seemed to look the other way when the story broke.

It was this indifference by the big media that made it easy for White House Press Secretary Mike McCurry to cavalierly dismiss the compelling evidence of homicide in a Cabinet secretary's death. At a December 17 press briefing, McCurry was asked, "Does the administration give any credence to these allegations that Ron Brown might have been shot?"

McCurry replied, "Absolutely none. Any credence is only given to those reports by entities associated with Richard Mellon Scaife [publisher of the *Pittsburgh Tribune-Review*], and we are right back into another one of these chasing a story that's been ginned up by people who no doubt, for whatever reason, hate the President of the United States."

Yet many of the people actively calling attention to the story did not "hate the President of the United States." Representative Maxine Waters (D-CA), the head of the Congressional Black Caucus at the time, asked the president to look into the new evidence. Leading forensic pathologist Dr. Cyril Wecht, a longtime Democrat, emphasized that there was "more than enough" evidence pointing to homicide. Clinton supporter Kweisi Mfume, president of the National Association for the Advancement of Colored People (NAACP), wrote a letter expressing his concerns to the president and wrote to Attorney-General Janet Reno, maintaining that "these allegations require an explanation."

Wilbur Tatum, publisher of a prominent African-American newspaper, *The Amsterdam News*, angrily complained, "All we want is the kind of investigation that the president would allow if his dog were run over under mysterious circumstances. Why should we ask less for Ron Brown that we would ask for a dog?" And CPO Kathleen Janoski, the AFIP's chief of forensic photography who endured threats and intimidation for speaking honestly about the hole she saw in Brown's skull, is a lifelong Democrat who worked for George McGovern in the 1972 presidential campaign and served as a volunteer for the Clinton White House for two years, answering the president's mail.

What is the reason for wanting to suppress information about the condition of Ron Brown's body? Perhaps it is nothing worse than a high-level attempt to avoid the embarrassing revelation of careless forensic practices as well as the failure to protect this high-ranking official in the first place. Perhaps it is an effort simply to avoid the burdensome complications of having to investigate a possible assassination.

Yet this obsession with secrecy creates the unfortunate appearance of something more ominous in the highest levels of government. As CPO Janoski pointed out, "When Brown's plane first crashed, I just figured it was just another one of those typical plane crashes that we're always called out to investigate. But the military is so intent on bullying and intimidating us into silence, that I'm starting to wonder if maybe there's more sinister motives at work." Joe Madison, a popular Washington radio-show host and NAACP board member who was pushing for an autopsy and exhumation at that time, expressed the same baffled exasperation with the administration's obstructive behavior. "I am just so disappointed in the response of the White House," he complained. "First of all, I don't know why they are being so defensive. No one has accused the president of any wrongdoing."

The Question of Motive

Why would powerful people want to eliminate Brown in the first place? One motive that has been suggested was the fear in certain quarters that Brown might cut a deal in upcoming investigations and incriminate others. As noted by Sam Smith in *The Progressive Review*, "At the time of his death, Brown was the target of a criminal investigation and there have been reports that not long before the plane crash Brown indicated that he might cooperate with prosecutors, warning that if he were going to take a fall he was not going to go alone."

The Commerce Secretary was being investigated on several fronts. Independent counsel Daniel Pearson was looking into allegations of personal financial violations as well as dealings involving the relationship of the Commerce Department and the Democratic National Committee (DNC) with the fund-raising activities of the Asian Pacific Advisory Council (APAC). Subpoenas were issued to Brown and numerous others a mere two weeks before his sudden death. Meanwhile, Larry Klayman's Judicial Watch conducted a parallel investigation, questioning the role of APAC's John Huang (whose involvement we will explore later).

In a profile on Klayman in the internet magazine *Salon*, reporter Joshua Micah Marshall explained, "In Klayman's version of events, there had been an uneasy confrontation between Brown and Clinton when he told the president that he would tell all unless Clinton shut down the independent counsel's investigation of the commerce secretary. Then Brown was unexpectedly asked to travel to Croatia ..."

Similarly, Ruddy and Hugh Sprunt reported in the *Pittsburgh Tribune Review*, "According to Nolanda Hill [Brown's former business partner], originally Brown was not scheduled to head up the trade mission to the Balkans that ended in his death. She says at the last minute—after Pearson's subpoenas were issued—the White House asked Brown to join the delegation."

Of course, the last-minute change might have been completely innocuous. The more ominous, and seemingly unlikely, possibility is that perhaps someone, plotting to deliver Brown overseas to make him easier prey, obtained this change of plans as a favor from someone high up—perhaps even an unsuspecting President Clinton—insisting that Brown's presence was essential to the success of the trade mission.

These reports echoed what Betty Muench's earlier reading had said: *"There will be this which did not want to go on this journey ... there will have been this in Ron which has a sense of fear of this trip. He will have tried to change this but that it was seemingly required of him. This was not his idea and yet it will seem to be on record as such ... this was a trip which was not necessary but that it was made to seem so and in that then he was set up ..."*

I requested a follow-up reading from Muench, emphasizing the new bullet-hole revelation and subsequent punishment of whistleblowers. Intrigued by these shocking new revelations, and wondering how he might have been *"set up,"* I asked for elaboration on the first reading's statement that *"there will have been this in Ron which was like a loose cannon and that then this is the way in which such problems are resolved by this administration,"* assured from past experience that these spirit guides handle these kinds of questions discreetly.

The new reading stated that another individual high up in the administration, but not the president, was involved in Brown's controversies, someone *"who will seem to have a facade that would belie the true force and ability to act. There will be this one who will seem to be involved in some way with Brown and who would have also been involved had Brown come forth as he would have had to do."*

"There will have been this implication in those affairs of government which will be outside the rules and that this person will have come into power and wanted to keep that power; but that also who did not want to go through shame and implication with Brown. There will be this which is eating at this person and that this will be revealed in a time when there will come forth a person outside the government who will [reveal it] ..."

According to this reading, it appears that a high-ranking official might have allowed others to "take care of" the problem, never imagining how far they would go, and now feels remorse.

Describing the influences responsible for the death of Ron Brown as well as that of Commerce employee Barbara Wise, the spirit guides pointed to hit squads based overseas. Could the Communist Chinese government or their gangster allies known as the triads have done the dirty work, thinking they were being of assistance to a certain corrupt individual or individuals in the Clinton Administration? *"There will be this which will seem to say that then the Oriental concept of power and what is then required would not prevent them from taking on this responsibility for this administration; and in that then it would seem in some ways to obligate this administration."*

"There will be this which will come out and it will show that there will have been collusion of a more covert kind ... collusion which was not intentional but only required one person to request some small favor which then became the ultimate favor but still implicating the seeker." Muench said she wonders if a mere off-the-cuff remark led to the ultimate deadly "favor."

"There is in all this then the necessity to look at the Oriental concept of power and life and overlay that onto the seeming intention of the democratic government of the U.S. This would say more clearly that indeed the Chinese will be deeply involved and it will be too late when this will come out. It will already have infiltrated covertly and overtly."

This is by no means a new and unique theory. As defense expert Charles Smith wrote in *WorldNetDaily*, "Nolanda Hill testified under oath that her lover and business partner, Ron Brown, feared for his life because of his dealings with the Chinese army."

According to these spirit guides, the transportation of Brown to his doom *"would not seem to involve the president directly but that this would come out of his administration would be something that would put additional strain on this administration. This is something however which is accepted in government and it has been done before and that there will be this now in all the cases involving members of this administration, that which will seem to be a mind set and that it has to do with power at all costs."*

The reading then turned to Brown's reported decision to tell all to the prosecutors. *"There will be this in Ron Brown which felt a kind of relief as if he had made up his mind before taking this airplane ride ... that he would then be relieved and he would accept the consequences no matter what. The family will go with the status quo and they do not want the name of the family head to be diminished further, the cloud of doubt is alright with them at this point as it would not then open up any proof. They however are not the ones holding up the further investigation of this one Ron."*

The powerful individual mentioned earlier as having been involved with Brown's controversial dealings *"will have now cleared the way for some other direction in all this."* This person *"will seem to hold the strings to guide this. Power is for some always power and it can be wielded even from a distance which will be a part of the problem of this administration. It draws to it too many of the same nature and in that then there is no one policy or guideline ... and many can do as they please."*

Bertie Catchings noted that "certain people not cooperating with this graft and corruption" were targets for elimination, "and I believe Ron Brown was one of these red, white, and blue Americans that just didn't want to go along with anything that wasn't in America's best interest, and so it was necessary that he be murdered."

Catchings' assessment may be somewhat generous to Brown, who some other observers would describe as looking out for his own best interests when he apparently decided to cut a self-protective deal with prosecutors. At the same time, the Commerce Department's excesses under his leadership occurred in the context of the intense mid-1990s competition between the United States and other nations for trade deals with the rapidly emerging Asian and South American markets. What Catchings calls "America's best interest" was indeed well-served in the form of the thriving economy that benefited American companies and employees. Brown played a vital role in nurturing the prosperous economy by enthusiastically pursuing new markets; at the same time, according to prosecutors he also might have had a hand in corruption that accompanied this aggressive, anything-goes commercial diplomacy, and he himself appears to have paid the ultimate price for it. And the same price might have been paid by an innocent bystander, an employee of the Commerce Department, later that year.

One More Senseless Death

Barbara Alice Wise worked for 14 years at the Commerce Department's International Trade Administration (ITA), where John Huang served as Assistant Deputy Secretary from 1994-95. She was last seen alive on the afternoon of November 27, 1996, the day before Thanksgiving. The 48-year-old employee apparently stayed and worked late that day; she was found dead on Friday, November 29 in a fourth floor office of the Commerce Department building in Washington, DC.

According to people who knew her, she had been in poor health. One neighbor told reporters that she "had been in the hospital a few times for internal bleeding," while another said that Wise "looked like she was very ill last week. She was walking very slowly to her car. She was very weak." An Associated Press story reported that District of Columbia police officers "have found no signs of foul play and believe that she died of natural causes." Yet she was partially naked and, according to a report in the *Washington Times*, "Ms. Wise's head, neck, and upper torso were covered with large multiple bruises."

Robert Cracknell cautioned against being too quick to suspect a connection between the deaths of Brown and Wise. He had a strong impression that she might have left behind a diary "which I strongly feel could throw a great deal of light on her private life and on this case."

Nancy Myer observed that Wise "had obtained some information that would have been politically damaging to people in control of her. She planned to turn it over to the FBI. She was murdered before she was able to do that."

"Documents that she had hidden in her office were also taken at the time of her death. Since she had not told anyone what she knew, the missing papers would not have been noted."

Myer saw Wise as "an honorable, decent human being who tried to do something courageous."

Bertie Catchings, who psychically sensed that "hands were used" to kill Sgt. Shelly Kelly after she survived the Balkans plane crash, said, "Barbara Alice Wise, I believe, was killed pretty much the same way … and there's a very good possibility that the same persons, or group or trio of people—there were either two or three people involved in all this—were actually the same person or persons that were involved in the killing of Barbara Alice Wise."

"Brown died in April, and he had confided a few pieces of information to Barbara Wise; or if he hadn't actually confided, somehow she had overheard conversation or found some scrap of paper, or maybe a combination of all of that—because I can see her with a piece of paper, that she's read something that is upsetting to her, a memo, and she's putting the pieces together a little bit too much … she'd become a danger just a little bit after she'd found out the information. She was killed by someone very professional who killed Sgt. Kelly the same way. It's a man with strong hands …"

Murder accomplished by the use of bare hands seems highly unusual and improbable, yet Catchings' conclusion is independently corroborated by Betty Muench's reading, which opens with an image of Wise overhearing something from the other side of a door: *There is a face in the center of a long vertical line on the right side. It will be as if there is this face which is dark with fear and anger and will seem to be hiding behind something. There will*

56

be this which is between her and some other activity. It is as if she will be caught in a situation in which she will have overheard much that will have occurred in that office on that night." Wise was last seen approximately 4 P.M. on Wednesday, November 27.

"There will be this which will have to do with a situation in which she will have been unintentionally present. There was no reason for her to be there. There will have been this which will have taken place and that then certain actions will have been taken against her."

Muench's reading echoed Catchings' sense of "someone very professional ... a man with strong hands." *"She was treated very methodically and that there will have been training in the one who will have battered her..."*

What was it that the killers hadn't wanted her to hear?

"There was much happening in that office at that time and there will have been information changing hands around the death of Ron Brown. There will have been much activity with several men present; there will have been the finding of information which will have been seemingly unimportant, but which was evidently felt to be important around the death of Brown."

"There will be in this then the wondering why this resulted in her death when she did not know any of these men and they did not seem to know her. There are those who assumed that she was involved in some way in that she will have been a trusted employee [assumed she was important and knowledgeable enough to have understood and acted upon what she overheard, thus posing a threat to the men she heard talking]. *In this she is an innocent victim and she died for no real reason to do with her own destiny plan."*

"Again this on the part of certain groups is overkill. Those who seemed to be in charge of this will have acted with methodical smoothness, trained men, and trained to kill as they did her. There is an Oriental influence in this in that she was killed in an Oriental way ... making then this connection between her death and Brown and the others."

International Terrorism?

This conclusion possibly points to the Communist Chinese infiltration into U.S. government corridors of power, specifically the Department of Commerce, which, according to some observers, manifested in the person of John Huang, a member of the political fund-raising Asian Pacific Advisory Council and president of Lippo Group USA. Lippo was owned by Mochtar Riady, the Indonesian tycoon who had simultaneous longstanding ties to Communist Chinese intelligence and to Bill Clinton and the Arkansas-based investment firm Stephens, Inc. Mochtar Riady's son James, who in 1984 became co-owner of Little Rock's Worthen Bank along with Jackson Stephens, became the biggest contributor to Clinton's 1992 presidential campaign. Throughout this relationship, Huang was the point man linking the China-connected Riady family to Clinton and other politicians in whom they were investing. In 1994, Clinton appointed Huang to work under Ron Brown as Assistant Deputy Secretary of the Commerce Department's International Trade Administration (ITA), where Barbara Wise worked; the following year Huang was given a fundraising position on the Democratic National Committee.

At the Commerce Department, from July 1994 to December 1995, Huang had access to intelligence secrets at the highest level, and according to Edward Timperlake and William C. Triplett II in *Year of the Rat*, "had kept his Top Secret security clearance for a year after he left Commerce for the DNC. We now know that during the 1996 campaign Huang was actively seeking campaign funds for the DNC from the Chinese and other foreigners who have ties to organized crime syndicates (Triads), narcotics trafficking, gambling, prostitution, the Chinese military, and all of Communist China's intelligence services. We also know that during that same period he could have legally received highly classified information."

When asked by Judicial Watch if he had ties to Chinese intelligence, Huang repeatedly invoked his Fifth Amendment right against self-incrimination.

In recent years, the Red Chinese government has become increasingly intertwined with the Chinese triad societies, "the world's largest criminal fraternity," according to Fredric Dannen, who did a three-part investigative report for *The New Republic* in 1997. "Of all the treacherous aspects of Hong Kong's reunification with China, the most treacherous—and the least noticed—is that it will seal what amounts to a cooperation pact between the triad societies and the Communist Party," Dannen wrote. "This dreadful alliance, of the world's largest criminal underground and the world's last great totalitarian power, has received surprisingly little attention in this country, even though the US Justice Department has identified triad racketeering as a significant global threat."

In light of this alarming reality, one might expect that any trade relationship with China be handled with the utmost caution. Instead, recklessness appears to have prevailed, as the Clinton team's China-related commerce dealings crossed over into Democratic Party fundraising, which seems to have included the acceptance of contributions flowing from questionable Asian sources, with the recipients indebting themselves in the process and, in the Huang scandal, allowing national security to be endangered.

Amazingly, even the highest-ranking American defense officials were tied up in business dealings with Communist China. As investigative reporter Bill Gertz notes in *Betrayal*, "Defense Secretary William Perry was linked to Chinese People's Liberation Army General Ding Henggao, head of the weapons technology acquisition bureaucracy until 1997. His successor, Defense Secretary William Cohen, had set up an international business consulting firm that was seeking trade with China at the time he was tapped for the post ..."

Deeper investigation appears warranted when, as Timperlake and Triplett remind us, "At least eighteen critical witnesses have fled the country," and "Another seventy-nine witnesses have taken the Fifth Amendment, deciding that telling what they know would tend to incriminate them."

But most infuriating of all is the possibility that the consequences include the .45-inch hole at the top of Ron Brown's head, which could very well be the work of hired assassins, and the similar tragic fate of other individuals on the plane as well as Barbara Wise.

But the murder trail does not necessarily lead only to Beijing. As in the Vincent Foster case, the key adjective here is "international." Catchings pointed to far-reaching connections that appear to go beyond the involvement of any single nation. Cracknell saw personal blackmail of Brown by a foreign country other than China as one crisis that was hanging over him at the time. Muench's reading emphasized a degree of American culpability in allegedly passing the buck to foreigners: *"There will be this then which will suggest that this will become a government of intrigue and that all will use this intrigue to make their own inroads. There will be many pawns along the way. Wise was a pawn and that then there will have been this then which will have been eliminated in such an easy way that there will have been no aspersions cast on anyone in the government. There will be this which will seem to say that the Oriental [Red Chinese and triad] concept of power and what is then required would not prevent them from taking on this responsibility for this administration, and in that then it would seem in some ways to obligate this administration."*

As mentioned earlier, the reading speaks of a high-ranking administration official who desperately wished to avoid being implicated by Brown's testimony and now feels horror over the actions that were taken to grant his wish.

Somewhat surprisingly, China's People's Liberation Army (PLA) has been quite candid about promoting a strategy of assassination and terrorism, as outlined in a book the PLA released entitled *Unrestricted Warfare*. As reported by J. Michael Waller in *Insight* magazine, "*Unrestricted Warfare* calls for widening the very idea of warfare to nearly every aspect of political, economic, cultural and social life in Western countries," a characterization which, if true, casts a new light on US trade with China in recent years and perhaps on Ron Brown's story in particular.

Yet, as the *Wall Street Journal* reported prior to China's acceptance into the World Trade Organization in late 2001, "Top business executives are issuing a blunt warning to federal lawmakers: Vote against the trade deal with China, and we will hold it against you when writing campaign checks. Phil Condit, chairman of

Boeing Co., and Robert N. Burt, chairman and chief executive of FMC Corp., said a coming vote to facilitate China's entry into the World Trade Organization will be a measure of every lawmaker's friendliness to business."

But the advantages to big business might have come at a heavy price for some unfortunate individuals in the U.S. While we may never know for sure how or why Ron Brown died, it is no secret that other individuals with knowledge of the same scandals have expressed fear for their lives. Chinagate witness Johnny Chung's claim that a gunman came to his Los Angeles office looking for him in March 1999 was confirmed by the FBI, which arrested the man. Before the attempt on Chung's life, John Huang had tried to warn the Justice Department that, in the words of an FBI summary of his account, "many PRC [People's Republic of China] unidentified factions believe Chung is a traitor" and might try to harm him for his cooperation with investigators. Chung said he had been warned before testifying, "If you keep your mouth shut, you and your family will be safe."

In October 1999, still guarded by several armed FBI agents, Chung told a Pasadena, California audience about his life under government protection, a life he his family spent mostly indoors. "I'm only allowed one hour under the sunshine," he said. Still defiant, he declared to his enemies, "You can try to kill me, but you cannot stop me from telling the truth."

Another key witness in the Independent Counsel's investigation of Ron Brown, Oklahoma businessman Ron Miller, died of a sudden illness in October 1997. Hospital officials termed the death "not fully explainable." According to legal consultant Stephen Dresch, who has been active in calling attention to the suspicious circumstances of Miller's death, Miller received a series of death threats during his final months.

It is in light of these disturbing circumstances that we examine the fate of Ron Brown and others on his flight, as well as Barbara Wise. The psychic detectives' general consensus that these deaths were not accidental echoes the suspicions raised by Lt. Col. Cogswell when he spoke out about the apparent bullet hole in Ronald Brown's skull at the end of 1997. When CPO Janoski, Lt. Col. Hause, and Air Force Major Parsons came forward to corroborate his claims in January 1998, bolstered by supporters ranging from the NAACP to Dr. Cyril Wecht urging an investigation, this bombshell of a story still did not even begin to make an impact in proportion to its importance. As a result, few people noticed or cared when Attorney-General Reno announced at the time that there would be no investigation.

But even in a nation that has come to resemble a dysfunctional family living in denial, a story this explosive sometimes can be kept alive through the efforts of a few concerned people until it finally attains critical mass and grabs the reluctant attention of the public. This appeared possible in early to mid January 1998, yet ultimately it was not to be. The country would be spared the rude awakening of having to fully deal with the suspicious death of Ron Brown, beloved husband and father, highest-ranking African-American official in America, for "salvation" was right around the corner. It arrived on January 18 in the form of a sexual gossip item involving a White House intern. The Ron Brown gunshot-wound story was thus eclipsed and conveniently consigned to oblivion.

Chapter 3:
Kurt Cobain and the Seattle Curse

"I'm not worried about what's going to happen when I'm thirty, because I'm never going to make it to thirty. You know what life is like after thirty—I don't want that."—Kurt Cobain

"There are plenty of things I would like to do when I'm older. At least, just have a family, that would satisfy me."—Kurt Cobain

In Akira Kurosawa's 1950 film *Rashomon*, witnesses to the same horrible crime—including the murder victim himself, speaking through a medium—tell differing versions of what happened. A remarkably similar phenomenon occurs here in the exploration of the death of rock icon Kurt Cobain, as psychic detectives and mediums describe essentially the same scene, yet characterize it in distinctly different ways.

This story encompasses much more than the violent death of one young man. The news that Cobain was found dead on April 8, 1994, an apparent suicide by shotgun, sent ripples of grief around the globe. After thousands of mourners attended the candlelight memorial in Seattle for the musician who had been called "the voice of his generation," one young fan went home and shot himself to death—the first of scores of copycat suicides worldwide.

To this day, a number of independent investigators and many Cobain fans insist his death was never properly investigated. Perhaps the Seattle authorities concluded so quickly that Cobain took his own life because, as an addict whose corpse contained an astonishingly high level of heroin, he was assumed to have been intent on destroying himself one way or another, like so many other young musicians who died drug-related deaths during that era: Shannon Hoon of Blind Melon, Jonathan Melvoin of Smashing Pumpkins, Stefanie Sargent of 7 Year Bitch, Sublime's Brad Nowell, and Hole's Kristen Pfaff—a friend of Cobain's who died ten weeks after he did, and whose case is also explored in this chapter.

As a result, there seems to be a tendency to dismiss the sudden death of any addicted rock star as merely one more senseless tragedy that was the victim's own fault—especially in the case of Cobain, who, just one month earlier, had lain comatose for 22 hours after an overdose in Rome, and whose name had become almost synonymous with self-destruction. Besides, as they announced to a shocked and saddened world, he left behind a suicide note. Yet the meaning and even the authorship of the most crucial portion of that note are still in dispute. What really happened?

Did Cobain Kill Himself?

Rarely has a gifted artist soared to prominence so meteorically and departed so soon. In early 1992, the rock band Nirvana—singer-songwriter-guitarist Kurt Donald Cobain, bassist Krist Novoselic, and drummer Dave Grohl—stood atop the music world following the release of their groundbreaking album *Nevermind*. Two years later, Cobain was found dead in a room above the garage of his Seattle home. According to the medical examiner's report, he had died on April 5, three days before the discovery of his body.

The conclusion of suicide, announced one day after Cobain's body was found, has been called into question by a number of reputable investigators. Although Cobain is said to have shot himself to death, no legible fingerprints were found on the shotgun. Dr. Cyril Wecht, a leading forensic expert, has maintained that no one with the level of heroin found in Cobain's blood—triple the lethal amount—could possibly have managed to kill himself with the shotgun. Dr. Wecht told *Unsolved Mysteries* that "for the great percentage of people, including addicts, [the level of heroin found in Cobain's body] would induce a state of unconsciousness quite quickly, in seconds, not even in minutes."

Moreover, Cobain was found with his sleeves rolled down and buttoned over his needle-marked arms, and his needle was put away in his kit. Could one man, alone, attend to such details, and then lift a shotgun and shoot himself to death, in the few drug-clouded seconds during which he faded into unconsciousness?

On the other hand, his life was filled with countless instances of self-destructive behavior, including an appalling number of near-fatal overdoses, lending support to psychic detective Robert Cracknell's conclusion that he took his own life.

"My psychic reaction is that it was suicide," Cracknell stated, "despite the damning evidence of forensic experts who state that the level of heroin found in subject's blood would have prevented him from killing himself with a shotgun. Who in truth knows, when one person is in such state of heightened awareness, albeit drug-induced, what he/she is capable of?"

Cracknell tuned in psychically as he looked at a picture of Cobain and noted, "The photograph shows a man who was clearly trying to establish an identity outside of the one given to him in his brief period of fame. I feel that he was definitely a practicing bisexual and this was causing him perhaps the greatest of anxieties."

Issues of identity almost inevitably would have plagued any young person whose career took off as suddenly as Cobain's did— not to mention someone who was so introspective and conflicted to begin with. In 1990, he was still a struggling musician; by the last week of 1991, he was a rich and famous international icon, an anti-establishment punk rocker who found himself rejected by many among his original fan base when he achieved the mainstream acceptance and material success that seemed the antithesis of what he stood for.

As for the sexual identity issue intuited by Cracknell, Cobain had spoken of his affairs with both men and women, and held strong opinions regarding what he saw as the destructive effect of stereotypical gender roles he had grown up with in small-town Aberdeen, Washington. His earliest and perhaps most enduring image of the typical American male was what he described in his journal as the "highly bigoted redneck snooze chewing deer shooting faggot killing logger types" he remembered from his hometown. "I definitely feel closer to the female side of the human being than I do the male—or the American idea of what a male is supposed to be," he declared. When he became a husband and father in 1992, Cobain committed himself to a life that presented him to the public as straight and conventional. Yet his choice might have caused him untold stress and second-guessing, if he indeed still had the homosexual tendencies he had described candidly to a gay magazine a few years earlier.

Androgyny, cross-dressing, and rape figured prominently in his work, both as personal themes and as elements of a broader plea for tolerance. In one of his final journal entries, Cobain drew a picture of a Nirvana T-shirt that featured a new symbol for the rock group—a seahorse having babies—accompanied by the inscription, "the male sea horse carries the children and gives them birth."

But the same deeply felt obsessions that drove his creativity also were the source of deep inner turmoil from which he sought relief. "The taking of drugs was, for him, almost an escape from the physical reality of his existence and a genuine attempt to achieve spirituality," Cracknell pointed out.

"The letter that he wrote is fascinating ... particularly in the words, "I LOVE YOU'... I do not believe that the final words 'I LOVE YOU' were addressed to one person, but rather to the complete circle of his friends and family, indicating also total frustration at not being understood."

The reading produced by medium Betty Muench's spirit group shows Cobain's death to have been a peculiar hybrid of assisted suicide and orchestrated homicide; he was indeed suicidal, yet received an appalling degree of assistance from others who took definite steps to end his life when his perception and judgment were impaired by heroin.

"There will come this which will work thru the dying process as Kurt Cobain he will live down the attention to this. There will come then for Kurt this which will permit him to forgive others who will

have been involved in his death. He dies because he wanted to die but that he will have had assistance. There will be this which will have permitted that he will have given permission for this to be so."

I asked about Cobain's alleged suicide note. Some observers have pointed out that he was planning to get out of the music business, and that the note—at least everything above his signature—reads like an apparent retirement letter to his fans. The meaning of the final lines, as well as their authorship, has generated passionate debate. After signing the note, "peace, love, empathy. Kurt Cobain," someone—probably Cobain—wrote, "Frances and Courtney, I'll be at your alter," in letters that are a bit larger. This is followed by a final message in letters that are much larger, in a handwriting that looks different from the rest of the note:

> Please keep going Courtney
> for Frances
> For her life which will be so much happier without me.
> I love you. I love you!

Muench's reading noted, *"As Kurt will work out the truth of the light that surrounds him and comes to see that it is the light of spirit and of love, then so he was trying to work this out in his mind as he wrote this letter. There is this which will have been distorted and delusional and thus it is not a valid so-called retirement letter nor a valid suicide note. It will be that he will have been rambling in his mind and he will have been erratic in his writing. As he will have seemingly come to the end and signs his name in very small letters indicating his sense of self-worth, it is as if he revives long enough to make his true case at the end. He will seem to indicate his unworthiness loud and clear at the end. Then with help he will have passed out of the earth plane."*

Psychic detective Bertie Catchings saw Cobain's hand in the major portion of the letter, but raised the possibility that someone else wrote the concluding declaration.

"I believe that he was murdered," Catchings stated, "and before I get into any more, I want to tell you that this note—there's a lot wrong with this handwriting. He was a man who was emotional, and he did the drugs, and he was poetic and he was sensitive ... but obviously he's just talking about love and his thoughts ... he's just talking about his feelings and he's not saying anything at all about suicide."

"And then you go down here to the last part of it," Catchings continued, "which says something about 'Keep going Courtney, for Frances, for her life, which will be so much happier without me—I love you, I love you.' That was not written at the same time and not by the same person and not with the same pen ... It looks like someone took this letter and made it into a suicide note because some of this printing was actually done by Kurt Cobain, but there was too much change in the words and scratching out—it's a very incoherent letter. It looks like Kurt quit writing this letter somewhere about the time that it says 'only because I love and feel for people too much, I guess' ... I believe that letter was tampered with."

Handwriting experts consulted by *Unsolved Mysteries* support Bertie Catchings' appraisal of the authorship of the final words written in large letters. One analyst, Marcel Matley, concluded, "The last four lines of the suicide letter, which include the words 'I love you, I love you,' were written by a different person." Another expert, Reginald Alton, studied the letter independently and concurred.

Yet even if the dramatic final four lines were written by Cobain, was he really talking about suicide? Is it possible that he was simply expressing his intention to walk away from it all—the music business, his marriage, and Seattle—while apologizing and asking forgiveness for leaving daughter Frances behind in the process, and reassuring Courtney Love that he supported her for their child's sake? Or did he mean that his plan was not merely to leave his career, his wife, and Seattle, but to leave this world entirely?

A second, less-known note that Cobain left behind appears to answer this crucial question. Courtney Love revealed part of it in an interview in the December 15, 1994 issue of *Rolling Stone*. It says, "You know I love you, I love Frances, I'm so sorry. Please don't follow me ... I'll be there, I'll protect you. I don't know where I'm going, I just can't be here anymore." Clearly, Cobain wished to get away from it all, but was *not* expressing any intention to take his own life.

As he explained in the better-known letter, he no longer found the music business gratifying, and was walking away from it. Nirvana was close to breaking up, and his decision to turn down a multimillion-dollar contract to headline the upcoming Lollapalooza tour added one more strain to his crumbling marriage.

When asked whether Cobain was suicidal, his best friend Dylan Carlson said, "No. He just wants to get away from all this. He doesn't like most of the people in the music business." Carlson explained, "Kurt was facing lots of pretty heavy things, but he was actually pretty upbeat. He was prepared to deal with things facing him."

Was Kurt's recent purchase of a shotgun, with Carlson's help, evidence of a suicidal intention? Not according to Carlson, who claimed that Cobain, like other major celebrities, feared intruders and simply wanted to protect himself. In an August 1993 interview, Cobain had explained, "Guns are protection. I don't have bodyguards. We know people who have been stalked or murdered. I'm not a very physical person. I wouldn't be able to stop an intruder without a gun."

His concerns were not unreasonable. In July 1993, punk rocker Mia Zapata of the Gits had been found strangled to death in Seattle. Although an arrest of a suspect in 2003, based on DNA evidence, indicated that the killing of Zapata had probably been a random street crime, all Cobain knew in 1993 was that a talented, charismatic leader of a Seattle rock band, someone a lot like himself, had been gruesomely murdered. Nirvana played in a benefit concert paying tribute to Zapata, whose murder led to the creation of the violence prevention charity Home Alive.

After purchasing the shotgun, Cobain went straight to rehab in Los Angeles—not the action one would expect of a man who was suicidal or hopeless.

On the other hand, on countless occasions Cobain had come close to death by injecting recklessly excessive doses of heroin. Any heroin addiction, even involving more "moderate" usage, tends to dramatically shorten one's life expectancy and could arguably be called suicidal by definition. Although his notorious tranquilizers-and-champagne overdose in Rome one month before his death might have been an accident, as the doctor who tended him maintained, it was merely one of many instances in which he rendered himself unconscious and nearly died.

Yet going into rehab as many times as he did, keenly aware of how exceedingly difficult and painful the detoxification process would be, could be seen as a valiant affirmation of health, sanity, and the preciousness of life. Cobain warns repeatedly and eloquently against drug use in his journals that were published in 2002; after depicting the horrors of heroin withdrawal, he concludes, "It's evil. Leave it alone." Trance medium Philip Solomon brought through a similar message from Kurt: *"You tell all them guys out there who think they're tough guys cause they put a few drugs in their body, they ain't tough, they're just plain stupid! Like I was stupid!!"*

Yet breaking the habit was an arduous uphill struggle. In February 1994, two months before he was found dead, he wrote that kicking heroin for the first time "is usually easy if you have pills. You basically sleep. Which is bad in my opinion because you think if its that easy I could get hooked and kick for the rest of my life. By the second and third time it becomes very different. It takes sometimes 5 times longer ... Every time you kick as time goes by it gets more uncomfortable ..."

And it is difficult to know the degree to which his many rehab attempts were genuine, rather than empty gestures to appease concerned loved ones (not to mention music business executives who had so much invested in him), as well as prevent Frances from being taken away again by the authorities. His final stay in the Exodus Center near Los Angeles—during which doctors and residents alike found him to be in good spirits—ended abruptly when he jumped the fence, flew back to Seattle, and went on a heroin binge.

He also bought a box of shotgun shells upon his return—according to some observers, evidence of suicidal intent. But Dylan Carlson, the man who knew Cobain best, maintains that the ammunition was simply for self-protection, an opinion supported by Cobain's loading of the shotgun with three shells, rather than the single shell that would be sufficient to commit suicide.

In the often bitter debate about whether or not this rock icon was suicidal, it appears that both sides are correct: the more one explores the accounts of his life, the clearer it becomes that two sides of Cobain were battling for his soul. He was a complex individual who could ricochet unpredictably between emotional extremes from day to day and even hour to hour. His cousin, Beverley Cobain, a psychiatric nurse, believes he suffered from manic depression. Some of his friends describe him as having been upbeat when they saw him during his final weeks; others say he was deteriorating and "not long for this world," so recklessly self-destructive that his usual heroin suppliers turned down his business. In addition, the genetic deck was stacked high against him—on his mother's side of the family, his great-grandfather had committed suicide; on his father's side, two uncles had killed themselves.

"I think it's possible that at some point that he had thought about suicide," Bertie Catchings noted. "He was very depressed about a lot of things." But she maintained that this forlorn, self-hating rock star did not kill himself.

As for psychic detective Nancy Myer, this was the one chapter for which she declined to do any readings. But silence itself can be a revealing answer to the question of whether this untimely death was more purely suicide or something more.

"I don't really believe that he intentionally killed himself," said Bertie Catchings. "He had taken some of that heroin in his system, and then I believe that someone came along and gave him more heroin in his system, and then I believe that someone came along and gave him more heroin and then shot him."

This description by Catchings of how Cobain died is remarkably similar to the scenario channeled by Muench in a reading that featured a symbol illustrating the key role of heroin in this tragedy, and the part allegedly played by other people in injecting him: *"There is this image on the left side ... it is like the 'baster' implement. It will have a round ball on the end of a tube but that this is dual; it is doubled. There is this which will suggest that this will be trying to reflect that there will have been this which was administered over a period of time and that there will be this which will have involved more than one person. This image will suggest that Kurt was 'basted' over and over and that then he will not have had any recognition of what he was about to do and what was about to be done to him."*

"There will have been this which will have already been done to him in reality, for it will have not allowed him to return to his own mind and to do those things to protect himself. Thus then this would suggest that this was intentionally done to him over a period of time in which then several people will have come and gone around him ..."

Although Cobain died on April 5 according to the coroner's report, someone attempted to use his credit card on April 6 and 8—a disturbing fact that tends to support the finding in this reading and others that during his final hours he was in the company of a person or persons who did not have his best interests at heart.

In addition to detailing this scene of Kurt Cobain seeking oblivion through drugs while receiving unseemly assistance on the road to self-destruction, Betty Muench's spirit guides also depicted the soul of Cobain as unwilling to admit to himself that there was more to the story—namely, that someone in another city manipulated the situation to ensure that he ended up dead (not that that was terribly difficult to do to a man who had overdosed several times in the recent past): *"There will be this which he was not capable of confronting. There will be this which he will have been kept in a state of confusion so that he would not confront. There will be this which will have been akin to deliberate drugging ... There will be this which will say that this would suggest an elaborate scheme but no ... it was merely someone taking advantage of the situation that existed ... the use of drugs and the use of people on drugs. This will be very easily done by those who know the ways of such things."*

Messages from Kurt

The spirit contact by medium Janet Cyford established a storyline in which we find Cobain recklessly overindulging in dangerous drugs, while also receiving final deadly "assistance" from someone else on the scene.

Cyford smiled when Cobain came through. "This is a nice guy, as he draws near to me," she commented, but she had a few seconds of difficulty in establishing a clear, coherent line of communication. "Come on, come on, thoughts are going all over the place … Never thought that he'd end up like this. I don't know whether this addiction had gone on for a long time … he's grinning about this as if, well, you know, his approach to it was well, let's find out what this is about, let's see whether it gets me hooked, or things like that … He knows it's stupid now, but he was sort of facing that, well let's try some more, let's see what people are saying about this, see what it's all about—a very cavalier attitude to it, you know, he's almost experimenting with it … this is something where he just went too far too soon."

This message from Cobain about his alarmingly casual attitude toward drugs—reckless even in comparison with other hard-core addicts—has been widely documented in chilling detail. In the Cobain biography *Heavier than Heaven*, author Charles R. Cross notes that "Kurt's interest was in escape, and the quicker and the more incapacitating, the better. As a result, there were many overdoses and near-death situations, as many as a dozen during 1993 alone." Cross quotes the recollection of Dylan Carlson, Cobain's best friend and a heroin addict himself: "I wanted to get high and still be able to do something, but he always wanted to do so much he couldn't do anything. He always wanted to do more than he needed to do."

Cyford's next message from Cobain went straight to the heart of the case.

"He didn't shoot himself," she declared.

"He was what he would have called a recreational drug user, but this is the first time he'd ever gone as far as this," Cyford explained, noting that he'd also taken something he had not taken before, "which put him in a state of mind where he didn't damn well know what he was doing with taking this much. Completely out of himself."

"Was he married?" she asked.

"Yes," I replied. Janet Cyford's question was not surprising, considering that she is a member of an older generation, with children who were born a few years before Cobain, whose name was no more than vaguely familiar to her. Yet this lack of knowledge of Generation X's most legendary celebrity is actually an advantage when it comes to conducting this kind of spirit contact, as it prevents prior knowledge and preconceptions from influencing the reading.

"This guy was of a very, very stubborn nature," she added. "If somebody told him he shouldn't do something, he'd go ahead and do it. A bit of a law unto his own self—and these are the things that he's telling me now as he looks back at himself."

This indeed sounds like the perversely contrary guy who, performing on *Saturday Night Live*, went ahead and did the one Nirvana song they had warned him was forbidden. In *Never Fade Away: The Kurt Cobain Story*, author Dave Thompson recalls, "There wasn't a teacher at Weatherwax High who didn't know about Kurt Cobain's stubbornness, the way he agreed to do one thing while he planned to do another …"

"This man was dead when they shot him," Cyford pointed out. "Someone did this to cover their own steps. I think that they brought the drugs to him, something like that … He's not given to me who it was. It was a guy, and when this guy finds out that this man's dead, *for goodness knows why*, but he thinks that if he manipulates it that he shot himself, it will be the end of it … Another guy brought drugs there, and they did them together. This was absolutely stupid—you know, nobody set out to kill him or anything like that; this wasn't a contract killing or something that needed to be covered up."

"You see, he's saying that he thinks that he shot himself up three times and didn't realize that he'd done that, but someone, when they realized that he was dead, decided that they'd shoot him so it'd look like a suicide. Now I don't know who this other person is. I'm looking at a much older man than this one, I don't feel that it was someone that was part of the band or anything like that. Maybe just a dealer."

"He knows that he was a mess. Had he parted from his wife? Was there something bad going on with her?"

During Cobain's final months, his relationship with Courtney

Love had deteriorated into violent quarrels that sometimes had to be settled by police intervention. He told friends that he intended to divorce Courtney, and she responded by telling their attorney to hire a vicious divorce lawyer. There were already signs that the coming breakup could be ugly: he wanted custody of Frances; she wanted to undo the prenuptial agreement; each suspected adultery by the other.

Rather than bring him a sense of relief, the prospect of ending his tempestuous marriage brought a deep sense of loss and depression, for Cobain still loved his wife; and guilt, because the last thing he wanted for Frances was the kind of pain he himself experienced in childhood when his own parents split up. (He never really got over the trauma, and his lingering family issues figure prominently in Nirvana's final album, In Utero, originally titled I Hate Myself and I Want to Die.)

"He just knows that he was an idiot. He knows that now ... these are the thoughts that I get from him, that he knows he messed just about everything up. You know, he could have had a far better career and a far better life if he'd have listened to the voice of reason ..."

"But there is something here that is important, that this guy's time was up. And a part of that irresponsibility was within his own almost unconscious self—of knowing, well, I won't be around very long so I'm not abiding by the rules ... His time was up, and it's almost as if he knew at some unrevealed level of himself that, you know, 'Kick over the traces, I won't be here for very long,' but now as he looks back at it, he realizes the pain that he left."

"Do you know whether there was a child, a daughter?"

"Yes," I replied.

"Right. The pain that he's left behind, that legacy that he's left behind—if he'd just used the talents that he had ... he would have left a better legacy and memory for that child."

"Is she about ten now?" Cyford asked.

I pictured Frances Cobain the way she appeared the last time I saw a photograph of her—about one year old, being carried around by her parents. I checked later and found out that she was born in 1992; this reading was conducted in 2001.

"He's a very lovely soul. That doesn't mean because they're a lovely soul, they know everything ... He's got no blame against this guy that shot him. The guy did that to try and—he thought he was doing the best thing ... In many respects the guy did this almost like to cover [Kurt's] name ... he'd be more like a hero that he'd shot himself because he was so unhappy about his marriage, rather than he wouldn't be a hero or be remembered if he just died of a drug overdose. That was the man's thinking as to why he shot him and made it look like a suicide."

There's no denying that, in some people's minds, there is something morbidly romantic about the dramatic self-destruction of a tormented or misunderstood soul. The likelihood that the shooter's judgment, like Cobain's, was clouded by drugs also might help explain his reasoning—or lack of it—at the time. In addition, if the shooter was a drug dealer, from his point of view a finding of suicide by shotgun had a crucial advantage over a fatal heroin overdose by a beloved celebrity, since the latter might have triggered a public outcry to find and punish Cobain's suppliers.

In trance medium Philip Solomon's spirit contact, intriguing messages came through regarding Cobain's life on earth and beyond. The more one observes the work of mediums, the clearer it becomes that individuals who have passed on are keenly aware of our physical dimension, knowing when, and for what purpose, their presence is being requested; not surprisingly, since Solomon's reading was the final one, Cobain's spirit apparently saw no good reason to cover the same ground again. Nevertheless, when Solomon asked whether Cobain killed himself, the answer that came through was illuminating: *"I told you man, I don't want to talk about these things. I killed myself. Course I killed myself. But I killed myself years before ... I'm happy where I am and it's better and I wouldn't want to be back in your world. I always said I would be dead before I was thirty and I was! Maybe it's to do with this [music] business."*

That last sentence might sound a bit like a generalization and a "they all do it" copout. Yet, as the "self-destructive death rocker" Kurt described in his final note, he was astonishingly typical of the grunge rock scene in Seattle. Of the four hot new bands from "America's latest music mecca" featured in the *New York Times* in November 1990—Mother Love Bone, Nirvana, Soundgarden, and Alice in Chains—only Soundgarden suffered no heroin-related fatality. Mother Love Bone, the group that later evolved into Pearl Jam, had already lost singer Andrew Wood to an overdose earlier that year. His death would inspire the song "Would?" by Alice in Chains, whose lead singer Layne Staley would fall into the same addiction trap and never escape, despite several rehab attempts. By the mid-nineties, for all practical purposes, Alice in Chains was history. Staley appeared on the cover of a 1996 issue of *Rolling Stone* with the headline, "The Needle and the Damage Done." In April 2002, he was found dead in his Seattle apartment, surrounded by his heroin paraphernalia.

Shortly after Cobain's death, his grieving mother, Wendy O'Connor, commented, "Now he's gone and joined that stupid club. I told him not to go and join that stupid club"—the club that included Janis Joplin, Jim Morrison, Jimi Hendrix, and other rock stars who died at the age of 27.

Ten weeks later, another prominent musician, a close friend of Cobain, would join them.

Kristen Marie Pfaff (1967-1994)

Kristen Pfaff, born three months after Cobain, was found dead in the bathtub of her Seattle apartment, with heroin in her system and drug paraphernalia at her side, on the morning of June 16, 1994, a little more than two months after Cobain's death. She had moved to Seattle the year before to become the new bass player for the band Hole, joining guitarist Eric Erlandson, drummer Patty Schemel, and the band's leader Courtney Love.

On June 15, Pfaff was packed up and ready to move back to her native Minnesota the next morning. Like Cobain, she had become entwined in the Seattle drug scene that was seemingly inseparable from the grunge-rock scene; and like Cobain, by 1994 she had had enough.

Pfaff hit rock bottom when her newly acquired heroin addiction landed her in the hospital in late 1993, then went into twelve-step recovery and appeared to have kicked the habit. As if to purge herself of Seattle poison while she packed, she put all belongings acquired in Seattle in a large trash bag to be discarded.

Cobain's untimely death was itself a powerful motivation for Pfaff to want to flee Seattle. Ironically, the emotional pain caused by his death was one factor that led her to take potent drugs during her final night, according to a reading by psychic detective Robert Cracknell, who felt that Pfaff and her friend Cobain "spent many hours together, enjoying a joint release from reality by taking drugs …"

"But she had to struggle to come to terms with Cobain's death," said Cracknell, who tends to see the victims' inner life in his readings. "Say what you will, whether it was suicide or accidental death, one clearly gets the feeling it made no difference to her, as long as she could experience the ultimate release."

When I met with medium Janet Cyford to do a reading on Kristen Pfaff, she knew nothing in advance about which case I wanted to cover on that day. I brought along a picture of Kristen accompanied by a brief description of the case. However, as Cyford had done on other occasions, she asked me to keep the picture and case description turned over, saying she would only refer to it if needed as a backup. As usual, it was not needed. Souls on the other side generally seem to know when and why their presence is being requested, and show up promptly for their appointment. "I'm getting a young woman," Cyford stated. "About five-foot-three, something like that. She has long brown hair and it's rather full, thick hair."

"Do you know whether she had a boyfriend?" Cyford asked. "Because she's talking about a young man there—in the afternoon and evening … I don't know where she was living at the time, but she was talking about the weather being very hot, being in sort of summer clothes—short top, short miniskirt." It was June 15, 1994.

"And it feels as if there's been some kind of argument or breakup with this guy some days before, or some time before, and he's coming to the place, and I get the impression of being on the top floor of somewhere—I don't know whether she lived in a house or whether she had a rented apartment there. I think it's rented—it's like an efficiency place ... And [the boyfriend] coming by, like making some overture to her of something for the last time."

Cyford paused, then added, "I think they did some drugs together, something he bought that was different, that she'd not tried before. Was she found with drugs in her?"

"Yes," I replied.

"I don't think he set out to do this, to kill her or anything like that. But, you know how people buy drugs sometimes and they're bad drugs? It was something like this." The message conveyed from Pfaff was that she was "doing the drugs with the ex-boyfriend really to get rid of him, to appease him in some way ..."

"And *this girl drowned*," said Cyford. "She drowned in that bathtub ... that was the cause of death ... It was the drugs, that she felt bad—you know, almost like fainting, losing consciousness. And this kid had a hard time when she got into spirit because she was so angry over this."

"And there was with her moving, there was something set up for her, there was an opportunity opening up for her, and—do you know anything about her parents? Were her parents where she was moving to?"

"Yes," I replied. "She was going back home."

"There's a gentleman in spirit with her that's either her grandfather on her father's side or her father. How many years do we go back with this?"

"1994," I replied.

"I think it's the grandfather that she's in spirit with. And nobody ... there wasn't any attempt to kill her. It was her own stupid fault of going back and using the drugs ... And the drugs wouldn't have killed her but ... if she'd have not been in the bathtub she'd have probably passed out and come round some time later. But she drowned."

"Do you know who Kirk is?" Cyford asked.

I replied that there was a *Kurt*, Kurt Cobain, whom she had done a reading on previously. "Maybe there's a Kirk also," I suggested.

"No, it's too similar," Cyford said. "It's Kurt."

"She has something about him?" I asked.

"Well, it's quite upbeat, actually, because she wants you to know they're still making music."

I asked if she is staying close with him on the other side.

"She's close with him. Did they play together before?"

"Maybe," I replied, "because I think he helped his wife's band. He wrote for them, he was involved with them …"

"Right, so he would have known of her. She's a very pretty girl. I don't think she was all that photogenic. You know, photographs or film didn't do that much justice to her. But there's almost a petiteness to her features …"

"I want to go back to this anger that she had, because it was almost like, through her own foolishness she missed out on an opportunity, but I don't think there are any accidents, I think we go when we're meant to go; I'm sure I've said that to you before. But *she's at peace now.*"

"She's asking me to pray for the mother and father … She's saying it wasn't wasted, her time wasn't wasted."

"She said she had lost a lot of weight as well," Cyford added, and that it "had been a difficult time in that Seattle area. I think she'd been there something up to five years or five months—I can't get whether it's months or years there, but she'd had enough."

Pfaff's stay in Seattle was brief. She moved there to join Hole in mid-1993, returned to Minneapolis in February 1994, shortly after completing drug rehabilitation, and temporarily toured with her old band Janitor Joe. Kurt Cobain's death that April might have been the final straw—when she returned to Seattle in June, it was to pack up her belongings and leave the city forever.

According to this reading, the last time she saw Cobain was in "a party situation, sort of after a show or something like that … and she thought that he looked very tired." Cobain "was quite spaced out on something—very overtired, you know, overworked …"

"She's saying about him that he was such a nice guy, but it became unreliable where his friends and colleagues were—he was the sort of guy that was in the moment with whoever he was with …

and there might be promises to two other friends, but … the person he was talking to at that moment, it would take over, so he became more and more unreliable as a friend. You couldn't rely on him to be where he said he would be, and he was getting worse and worse …"

"She didn't have time to find out the truth about [Cobain's death]. She wasn't surprised, because he was on a downward slide." But her thoughts mainly seem to be about her family. "It's not distress, it's sadness where her mom and dad are concerned … Because they've never recovered from it." According to this reading, Kristen is concerned especially about easing her mother's grief—in part, for her mother's own sake; and in part, because the enormity of the grief for Kristen could have the effect of devoting a disproportionate share of parental attention to her, to the possible detriment of their son.

In contrast with the finding of accidental death in this spirit contact, psychic detective Bertie Catchings said she believes that Pfaff "was fed up with the whole deal, and she wanted to go home," but that someone "actually wanted her to die."

Catchings emphasized that with Pfaff, as with Cobain, "it was personal reasons—wasn't being silenced for information so much as that she had rubbed some people the wrong way." And she sees both their deaths as having a connection with the shadowy world of dangerous illegal drugs, in which life is cheap and the casualties are high.

If this is accurate, what motive might there have been for murdering Kristen Pfaff? A possible answer comes in the Muench reading, in which we receive a message that Pfaff was one of several people present at the scene of Cobain's death, and was silenced to keep her from incriminating others who played a role in ending Cobain's life.

The reading noted, "*there is not so much intrigue in this as might seem but that there will have been others who will have been involved [in Cobain's death] and involved in ways that will not permit excuse. There will then be this which seemed to them to have to be done—a consensus all around.*"

"*There will be this which will have included Kristen but that she will not have been the only one and she too will have lost cognizance of her predicament."*

So according to this storyline, Pfaff might have been one of several people who either assisted Cobain in getting high or failed to stop him from overdosing. She *"will have wanted to stop him but that she could not. This one will have then in her altered state have bought into the idea and will have assisted him then."*

This is a good point at which to stop and remember to approach all these readings with caution. Communications between this world and the spirit world can be hazy—and this includes automatic-writing mediumship that produces detailed narratives that look so solid and compelling on paper. Even with these messages coming through a highly accomplished medium, possible errors could include confusing Kristen with a different woman having a similar name (Kurt spent a good portion of his final days with young woman named Caitlin, who provided him with heroin), or seeing Kurt and Kristen taking drugs together on a different occasion, but mistakenly describing this as having occurred on Kurt's final night.

But what would have been the motive for silencing Pfaff? If this scenario is true, why would other people fear her speaking out, when in doing so she would incriminate herself along with them? According to Muench's reading, an attempt to pin the whole blame on her resulted in (unfounded) fears that she would tell the full story, emphasizing the insignificance of her own role in order to clear her name.

Muench's reading (in 1997) described Kristen Pfaff's condition: *"There is this which will suggest that she will feel isolated but that is the feeling she will have had also in life. She will have felt this so intensely that she will have assigned her life over to drugs and behavior which will not have been approved of. While she was not truly this kind of person, she will have been lost in that ..."*

"There is this which gives her light now and that this will have to do with someone asking for her [this question through a medium], for it is as if when she will have died others will have simply dismissed her and not thought of her any further."

This brings to mind the seeming emotional deadness of Pfaff's peers as perceived by her father when her family arrived in Seattle after her death. Norm Pfaff told the *Seattle Weekly*, "There was no sign of the type of remorse you would look for in a person who'd lost someone they care about. It could have been that Kristen died or somebody missed a bus." Kristen's mother Janet said, "I don't know what's going on in that Seattle scene, but there's something wrong, terribly wrong." The Pfaffs made it clear that Kristen's bandmates were not welcome at the funeral, echoing Kristen's own final rejection of Seattle.

"There is this inquiry which will seem to give her some movement and that this will be as if to get her to think about her life and getting her now to talk about her death."

The reading went on to describe someone sneaking in to drown her—something that could have been done when she was alone in her apartment from approximately 9 P.M. to 9 A.M.—but characterized her as in a state of diminished awareness. A key sentence might help explain how this reading can be reconciled with others that found an accidental overdose: *"She was not alert or aware and she will not have been anymore enlightened then than now ..."*

So Kristen indeed might have been nearly or completely unconscious at the time. Just as in the case of Vincent Foster, who is said to still be confused as to the facts surrounding his death, perhaps she knows no more today in the spirit world than she knew then.

"She did not have a sense of self-love and that this then for a long time after her dying was felt to be justice ... that she might indeed have had something to do with Kurt's death but that in reality she did not anymore than anyone else who knew him and could have stopped him. There will be this then which will suggest that Kurt wanted to die but that he did not want to have it be very messy. Ultimately there was some kind of help for him in this action but that Kristen was not the one."

"There was someone else on the scene and that is the reason for wanting to silence her and not wanting her to remember. She will have known of someone then as she felt it at the time of her own

death. Incrimination did not concern her but had there been any kind of an in-depth investigation of this Kurt death then there would have been found others involved and that Kristen then could not have taken this on herself. It would have been refuted by the investigation which was not thorough, as when in the case of drug deaths, there is not usually a deep investigation no matter what the stature of the victim. There will be this then which simply washes its hands and the police can then be called 'Pilate' and they can be free of this."

Even if there had been a thorough investigation of Cobain's death, Pfaff had been in too drugged a state to be a helpful witness, according to this reading. *"Kristen would not have remembered, she would not have known that there was someone there in that she would have been passed out and in that she would not have focused on them very well anyway. She will have been sick of something else and that too will have added to her focusing problem. There will be in this then the killing of someone [Kristen] for reasons that were not necessary ..."*

Can these different readings be reconciled? Perhaps. Is it possible, for instance, that Pfaff was already dead, not merely unconscious, when someone, unaware she was dead, took definite steps to "kill" her? It is certainly possible in the case of a heroin user—in fact, this would be a repeat of what happened when an already-dead Kurt Cobain was shot, according to Janet Cyford's spirit communication (a conclusion powerfully reinforced by the discovery that Cobain had three times the lethal amount of heroin in his system when he was shot)—and it would explain how Kristen's spirit says she died accidentally, while some psychic detectives see foul play.

The extreme reluctance of people in spirit to "point a finger" might also help explain the disparity, at least in part. Another possibility, of course, is that one or more of the psychics are in error or misinterpreted what they perceived. As much as we desire clarity, it is not to be found in this particular case; the readings on Kristen Pfaff, taken together, are inconclusive, perhaps creating more questions than answers about her death and how it may or may not relate to Cobain's death. The only thing that is certain is the heartbreaking prescience of some of her friends' warnings about the astonishingly high drug fatality rate of young rock musicians in Seattle when she was contemplating whether to move there.

A Glimpse Beyond

In 1990, Kurt Cobain was a rising yet poor musician who applied for a job cleaning dog cages in a kennel and was turned down. By the last week of 1991, Nirvana's *Nevermind* was at the top of the charts and Cobain was an object of worship worldwide. In 1992, he married the love of his life and became the father of a daughter he adored.

He had known idyllic happiness before, when he was a child, and it came to an ugly, gut-wrenching end at the age of nine when he saw his parents divorce. He never moved beyond the feelings of rejection, betrayal, and sorrow. Looking at life through a lens darkened and distorted by his unresolved trauma and his untreated depression—further aggravated by the mysterious stomach pain that fame and fortune could do nothing to relieve—he appeared to believe that when abundant blessings poured into his life, he was simply being set up for another cruel twist of fate. He obsessively feared that Frances would be born deformed; when she was born healthy and normal, he failed to take it as a hint that his pessimistic and fearful outlook might be mistaken. As he wrote in his final note, he had "a daughter who reminds me too much of what I used to be. Full of love and joy kissing every person she meets because everyone is good and will do her no harm. And that terrifies me to the point to where I can barely function. I can't stand the thought of Frances becoming the miserable self-destructive, death rocker that I've become …"

Medium Betty Muench's reading, done in 1997, found Cobain to be in an infinitely better place, safe and loved, but temporarily persisting in his self-loathing.

"There will be this which will seem to be holding onto thoughts of self-deprecation. There is this which will seem to deny the higher light and he will seem to keep trying to create a hell for him to be in. This is not the way of higher spirit and they allow him this for this time but that indeed he will rise out of this and he will give up this denial

of his being. There is this from his soul level which will suggest that this one is truly powerful and gifted and that the milieu that he will have found himself in on earth will have been beneath his ability. In that then he will not have been true to himself and thus the self-deprecation. There will be this which he will come to realize. He will learn that he will have greater abilities still and that then he will re-manifest these in a way that will satisfy his soul."

Whatever difficulty Cobain and Pfaff might have experienced crossing over in a drug-impaired state was only temporary, for they are in a place of limitless love and support. Although they do not experience time in the same way we do, it is worth noting that Janet Cyford's spirit contact four years later, in 2001, found Pfaff in positive spirits, conveying an upbeat message about herself and Cobain, and an assurance that "she's at peace now."

"It seems as if the two of them are very close together now," Cyford noted. "[Kristen] said earlier, 'we're still making music.' And they do shed along with the physical body, the personality insofar as he might have that craving for drugs but not access to them, so that would be overcome in time there ... But it seems as if this guy was very loved—even the love that came from his fans this side, their grief, would have helped him ... the outpouring of grief, you know, it's a good energy. It supports him. Whereas if he had been just a Joe Blokes—a guy like that, unless there were supportive family members around him ... but he was loved, loved this side, adored this side by so many fans and loved by people in spirit that knew him, that he had a good opportunity to get on his feet there."

"And then, he helped her, even though it was just a couple months [between their deaths] ..."

Healing awaited Cobain as soon as he crossed over. In trance medium Philip Solomon's spirit contact, Cobain said, *"... I had to spend quite a bit of time getting myself well when I came over here. You know, I always had a bad pain in my stomach. That's why I took heroin really—for the pain in my stomach, but nobody would ever believe that so don't bother to tell them. And coughing—I always had a rotten cough. Can you imagine a singer having a cough?! Don't have none of them problems here, man! Had to spend some time in the halls of healing though."* Drugs such as heroin apparently pollute not only the physical body, but even the astral body that survives death; fortunately, in the higher realms, "detoxification" in healing sanctuaries awaits anyone who leaves the physical world in a drug-clouded state.

Cobain continues to leave his mark in a way that rivals and sometimes surpasses the charismatic legacy of Elvis Presley. In a survey of 500 rock musicians and critics who voted for VH1's 100 Greatest Albums of Rock & Roll, announced in 2001, Nirvana's *Nevermind* came in second, behind the Beatles' *Revolver;* outpolling other Beatles albums in the top ten — *Rubber Soul, Abbey Road,* and *Sgt. Pepper's Lonely Hearts Club Band* — as well as other masterpieces near the top, including the Beach Boys' *Pet Sounds,* Marvin Gaye's *What's Going On,* and Bob Dylan's *Blonde on Blonde.* In late 2002 and early 2003, Cobain ranked impressively high on the book and record charts with the release of his *Journals* as well as *Nirvana,* a greatest hits collection that included a previously unreleased song.

He also left his mark on the culture in other ways he never intended and could not control — the increase in the popularity of heroin during the 1990s, a trend he contributed to despite his attempt to discourage fans from drug use by lying to interviewers that he had kicked his addiction and had no use for heroin; and the copycat suicides, many by gun, after his body was found (even though, ironically, it is extremely unlikely he shot himself). And Cobain's continuing influence was clearly in evidence when, shortly after his death, a music critic faulted a new grunge rock album for not expressing enough self-loathing.

In dramatic contrast with such a dysfunctional world, there is no pain, loneliness, or negativity in the place where he now resides — "the other side," or Heaven, or the second level, as it is referred to in medium Philip Solomon's work — the astral realm that countless individuals who return from near-death experiences characterize as absolutely real and too beautiful to describe. Beyond Heaven is the third level, Nirvana, where an even more ecstatic vibration of light, love, beauty, and truth is experienced, as we learn from spirit communication conducted by Solomon and others; And beyond

Nirvana there are said to be additional levels of increasingly glorious bliss—an encouraging thought on days when life looks bleak.

Chapter 4:
POW Activists—Final
Casualties of the Vietnam War?

"There is no serviceman or -woman anywhere in the world who doubts for a moment America's resolve to care for them if they are lost."—Pete Peterson, US ambassador to Vietnam and former prisoner of war

"The willingness with which our young people are likely to serve in any war, no matter how justified, shall be directly proportional to how they perceived the veterans of earlier wars were treated and appreciated by their nation."—President George Washington

"There are no more prisoners in Southeast Asia."

So said an official communication from the U.S. State Department to the Department of Defense on April 12, 1973. But if all living American prisoners of war were returned that year, why did an Air Force general maintain that intelligence experts felt "shock and sadness" that so many known prisoners were clearly left behind? Why did a congressman and former high-level aide to President Ronald Reagan claim in mid-2002 that Reagan privately admitted that hundreds of abandoned American prisoners were still languishing in Vietnam at the end of his eight-year term? Why were citizens who attempted to investigate or present evidence allegedly harassed and intimidated? And what are we to make of the tragic, untimely deaths suffered by certain individuals actively involved in this issue—are they coincidence, or something more?

The CIA Patriot

The mystery of Jerry "Hog" Daniels' death appears to have a possible connection to a top-secret foray deep into Laos in 1981. CIA agent Daniels and contract agent Scott Barnes, accompanied by about 30 of Laotian General Vang Pao's armed Hmong guerrillas, allegedly found a walled compound outside of which Caucasian prisoners worked under armed guard. As Barnes recounts in his book *Bohica*, he and Daniels, in shock at the discovery, snapped as many pictures as they could while the prisoners were in view. "They were thin and filthy and appeared to be in poor health," Barnes recalls. Barnes and Daniels confirmed that the men were indeed Americans by picking up their conversations with a listening device.

Daniels "began to cry. 'They're here! We really did leave them behind!' In anger he hit the ground with his fist. '*I don't believe it! I didn't expect this!*'"

"I wept with him."

Their Laotian interpreter made a suggestion: "Why not hit now? We've got enough armed men." The devotion of the Laotian Hmong tribesmen to their American allies seems to stand in dramatic contrast to the attitude of U.S. authorities toward their own men, as we shall see.

But Daniels declined the suggestion. "We're not here to rescue. We're here to confirm."

"But we keep telling your government and they haven't done anything. We've got enough people here not to take them out," the interpreter insisted. But the difficult logistics, coupled with the weakened state of the American prisoners, ruled out an impromptu rescue.

The two men divided the film. Barnes mailed his film to Daniel C. Arnold, CIA Station Chief, in Washington, DC. He was later told that the negatives had been accidentally destroyed in processing. Daniels delivered his film to the U.S. Embassy in Bangkok. Six months later, Daniels died of carbon monoxide poisoning in his Bangkok apartment. When Daniels' body was brought back to Montana for burial, Vang Pao and his men, to whom Daniels had been a devoted friend, played a prominent role in the funeral.

Was Daniels' death an accident or murder? No clear consensus emerges on this point, and there might be too many complex factors at work for us to see these events in a clear context.

"I don't get any impression of foul play in Mr. Daniels' death," psychic detective Nancy Myer observed. "There was no concern about what he had discovered in Laos as it was not believed by the general public."

Indeed, most of the public either lacks interest in the POW issue or regards such evidence as politically motivated conspiracy theory not worthy of consideration. Faced with this level of skepticism and apathy, would Daniels' purported photographs of live prisoners really carry much persuasive weight? Skeptics could question whether they actually showed American prisoners currently being held. And the most dramatic part of the story—the two men allegedly hearing English being spoken by the prisoners—was not part of the evidence they brought back. The photographs alone were arguably not much of a threat to anyone, and even if Daniels was involved in issues of controversy, this does not rule out his dying accidentally.

"At the time of his death I do feel he was working on another case," Myer pointed out. "But I sense the death was a genuine accident due to an improperly vented heater. The chimney in it may have been dirty and partially blocked."

Robert Cracknell saw the Daniels case as ultimately difficult for us to ever comprehend because of the complex influences involved and the foreign culture in which the mystery is set.

"I find this case totally fascinating!" he declared. "And though I am no stranger to mysteries or unusual deaths I find this one to be akin to a major Hollywood production. It also brings me to accept that though there is not, and never will be any true psychological reasoning behind men's actions, I am painfully aware of the fact it is a culture about which I am not familiar ..."

"I feel as though I am writing a film script here ... It is so full of twists and turns, involving senior officials, intrigue, and official secrets that one wonders whether or not the truth will ever emerge. Here is my script: The CIA and American government knew of and already had evidence about prisoners of war still being incarcerated.

The odd thing, however, is that Jerrold Daniels and Scott Barnes took part in a secret mission. I cannot believe this was on behalf of the CIA, who didn't want evidence to emerge. Neither did the military. The Laos—for want of better words—Secret Service possibly made attempts to retaliate with counter allegations of an American retaliation during the war, including evidence of massacre and burial grounds uncovered—proving that there were massacres by the American forces of innocent villages."

"Daniels was killed by Laos agents as he was the greater danger and also as a clear warning to the CIA that they knew all about their operations and their agents. From thereon in there had to be official meddling in the destruction of half of the film that was sent to the CIA laboratory. But what of the half that Daniels delivered to the American Embassy in Thailand? ..."

"I am sure that this story of prisoners of war still being kept had been circulating for some time, similar to the story of the alien's body and the flying saucer, which had been discovered and was kept under military secrecy. But the whole thing would become one of national security, as the facts known would show to the world (and more important, to the families of the prisoners of war) that they had deliberately colluded with the Laos authorities to cover up the facts about prisoner of war camps. Could it be that the prisoners of war being held were the only evidence that the Laos authorities had that they, the prisoners, were responsible for random, obscene killings and the annihilation of entire villages? So a state of quid pro quo had to exist. 'You keep quiet and we'll keep quiet!'"

A reading by Janet Cyford, which also appears to lead us to Southeast Asian government authorities, began with a surprise, as she described her spirit connection "saying to me that President Clinton had looked into this when he was on his visit out there ... Someone's showing me that there's photographs that exist in a government office in Thailand, and President Clinton—although this wasn't in the news or anything like that—had talked about this when he was out there. There's something coming to the surface about the photographs that are left. They're not very good, they're not very clear, although they were taken with quite good equipment, they're not conclusive, someone's telling me ... there was a lot of good work that he did out there in improving relationships. There's a lot of people that were alive at that time that suppressed things, but now are too old to do anything about it or passed into spirit."

"I feel as if I've got someone speaking for him," Cyford said, and described "a contact Jerry had made" who was responsible for his death, a Southeast Asian official, "very heavy-set. He's saying something about being tricked into this ... it was a red herring; the heavy-set man wanted to talk to him about these photographs. I think at that time he'd still got photographs, or he'd still got film ... He's saying there's only two of these people left alive now in this camp. Now, I think I'm looking at him ... he was injected with something ... he's talking about six people that they took photographs of in that camp. I think they could see that—they couldn't identify them, but they thought that one of the people there was a colonel or quite high up ... that man is in spirit now, there's only two of them left alive and there's some dementia there; I don't think they know who they are ... They were heavily drugged, mind-altering drugs ... because if they had known who they were, they could certainly not be so passive about staying there."

"He's saying nobody would believe him. But truth does come out; it's a spiritual law ... if you wait long enough, truth comes out—something to do with Bill Clinton himself asking questions about the prisoners of war ..."

"That place where the photographs were taken is not there any longer ... there's only two [prisoners left]—as he says, getting better treatment now then they've ever had, but their minds are gone completely. Six have passed over."

A reading by Betty Muench found that *"there will be in Jerry ... the desire to suggest ... that he will have indeed been used and dispensed with by a higher power and in that then he will seem to be now holding back and not going forward in his evolution into another life, another lifetime. There will be this which will suggest that Jerry will be one to want to convey a truth and that this will be a part of his seeming betrayal."*

This reading also included an assertion that might sound

outlandish, yet turns up elsewhere in POW research: *"There will be this which confirms the misuse of prisoners of war and in that then there will be this which will show that many were used for a kind of slave labor and that this will also then suggest that they could not indeed be allowed to escape or be released for many reasons. There will be this which will show that those who will be a part of the cause of this, those who are in power within several governments and who will be benefiting from this situation, will all be those who will be able to control this situation from afar."*

The mention of *"those who are in power within several governments and who will be benefiting from this situation"* echoes the shocking allegations of American POWs being used in connection with the covert drug trade.

"This is elaborate and many have been lost in the need to preserve the secrecy and this operation. The cry for human rights in certain places will be only a smoke screen for other activity which will seem indeed to want certain human rights observed but not others. There will be an uncovering of all this as now there are too many involved and that this will explode very soon and that then Jerry will feel vindicated—in his loyalty to those who served their country and then were so maliciously used by parts of their own governments."

"Jerry will have known of the risk he was taking but that he also knew that anyone he brought this out to within this system will have been able to stop the information from reaching its target. He was playing by the rules and he will have been betrayed."

Bertie Catchings stated that Daniels' death by carbon monoxide poisoning was a case of murder. "I think he's a fine man, that he was very patriotic," said Catchings, but when he was seen as "a nuisance" by covert operatives, "he was eliminated."

The General

What are we to make of the violent death of Brigadier General Bobby Charles Robinson, a behind-the-scenes participant in the Bohica mission? Was it suicide, foul play related to the POW issue, or foul play connected to another issue? On January 14, 1985, the 52-year-old deputy executive director for chemical and nuclear matters for the Army Materiel Command died of a gunshot wound at his home in Fairfax County, Virginia. A brief *Washington Post* article the next day was headlined "Army General Kills Himself."

General Robinson was also involved in controversies apart from the POW issue, primarily in his area of expertise, chemical warfare. In 1998, after CNN reported and then retracted a story that the CIA used Sarin gas to kill American deserters and defectors in Southeast Asia, investigative reporter Michael C. Ruppert wrote that "Robinson was known to have been involved in moving Sarin supplies into the region at the time. [POW researcher William] Stevenson confirmed this. Sources postulated a cover story to Stevenson that Robinson had been planting Sarin gas to blame the Soviets for its use and thus motivate Congress to increase chemical warfare budgets. Such operations are not unusual in covert operations and are hardly grounds for a suicide. As one source put it to me, 'It's much more likely that Robinson could have exposed the use of his Sarin to kill Americans and he had to be killed— especially if he found out what his precious chemical agents were used for.'" Such allegations, involving covert activities of decades ago, are difficult to confirm. Therefore, CNN's retraction of the story is understandable.

Bertie Catchings saw this case as a murder, although she did not psychically pick up on details as to circumstances and motives. Robert Cracknell expressed concern about the prejudicing effect of the other cases on this one, which might create an unwarranted leaning toward seeing a conspiracy. "The main psychic impressions have already been stated in the opening case of Jerrold Daniels, who was a CIA agent," he noted. "To bring in other cases where the victims also had CIA connections can only bring the conscious mind into play. The dividing line between the psychic and conscious mind is extremely thin."

Medium Janet Cyford tuned in to this mystery and said, "The scene that I have is of a gentleman, quite heavy-set actually, walking to a window as he hears—I don't know whether it's a car that's drawn up, or some noise outside. He's got a newspaper in his hand, he's taken his glasses off, and it feels to me as if … there's a great explosion of light ... there's a voice, a woman's voice, in the background, as if it calls out to him, 'What was that?' or 'Who was that?' Someone crossing—it feels as if it's the back of the house—there's someone crossing the lawn that he recognizes—there's three men there. The one in the middle, he believes he recognizes, feels that he knows him enough to go to open the door. He directs the man to the side of the house to come into the place ..."

"The man that he feels that he knows, he's known for—the connection to him goes back a long, long way, many years ..."

"I've not got him," Cyford explained. "Someone [in spirit] is going over this for me ... This man was shot from behind ... Now, I don't know what the connection is here ... This is strange—I'm sorry, this is going to confuse you a bit. One of the men ... not the one he thought he knew, wanted to know why he'd done such and such at some other time in his career, and it seemed as a very unpleasant man as well, as if he'd—I don't know whether he'd shot the gun or what—but he had a great grudge against him for something ..."

"There's a lot of confusion in this man's mind even today," she points out, adding, "He'd got a rather cocky way with him as well ... superiority about him." If true, this trait is probably not unusual in a general, and arguably even a positive and useful quality at times. "I don't think it's got anything to do with his position at that time; it was a decision he had made back years before that was the bone of contention with the man that shot him."

A reading by Betty Muench shows the general to have been murdered. "*This man was a man of his men. He would not take his own life. There will be this which will show that he will have placed the well-being of his men over his career ambitions and in that then there will be this which will have caused him to speak out for the men and in that time then he will have been shown that he must sacrifice those that will have been already sacrificed. He could not fight for the release of certain men ... There will be this which will show that he will have had in his mind the freedom of his men and those that will have been left behind. He considered all military 'his men.'*"

"*There will be this which will suggest that he will have come across certain information which will have shown an activity which was not of a military nature and that it will have had to do more with his own government than the government of any other country. In that then he will have spoken out and in that then he sealed his own fate."*

Here we get a further glimpse into the nature of the alleged forced labor revealed earlier in the Daniels reading. *"There will be this which will suggest that the covert activity of the government will have involved not only drug traffic but other people traffic as well. Those who could think and do will have been sacrificed to be held into work that required certain skills and it is as if those skilled people will have been American prisoners and then converted into this other work, using their military skills but also certain skills derived thru formal education. Look for a kind of theme in the kinds of educations that will have been behind those prisoners claimed to have been killed or missing in the war."*

The skills referred to here might tend to be technological and largely aviation-related—the expertise not only of downed pilots but their "backseaters" as well. As author Nigel Cawthorne notes in *The Bamboo Cage*, "Very few of the highly trained backseat weapons officers were among the returnees."

The reading continued, *"There will be those still alive who would not now go back (home) fearing some other kind of retribution. They are renegades now and cannot go back to their former lives and as men will be persuaded on the basis of their own ego-involvement in what they now do. Not high morality involved but survival."*

So even if such prisoners were willing to risk their own lives to escape, perhaps they feared something worse, *"some other kind of retribution"* if they were to return to the United States. What is being referred to here? Perhaps we can gain some insight by exploring the fate of a brave woman who sought the truth about her captured husband.

The Prisoner's Wife

Marian Shelton co-founded the League of Families with Dorothy McDaniel, wife of POW Eugene "Red" McDaniel, and spent decades fighting to learn the fate of her husband, Colonel Charles

Shelton, who was shot down over Laos in 1968.

Born Dorothy Marian Vollman in Owensboro, Kentucky, she first met Charles Shelton in Owensboro in the summer of 1946. Five years later they were married, and in 1954 Charles began his Air Force career, which brought the family to Okinawa in 1964. Capt. Shelton was shot down over Laos while flying a mission on his thirty-third birthday, April 29, 1965, and parachuted safely from his RF101C photo-reconnaissance plane, but did not return in the 1973 POW release. Marian's efforts on behalf of her missing husband brought her to Southeast Asia in 1973 and even to Afghanistan in 1989 as a participant in an effort to exchange Soviet POWs for Mujahedeen prisoners and American POWs.

Mrs. Shelton eventually became an ally of Scott Barnes, who wrote in *Bohica*, "I thank God ... for Marian Shelton, who, even though she lives far away, is now my closest friend and most loyal supporter." On October 4, 1990, Mrs. Shelton was found dead of a gunshot wound at her home near San Diego. Her death was ruled a suicide.

The thought of a distraught POW wife taking her own life after 22 years of a fruitless quest for the truth is troubling enough, but might the truth be something even more horrifying? Or is it possible to read too much into this case because of the nature of other cases? Robert Cracknell was blunt about the prejudicing influence of one case on another. "This now becomes difficult as you have given me the [Daniels] case ..." he explained. "As stated on the main case— one can easily weave into a web of intrigue the reasons for other deaths." He found this case a difficult one to pick up on psychically, and did not venture a definitive conclusion.

Nancy Myer's answer, if true, also serves to caution us against being too quick to link cases that might in fact have no common bond.

"Ms. Shelton was engaged in an argument with a young man in his early twenties at the time of her death," she explained. "She knew the young man well. He had done work for her on several occasions. The argument involved money that he felt she owed him." She became frightened by his bizarre behavior and tried to call 911. The young man tried to restrain her. They struggled and a shotgun accidentally discharged, killing Ms. Shelton."

"This is an accidental homicide."

"I sense that this death tormented the young man ever since it happened. He wants to come forward but he's afraid that no one will believe him that it was an accident. He liked Ms. Shelton and only intended to get the money he felt was his. He meant her no harm."

This psychic vision of an unintentional killing is seemingly echoed in a phrase that came through repeatedly in Janet Cyford's reading—"a stray bullet."

"The husband and wife are both in spirit," Cyford noted as she tuned in, but found herself drawn initially to the spirit of Charles Shelton "because there's a very bright energy here with him." And she liked his voice. "Do you know where this man—whereabouts in this country he came from? Because there's an accent here, a drawl he's got."

The message that came through was that Marian's death was not a suicide. "She was shot but I don't know whether it had anything to do with this or not. Was that the prognosis, that she had taken her own life? Because he's talking about a stray bullet ... This wasn't suicide. He can't find the source of the bullet. Like a stray bullet, he's saying."

Like so many contactees on the other side, the spirit of Charles Shelton quickly changed the subject from death to life, with Cyford bringing through the message that "these two would have known one another when they were youngsters growing up, and he's so proud of her ... they'd been together all their lives."

Indeed, when they first met, he was 16 years old and she was a month short of 13—the beginning of a rare lifetime partnership.

"I don't know where to go now, 'cause his thoughts are jumping about so much. He's talking about this—I need to go back over this—does anyone know anything about him when he became a prisoner of war? Because there's something about his foot, a bad break in his leg, as if there was gangrene setting in or something dreadful like that, that he died of out there. He's saying he didn't last long out there ... dreadful conditions, he's talking about ... no medical help ... and it's almost as if he doesn't want to go into that. All he's concerned about is that she's with him."

"And this business about the stray bullet ... but again this wasn't looked into enough ... She wasn't like that. She would never have done that. If there was a time that she felt like suicide, it's when he was first lost out there ... But the two of them are together, and if there's concern, it's about the family ..."

"I wonder if there's two daughters, one of them being quite young [when he disappeared] and, you know, the memories of her father are not so clear. There's a daughter who looks very much like her mother. I don't know who looked into this woman's murder, but they didn't do enough. And when I say to him, 'Do you know, had it got anything to do with what she was digging into, and he goes, well, of course, you know, she stirred up a lot of—she wouldn't let the mud settle. And he can't point any finger at who did it or who didn't do it, but ...he doesn't know who it was that did it ..."

Janet Cyford's voice brightened as she enthusiastically shared that "this is such a lovely personality, this man—I want to say 'simple'—I don't mean that in a derogatory sense, that he wasn't educated or—but it was the simple things of life that mattered—very gallant, a real gentleman in his way...And all he's concerned about is that she's with him."

Examining pictures of Marian Shelton, Bertie Catchings saw a drug-trafficking connection, with the killers trying to send a message to Mrs. Shelton's friend Scott Barnes. Marian's association with Barnes put her in the way of danger. "If you decide to cross the river that's got alligators in it, you don't want to die, but a lot of people say that's suicide to go across there ... [Barnes] has had a lot of threats on his life, and it could be that some of the people ... would rather he not be dead, because they might could use him in some kind of way, but maybe control him a little more to make a believer out of him; they do like in *The Godfather*, they try to make this man an offer, and they kill his horse."

"She was killed either directly or indirectly because of drugs. There are certain little laws of retribution, that if you don't cooperate or if you offend someone, that you have to pay one way or another. And it probably wasn't her connection, but she found out information she shouldn't've found out—and this guy that wrote this book [Barnes] knew a lot of things about drug-related people, and he associated with people that associate with drug-related people; and the drug lords were offended, and someone had to die, and Dorothy [Marian's actual first name] was a good prospect."

"I don't think that she was a great threat to anybody ... But her death might intimidate others who might care for her or feel that she was useful," Catchings pointed out.

"I don't know which group might have anything to do with it, but my feelings are it would come from a group across the ocean there—somewhere on the Asian side—Laos or Cambodia."

"She is an innocent victim," Catchings continued. "She didn't do anything wrong, except cross a river that had alligators in it. And that's exactly why, technically, it's almost humorous, ludicrous, for them to say she committed suicide. Because, you cross that river, you get involved with that kind of people ... if you hang out where some of these alligators are, then one day one of them's going to bite you—I don't care how pure and sweet you are."

Catchings also studied a photograph of Col. Charles Shelton and commented, "I believe that her husband's dead ... My feelings are that he was a very honorable colonel, and that he didn't wish to cooperate with [his communist captors] ... And when he was of no more use to them, they didn't give him the best medical conditions, and I think he had different illnesses, and I think he'd been bruised and beaten and harmed, and probably when he was missing he was injured. And I think the man just didn't have a chance. I don't think they took a gun and shot him—just poor living conditions—lack of proper food and exercise, and physical and mental pressure, and the confinement, it just killed him. I think he's been dead for a good while."

But the suffering of the Shelton family did not stop there. The oldest of their five children, Air Force chaplain Charles Shelton, Jr., endured harassment in 1987 for showing concern over the fate of his father and other POWs. After mentioning in a speech the possibility

101

of live American prisoners left behind in Southeast Asia, Father Shelton was warned to keep his mouth shut, and immediately became a pariah; in addition, charges of sexual misconduct were suddenly leveled at him. His impeccable reputation brought shows of support that helped him to prevail against the false allegations, but the ordeal was one more devastating example of the Shelton family enduring punishment in return for their service and devotion to country.

According to a reading by Betty Muench, Marian Shelton's assassin *"was meeting with her in order to relay some information to her ... something she wanted to know about and that this meeting will have been a sham ... There will be this which will suggest that indeed this was a murder and that there will have been a situation which will have only had to do with her main concern and that will have been this work that she will have been doing. She will have been told much in that meeting and then she was dismissed in this fashion, as if to satisfy something in her curiosity and then to end her life."*

The killer *"was as a messenger. She was told many things which would seem to confirm Barnes' work ... there will be this which will have been easy for the assassin for indeed this was an assassination of the first order, meaning this will have come down from a higher source ... there will have been this which will have seemingly confirmed much of what Dorothy had learned thru Barnes and that this was very important to her."*

"There will be this which will have also confirmed information about her husband who will have survived longer than was claimed, and who will have been brought into a conspiracy out of his need to find a way back. Once she will have learned of all this, there will have been a kind of release in her and when her life then was threatened she will not have resisted. She almost welcomed death in that she will have been so sorrowful and ashamed of the system which allowed this kind of energy to occur—supposedly in a democracy where truth is supposed to be so valued."

Marian Shelton was buried in Arlington National Cemetery on October 12, 1990. On October 4, 1994, at the request of their children, Charles Shelton's status was officially changed from prisoner of war to killed in action. In what appears to have been an eerie understatement, the Reverend Charles E. Shelton, Jr., declared, "We no longer had the emotional resources to pursue the POW-MIA issue because of the stress. This issue kills people. That has been our experience. Our family has sacrificed enough. And not everybody is playing fair."

Other families of POWs and MIAs "exhibit symptoms of extreme paranoia, as well they might," states Nigel Cawthorne in his 1990 book *The Bamboo Cage*. Cawthorne notes that in addition to Mrs. Shelton, who "believed her home to be bugged," other families of missing men "have stories of mysterious break-ins, disappearing papers and the inevitable toll on health of long years of worry."

And authors Mark Sauter and Jim Sanders, reporting their findings in *The Men We Left Behind*, conclude, "US government agencies, up to and including the White House, have engaged in what can only be described as 'dirty tricks' against POW family members and activists. There is evidence that both the DIA and White House engaged in illegal domestic intelligence gathering on the activities of American citizens."

On September 18, 1999, in a ceremony attended by approximately 2,000 people, the Colonel Charles E. Shelton Freedom Memorial in Honor of Prisoners of War and Missing in Action of All Wars was dedicated in Owensboro, Kentucky, near the park where Charles and Marian first met. Captain Eugene McDaniel, a former POW who had worked alongside Marian, told the crowd, "I don't know about you, but I have had a real problem with forgiveness. It was easy for me to forgive my Vietnamese guards, those who tortured me, and I did forgive them. But it has been infinitely harder for me to forgive those in my own country who could act on behalf of our abandoned men and who don't, those who know the truth and refuse to admit it, those who could bring justice to bear and refuse to do it. In fact, I'm still working on forgiveness, asking God to teach me to forgive those who have continued to ignore the truth about our men."

The Movie Producer

On July 15, 1991, 45-year-old Roland Jon Emr—a movie producer with ties to the POW issue—and his 20-year-old son Roger were gunned down in their car in broad daylight at a traffic light in Culver City, Calfornia; a friend, Sue Fellows, was slightly wounded; Roland's 71-year-old mother Renee was not hurt. Roland's 71-year-old father Arthur was shot to death in his Phoenix, Arizona home the same day.

How did a moviemaker get involved in the prisoner issue? Roland Jon Emr, known as Jon, had teamed with his mother Renee to produce a television movie called *The Last POW? The Bobby Garwood Story*. Renee and Jon also had bought the rights to Scott Barnes' *Bohica*; according to Barnes, four of the six films to which Emr claimed to have the rights had POW themes.

A *Los Angeles Times* report on the killings quoted Culver City Police Detective Hank Davies on possible motives: "There's plenty of people who were upset with Emr," the detective said. "From what many people have told me, he was a con artist. There are plenty of people who have motives. I'd say millions was skimmed."

Emr's enemies came to include Barnes himself, who alleged "millions lost through [Roland Emr's] scams" in the 1980s. The animosity was mutual; Renee Emr called Barnes "as shrewd as they come, and as evil. You have never been harassed until he comes after you."

It is difficult to determine who, if anyone, is in the right in this ugly squabble; yet it naturally draws one's attention that Jon Emr, like Marian Shelton, had worked to call attention to the POW issue, and then died violently.

Renee Emr, survivor of the massacre at Sepulveda Boulevard and Slauson Avenue, identified the killer as Robert Michael Allen, Jon Emr's bodyguard. Allen's motive was said to be anger at Jon for allegedly promising Allen a substantial interest in a planned film on James Dean and then reneging.

Allen was on the FBI's Ten Most Wanted list for 15 months, until his remains and those of his girlfriend Susan Lynn Calkins were found in the desert by hikers on November 22, 1992. Near the skeletons was a zippered bag containing two guns, one of which was shown by laboratory tests to be the one used to kill the Emrs. Police ruled the deaths of Allen and Calkins a murder-suicide.

But as writer Fred Schruers points out in a *Premiere* magazine article, some people "wonder if he was killed by conspirators who indeed had hired him to take out Emr. As [discoverer of the bodies Steve] Snow ... asks: 'If he killed himself, how did he get out there without a vehicle ... ? And if he shot himself with one of those guns, how the hell did it end up back inside that zippered-up bag?'"

According to Nancy Myer, Allen played a role but did not act alone. "These deaths are all related to a business deal that went sour," she pointed out. "The former bodyguard was hired for his knowledge of the patterns of the Emrs and so that the killers could get close. Robert Allen was willing to participate in the murders because he parted on bad terms with the Emrs."

"The man who ordered these murders had a deal with Roland Emr involving the production of a script and the movie property made from that script. In the opinion of the killer, Emr ripped him off. Instead of seeking help from the courts this man hired a killer to take out his anger for him. He then had the killer eliminated so that it could not trace back to him."

"I believe that two detectives surfaced information relative to threats over this movie deal but they did not realize how significant the information was to their case," Myer noted. "I think they ended up suspecting that it was drug-related."

"I have the feeling that the man who ordered these murders has since died of cardiac problems."

Robert Cracknell also felt that a business-deal motive was behind these murders, stating, "I believe the killings of the Emr family were as stated and the investigation facts correct; that any involvement with prisoners of war was a coincidence."

He emphasized that while "it would be so easy to weave circumstances and vague connections to tie in and strengthen a definite connection," there is little logical reason to believe that a POW movie based on a book would be a threat to anyone. "The book has been published. The fact that they are considering making a film about it is not going to make a scrap of difference. The truth, albeit somewhat short, is now public knowledge. There are POW camps containing live Americans in Laos, as there well may be live Americans being held in Russian prisons ..."

Looking at the tragic reality of decades of imprisonment, he added, "The families of the men missing surely have a right to know the truth—but would it be viable for them to suddenly be reunited with the men after so many years of brainwashing, both politically and mentally? In fact, do they now consider themselves to be Americans?"

This last point was echoed by Bertie Catchings when she discussed the issue of rescuing or purchasing the freedom of POWs after decades of captivity. "I think some of the young men were not well," she observed, "and they didn't know what was going on, their minds were deranged, maybe a few of the men chose to marry and live over there ... And you are assuming—or a lot of the people that are wondering about it are assuming—that each person has got the mental capacity that you might have at this time, but some of these people were brainwashed. Just from living in a strange, bad situation, they might feel like, 'Well, who would want me back home anyway?'"

Like Cracknell, the spirit of Jon Emr sees no logical reason why his movies would be considered important enough to make him a target, according to a reading by medium Janet Cyford.

"Oh, this is like a knotted ball of string," she said as she tuned in first to the most incomprehensible of the three murders, that of Jon's father, Arthur Charles Emr. "Someone that this Allen knew killed Arthur Charles," she noted. "This man was—he was a real 'bigshot,' this Allen—big mouth, and so was she [Calkins]. And it was used against him ... There was money that changed hands for this."

As for Jon, she pointed out that "the film that he was making ... since he's been in spirit, he couldn't understand why they would've made such a fuss about what he was making ..."

Allen's grudge against Emr was used by others who found it convenient to hire him as an assassin. "You've only got to drop the word in the right ear of the person to incite anger." Yet, according to this reading, Allen's gripe against Emr was not a legitimate grievance over having been cheated, but had more to do with simple impatience; he wanted Emr to move ahead with the James Dean movie, in which he had a shared interest. But "it was put off for what [Emr] was doing [other projects, usually with POW themes], and he wanted it to be faster than that ... He wanted the James Dean thing done ... He was used to getting his way, this one. There were people there that could verify that he was a piece of work, this man—a nice English expression for you—you know, *disgusting* piece of work."

"All I can say from this guy—he cannot understand why what he was doing would have taken his own life."

And the spirit of Jon expresses concern for his remaining son, still haunted by the killings and lacking a solid foundation, "as if he's restless, as if he can't settle anywhere."

An intriguing image came through in the reading. "I'm looking at a large vehicle that would have been—it's as if this vehicle moves dirt, as if it comes into some area and the dirt is red in my vision, the dirt is put in the back of this big heavy vehicle, it's got enormous tires ... I'm told this is something that was going on at that time ... if something's unearthed, then I'm wondering whether this is a symbolic picture ... no, it's too real for that. It's some construction going on, and it seems like it's in desert land ... there's being a body uncovered that was something to do with this man's death ... I don't know what that person has got to do with this."

Here we are presented with a difficulty that occurs repeatedly in mediumship—what information being conveyed is symbolic, and what is real? If it is real, as Cyford believed it probably is, the desert image brings to mind the bodies of Allen and Calkins being found in the desert. But what about the construction image? Is this a related part of the story that has yet to come to light?

But she conveyed a message from Jon that "there are a lot of layers of this," of which Robert Michael Allen and his grudge are but one. "It doesn't seem as if there's really any reason ... why he should have been shot like this ... I'm being shown an argument

... this guy I would've said was a very placid, easygoing fellow, but he'd got a temper as well—a real bad altercation ... he was more determined to go on with the story of the POWs, because they were telling him to stop it. I'm being told I can't give you any direct link to who was at the back of this ..."

"But with this man, his only concern is about his younger son. There's an older man that's still alive that worries about this younger boy—well, he's a man now ... He's saying they hadn't even got very far into [the POW issue] ... what they were worried about, was how far he would go into touching the truth ..."

"... and when he wouldn't back down—because money was being withdrawn—it was decided that they'd have to shut him up completely ... That was the first threat—that money wouldn't be put up for him to continue in that vein. He'd come across a POW that had got some things to say. They were afraid of what he was going to uncover, and it was like, don't let him go any further with it."

In a reading by Betty Muench, the spirit of Emr was found to be offended by the speculations pointing to business fraud on his part as the reason for his death.

"There is an immediate sense of indignation and that this will come from the source which is Roland. There will be this which will show that he will not concur with those theories which will have to do with any kind of scam. There will be this which will show that he will be one to hold this indignation very strongly still and that this will be because of the killing of his son and his father and that there will be this which will not have caused him alone to be indignant, to be this over his own death, but the indignation was over the killing of the rest of the family."

According to this reading, Emr had learned POW-related facts from Barnes, and let his father and son in on this information, thereby resulting in their deaths as well as his own. "There is this which he indeed did share with the father and the son and that there will have been this which was among them like a bonding energy around this information primarily provided by Barnes' information. There will be this which was thought to be very important and valuable *and that he will have wanted to make this film but that he will have been thwarted at every turn and when there will have been one last imposition on him around this, then he became very secretive and that is when others will have suspected he was withholding which then appeared to be dishonesty. At this point Roland did not know who to trust and this will have made it seem very much more of a connivance. There is in him a denial of anything to do with any kind of cheating and that is one source of his indignation but that indeed he will have confided in his son and father and for that he is also sorry. He would not have done so had he thought that someone would have taken them all out of the earth life and then proceed to take out others who were not really involved."*

After the reading, Muench commented on Roland Jon Emr's denial of wrongdoing: "Usually in spirit, people do not try to perpetuate a fraud and so I believe him in this ..."

If this is true, then the misconstrued secretiveness on the part of Emr described in the previous paragraph might well have caused miscommunication, as people mistook the secretiveness for something worse. Another unintentional provocation may have its source in his ebullient personality, his salesman's ability to convince potential investors and perhaps even himself that "we're all going to get rich" and then fail to deliver. His apparent inflation of false hopes on the part of bodyguard Robert Michael Allen with regard to the planned James Dean movie might be what led Allen to turn against Emr as an assassin-for-hire.

Allen himself was apparently eliminated because he could incriminate others if he were to talk, Nancy Myer pointed out earlier. His supposed murder of Susan Lynn Calkins followed by suicide was in reality a double murder by the people who hired Allen to kill the Emrs, according to Bertie Catchings.

"It was not suicide. It's just like, if you wanted somebody to be dead, you went out and hired somebody and paid them a large amount of money so that you wouldn't be there when the crime took place ... That person knows that you were responsible for him doing that, and he can keep milking you for money," said Catchings, who added that they probably planned all along to silence Allen.

The deaths in the Emr case, she noted, "were brought about because they were getting too close to the truth. That's why I told you the wife of the POW, I believe, was killed not so much for anything she did, but it was sending a message to Barnes to back off and try to keep his mouth shut and not get too close to the truth." She emphasized that in the case of the Southeast Asia Golden Triangle drug-trafficking machine, "spending 1 million a day is nothing to them, so when people covet money so much, what's a few deaths of people that threaten their business? It's just 'good business.'"

The Muench reading pointed to hired killers acting under the direction of one ringleader. The conclusion is poignant: "*Roland is available and will be available to offer any kind of energy to this investigation but that he at times, even in spirit, will feel the sadness of defeat by those so-called powers that be and that there will be this which will seem to be unsolvable even from those higher levels of spirit. There is in the workings of conspiracy that which will leave a long line of negative energy and negative karmic patterns which in this time Roland, while indignant, still knows is truth.*" So there will ultimately be justice in the form of inescapable karma for the wrongdoers, even though earthly justice appears impossible in this case.

"*There will be this which he will have some guilt in around the father and the son and that has to do with his gaining their support and their interest in his cause and that his cause may have been the cause of their demise. In that then he grieves strongly but that he is also very much angry about this and this is what he works on at this time …*"

"*This sense of indignation is for Roland at this time probably very good for him… helps him to focus and remain available. Ultimately he will want to move into spirit and seek his true soul which is much more than the personality of Roland, so that ultimately he will want to move on …*"

Forsaken American Troops: An Open Secret

How did so many American prisoners get stranded in Southeast Asia in the first place? In *The Men We Left Behind*, investigators

Mark Sauter and Jim Sanders tell us that in early 1973, "Hanoi released lists of American POWs held in North and South Vietnam. The lists were minus the names of many men known or suspected to be in enemy hands. Air Force General Eugene Tighe, later director of the DIA [Defense Intelligence Agency], remembers that intelligence experts felt 'shock and sadness' at the incomplete prisoner lists. Not only were the lists from Vietnam incomplete, the lists did not include any POWs from Laos."

Simply stated, the North Vietnamese were holding most of the remaining men for ransom. But the reality of this hostage crisis was shrouded in euphemistic language: According to the agreement worked out at the Paris peace talks, Hanoi would get "reparations" or "reconstructive aid" for damage done to their country by the American military machine; in return, the United States would receive what was diplomatically termed cooperation or progress on the prisoner issue, i.e., return of the hostages.

France had found itself in the same situation after its defeat at Dien Bien Phu in 1954, and bought back its men gradually over the years. The payments were purportedly for humanitarian aid. "They kept on paying and men kept on coming out," reports Nigel Cawthorne. "Over the next 16 years more than 1,000 Frenchmen and French Legionnaires came back from the dead." Returns continued up until the mid-1970s. (But the French had listed 9,537 men as prisoners. What became of the rest?)

In a letter to the North Vietnamese government, President Richard Nixon promised $3.25 billion in "aid." But he faced the unhappy task of presenting this bitter pill to Congress at an especially inopportune time. Newspaper reports of communist torture of the returned prisoners produced a national sense of outrage that diminished the prospect of a multi-billion-dollar aid package to the communist war criminals. And the president himself was losing clout. "Certainly the US Treasury held enough cash to purchase the POWs ... ," Sauter and Sanders note. "But it was political capital that the Nixon Administration lacked. Heading into the Watergate crisis, Nixon and his advisors believed it too sensitive politically to tell the truth about the Paris negotiations and the secret wars in Laos and Cambodia. Nixon and Kissinger even concealed from Congress the fact that they had promised specific amounts of aid to Hanoi."

"In the end, rather than pay for unpatriated US POWs, the Nixon Administration chose to deny their existence."

Thus began the government's cover-up of its abandonment of our men, a policy that, once instituted in the bureaucracy, continued through all succeeding administrations. The enemy ceased to be Hanoi and instead became POW experts wishing to share intelligence, prisoners' families digging for the truth, and refugees and defectors bringing back evidence of live Americans left behind. As stated in a summary of a report by Gen. Eugene Tighe, "The POW office only pursues leads that will help discredit the source."

And the general expressed his bafflement that the same intelligence that is classified and kept from the prisoners' families is given to the North Vietnamese communists by U.S. delegates. Similarly, Army Colonel Millard Peck, chief of the Defense Intelligence Agency's special office for POW/MIA affairs, reached the disturbing conclusion that his agency had a "mind-set to debunk" reports of live American troops left behind.

Imagine the men waiting in vain to return to their families, eventually falling into hopelessness as they realize the finality of their abandonment. Vietnam veteran Dannion Brinkley, who experienced a richly detailed near-death experience after being hit by lightning in 1975, writes in his bestselling book *Saved By the Light* about the "boxes of knowledge" he was shown in the afterlife, the first three of which "showed the mood of America in the aftermath of the war in Southeast Asia. They revealed scenes of spiritual loss in our country that were byproducts of that war, which weakened the structure of America and eventually the world."

"The scenes were of prisoners of war, weak and wasted from hunger, as they waited in the rugged prisons of North Vietnam for American ambassadors to come and free them. I could feel their fear and then despair when they realized one by one that no help would be forthcoming and that they would live out their remaining years as slaves in jungle prisons ..."

"The MIAs ... were used as a starting point in the visions to show an America that was slipping into spiritual decline."

Evidence shows that other American POWs were shipped to the Soviet Union, China, and other communist nations, even after the war ended, to be exploited for their technological knowledge. Valuable men such as these were never returned. No less an authority than Russian President Boris Yeltsin has supplied corroboration, telling NBC in 1992, "Our archives have shown this to be true. Some of them were transferred to the territory of the former USSR and were kept in labor camps. We don't have complete data and can only surmise that some of them may still be alive."

Instead of seizing on this remarkably candid admission as a rare window to the truth—and perhaps even to the recovery of prisoners—the U.S. government immediately downplayed Yeltsin's comments. Such revelations would have shined an unwelcome light on high-level failures, and also would have clashed with one of the key aims of U.S. foreign policy during the 1990s, the normalization of relations with Vietnam as part of a rush to establish trade, over the dead bodies—and perhaps in some cases, live bodies—of the POWs, a development that appears to have had little to do with forgiveness and much to do with the almighty dollar.

In the end, combining the psychic readings with the known facts, no definite consensus emerges on the cause of these deaths and whether they ultimately share a common connection. Considering that thousands of people have connections to the many men left behind—and that hundreds became active in the POW issue— could the tragic fates of a handful of them be no more than a coincidence that we should not read too much into?

At this late date, all we can do is pray for the forsaken prisoners and lost activists and take our only comfort in a higher, truer perspective—that although they are lost to us, they are never lost to our omnipresent and loving Creator.

Chapter 5:
Judi Bari and Leroy Jackson — Who Is Targeting Environmental Activists?

"... many of these people [environmentalists] have done us an essential service in helping us preserve and protect our green zones and our cities, our water and our air." —Reverend Billy Graham, *Approaching Hoofbeats*

"If the troubles from environmentalists cannot be solved in the jury box or at the ballot box, perhaps the cartridge box should be used." —Former Secretary of the Interior James Watt

Miraculously, the motion-triggered bomb that exploded under the car seat of environmentalist Judi Bari as she drove down an Oakland street on May 24, 1990 did not kill her. But she spent the remainder of her life in agony from the blast, and later suffered the ravages of breast cancer that spread through her already-broken body. Judi Bari died on Sunday, March 3, 1997, leaving behind two young daughters.

At the time of her death, the 1990 bombing remained unsolved. Was it a conspiracy by powerful interests or the act of a small group or someone acting alone? And what really happened in the similar case of New Mexico environmental activist Leroy Jackson, who was found dead—allegedly of a drug overdose—shortly before he was to brief federal officials on logging company corruption?

114

The Attempted Murder of Judi Bari

Judith Beatrice Bari was working as a carpenter in northern California when she joined the radical environmental organization EarthFirst. By force of her intense, committed personality, this petite activist eventually molded the once-violent organization along the lines of her own militant yet stubbornly nonviolent vision.

One of Bari's strengths, which made her particularly threatening to the lumber interests, was her ability to reach out and connect with timber workers. At the time of the car-bomb explosion, she was beginning to turn these enemies into friends by emphasizing common interests and demonstrating solidarity with blue-collar workers. She won friends among their ranks when she fought on behalf of lumber workers who were exposed to hazardous chemicals. Earlier in her life, Bari worked as a union activist who played a leading role in two strikes.

In the spring of 1990, the 40-year-old Bari was making plans for "Redwood Summer"—a timber conservation protest campaign modeled on Freedom Summer in Mississippi in 1964—which she hoped would draw volunteers from around the country. She declared that "... because of the stranglehold of the timber companies on our local economic and social structure (which we found parallel to the stranglehold of the racists in Mississippi), as long as the crisis remained local, we didn't think we would be able to stop either the violence against us or the violence against the forest." As had been done three decades earlier, she hoped to draw the attention—and the conscience—of the nation to the crisis. "We felt that if the people of the United States knew that they were clear-cutting the Redwoods and beating up the activists that they would be appalled ..."

But as fate would have it, the strongest parallel of Redwood Summer to Freedom Summer would be the acts of bloodshed. In the late morning of May 24, 1990, Judi Bari was driving a white Subaru station wagon down an Oakland street, accompanied by boyfriend and fellow activist Darryl Cherney, when a car bomb hidden under her seat exploded.

115

"I felt it rip through me with a force more powerful and terrible than anything," she later recalled. "It blew right through my car seat, shattering my pelvis, crushing my lower backbone, and leaving me instantly paralyzed. I couldn't feel my legs but desperate pain filled my body. I could feel the life force draining from me, and I knew I was dying ..." Cherney sustained injuries to his face—including an eye injury—from flying glass.

The Oakland Fire Department had to use the Jaws of Life to cut through the front door to get to Bari. According to the report of Michele Griki, a civilian evidence technician with the Oakland Police Department, a bomb had exploded under the seat, suggesting an assassination attempt. But an FBI team quickly entered the case and persuaded the Oakland Police Department that Bari and Cherney were dangerous radicals, "the type of people" to be transporting a bomb. In fact, EarthFirst had never had a bomb-related incident in its history.

And the authorities did not seem troubled by the illogical nature of the scenario they were advancing—that someone would place an armed, motion-triggered bomb under a car seat and then go drive the car. Few in the media expressed skepticism regarding the official storyline, an unfortunate phenomenon that would be repeated six years later when an innocent man, security guard Richard Jewell, became the FBI's chief suspect in the Atlanta Olympic bombing. ("Jewell fits the profile of a lone bomber," wrote the *Atlanta Journal and Constitution*, and NBC News added that there was "probably enough to convict him.")

The two victims were charged with "illegal possession of explosives," but in mid-July, the district attorney concluded there was no basis for prosecution. Incredibly, the authorities showed no interest in finding the actual bomber or bombers still on the loose.

So who really committed this crime? Bari said she suspected it was a hit man hired by the lumber interests. A hate group was another possibility; she and Cherney had received a flood of death threats shortly before the car bombing. Reporting the threats to police and the FBI had done no good. The timber industry and hate groups seemed to overlap, according to Bari, who claimed that the timber interests spread alarming misinformation to incite lumber workers and the general public to take action against her. She recalled that "we were calling for people to come in from all over the country to engage in non-violent civil disobedience to stop the over-cutting; and the timber industry was mounting a campaign to portray us as violent, and to whip up hatred against us. This included my receipt of increasingly frightening death threats, and the fake press releases that were being distributed not only to the press, but were being passed out in the lumber mills and on the logging jobs. The fake press releases had the Earth First logo on them—but they weren't written by us, and in contrast to what we were really saying, they were calling for violence and tree spiking...."

In an interview with *Albion Monitor*, Bari voiced her suspicion of a high-level conspiracy, pointing to another bombing that occurred in May 1990 as part of what she described as a high-level plot to frame and destroy her.

"Two weeks before I was bombed in Oakland, a bomb partially exploded at the Cloverdale L-P [Louisiana-Pacific] mill," she noted. "This bomb turned out to have the identical construction of the bomb in my car, absent the motion device. It had the timer, it had the same kind of colors of wires, it had the same solder—they tested the solder, it was from the same tube of solder. They tested the tape, it was from the same roll of tape ... Placed nearby—and this is a strange thing for somebody who intended to burn down a mill—was a cardboard sign that said 'L-P Screws Millworkers.'"

The bomb exploded, just barely—not enough to ignite the gas can and burn down the lumber mill. In Bari's view, the bomb was designed to fail; if it were really intended to burn down the mill, what would be the point of placing alongside it a cardboard sign that would be destroyed in the fire? The sign, according to Bari, was meant to be seen with the partially exploded bomb, creating a terrorist-bomber image of Bari and her colleagues that could be used to arrest Bari as the chief suspect two weeks later when an identical bomb would explode in her car.

Yet, according to the psychic readings on this case, the culprit is neither the lumber industry nor rogue agents of the FBI, as some of

Bari's supporters suspected.

"I don't think it was something that the logging people as a whole or as a group appeared to know about," said Bertie Catchings, who examined photographs of Bari and the car wreckage. "I think that one or two people that were angry, that had an extremely violent nature, just decided to do this."

It was "someone involved with a hate group that did indeed fix the bomb," Catchings noted, "and I do not believe that they [Bari and Cherney] tried to rig it themselves." Catchings seemed to hint at a connection between some logging people and hate groups— ideological allies with a basic awareness of one other's activities in the small-town environment—intuiting that "probably there were people among the logging people that knew who did this, and they talked to the guilty people and explained to them that they'd better not do this anymore ..."

Her reading suggests that perhaps some people in the lumber industry knew of and tolerated efforts by hate groups to sabotage Bari through false propaganda and intimidation, but did not know that one or two individuals would carry their hatred to the extreme of attempted murder.

Nancy Myer also saw Bari incurring the wrath of violent individuals who then took the law into their own hands. "During the course of Ms. Bari's work on behalf of the environment I have the sense that she had a number of encounters with what I can only call a mountain family," she points out. "They lived in primitive conditions and did not exactly believe in or adhere to local laws. They are descendants from settlers going way back."

"She had an argument with two of the men from this clan several weeks before her death." Myer believes that Bari was targeted "as a direct result of that disagreement and not the environmental issues."

"The mountain family has connections with two different militia groups. That is where they got the expertise for the detonators and the materials for the bomb."

"This is a close-knit group that a lot of local people are afraid of. I doubt that anyone will ever give them up."

Myer's vision of the car-bomber(s) having targeted Bari for

reasons other than her controversial environmental campaign comes as a bit of a surprise. But her psychic opinion is echoed in Robert Cracknell's reading, in which he conveyed his strong impression that "she would take up any cause," specifying the abortion issue in particular. Shortly before the bombing, she had indeed infuriated some pro-life activists by counter-demonstrating against them. Expecting to encounter crude, bullying behavior on the part of the anti-abortion activists, Bari proceeded to behave like a crude bully herself, joining Cherney and others in singing provocative pro-abortion songs that outraged pro-life demonstrators trying to shut down the abortion clinic.

A chilling letter to *The Press Democrat* in Santa Rosa from "The Lord's Avenger"—claiming credit for the bombing of Bari and Cherney, as well as the attempted bombing at the Cloverdale Louisiana Pacific sawmill—attacked Bari for her support of a "baby-killing clinic." The letter writer's accurate description of the two bombs, information that was not available to the public, make him or her a key suspect in this still-unsolved case.

"I believe that the bombers were not professionals as such, i.e. 'for hire.'" Cracknell explained. "I think the more likely scenario is that she may well have been in the area of the explosion for some time and had possibly stirred up local feelings against her, (a) by her lifestyle in general or (b) because of her current protest campaign. I get the feeling that maybe a local election was taking place at the time and the impression of a group of men who lived hard and drank hard, whose concept of a woman was that she should be dressed and 'frilled-up' like a woman (her place being in the kitchen, or the bed). This group of men, possibly under the influence of alcohol, constructed a home-made bomb, which I believe was not meant to kill; the intention simply being to frighten her and to get her to leave the area."

The misogynistic attitude that Robert Cracknell sensed on the part of the bombers is reflected in the Lord's Avenger letter (a piece of evidence I did not share with Cracknell), which declared, "Let the woman learn in silence, but suffer not a woman to teach or to usurp authority from the man." As Bari recalled, the letter writer also announced "that the Lord told him to bomb me when I spoke at the abortion clinic the year before. That he saw 'Satan's flame shooting from [my] mouth and ears, proving that this was no natural woman born of Ruth.'" Bari raised questions about the authenticity of the Lord's Avenger letter, suggesting that it might have been authored not by a lone religious terrorist, but by FBI officials to create a new suspect and thus deflect attention away from the negative publicity resulting from their disastrous framing of Bari and Cherney. She noted that in addition to the bomber, the FBI was the only other entity that could describe the way the bomb was constructed.

But the psychic readings on this case tend to support the authenticity of the Lord's Avenger letter, along with the conclusion that two angry individuals, rather than a corrupt element of a government agency or corporation, committed this terrorist act. Medium Betty Muench's reading presented a picture similar to that perceived by the three psychic detectives.

As in Nancy Myer's psychic vision, the bombers are described as a pair of angry men. *This was done by two men who will have been especially hateful of her work and her attention that she was receiving ... two men alive today and unemployed, aging, bitter, and very ill with life-threatening disease. A sorrowful payment for their attempt on others' lives.*

Medium Janet Cyford began her reading by asking, "Is there a daughter left? Someone's talking about their daughter."

Judi Bari left behind two young daughters when she died.

"It's as if she's trying to find out in her mind, wondering in her mind, how they got to put that bomb in the car, because she went back over in her mind—where did she leave it, where was it? ... I feel that I'm looking at it in the front of where she lived, looking down on it ... but remembering that she parked it in a parking lot somewhere. She certainly had nothing to do with it. Someone else put it there," but she still wonders 'how on earth did they get it in there?'"

A message also came through that "if this had not been such a flimsy car, she would have been hurt far more," as the heavier construction of a larger and more solid vehicle would have held more of the deadly power of the blast within the car.

Cyford said that the spirit of Judi Bari conveyed an image of "someone pushing into her ... and threatening her," local individuals "who would have been losing their jobs or lost out in this anti-logging campaign. Someone's saying to her, 'We're going to shut you up.'—and that's someone that almost knocks her over, walks into her on the street, but this guy here, you know, the police would do nothing ... there's no protection."

This account matches what Judi Bari said about her attempts to get help from law enforcement following threats on her life, when she maintained a Mendocino county deputy told her, "If you turn up dead, we'll investigate." She then took the death threats to the Board of Supervisors, where, she later claimed, one of the supervisors simply told her, "You brought it on yourself, Judi."

Bari's anti-logging organization, according to this reading, "was beginning to unearth plans that the logging companies had that eventually did get stopped—they were gonna do far more; even though she went through all this, it did what she set out to do, and stopped a lot of logging going on."

"This business with the bomb—she can't point the finger at individuals, but it was not done by the FBI, it was done by ... the people that wanted her to stop organizing or being part of this organization ... with hindsight, the very fact that the bomb was put in the car and all the media attention it got brought more attention to what she was trying to do."

Cyford emphasized, however, that even in the case of a highly committed activist like Bari, "there doesn't seem to be that feeling of 'they've still got to carry on with this.' She just is, as a mother would be, concerned about her children ... It seems as if they were quite young at that time." Judi Bari's daughters Lisa and Jessica would have been 8 and 4 years old in 1990, when she was disabled for life by the bombing; and 15 and 11 the year their mother died of cancer.

The long fight for justice by Bari's supporters ultimately brought victory and vindication. On June 11, 2002, in an article entitled, "Earth First activists win case; FBI, cops must pay $4.4 million for actions after car bombing," *San Francisco Chronicle* writers Jim Herron Zamora and Henry K. Lee reported:

> A federal jury in Oakland today awarded $4.4 million in damages to two Earth First organizers who were injured in a 1990 car-bomb blast, agreeing with plaintiffs' arguments that FBI agents and Oakland police violated their civil rights by focusing on them as suspects.
>
> The eight-woman, two-man jury awarded $2.9 million to the estate of the late Judi Bari and $1.5 million to Darryl Cherney, finding the federal agents and police officers liable for violating the former couple's First and Fourth amendment rights ...
>
> "We lived for years under the cloud of suspicion—Judi died without ever being officially exonerated," [Cherney] said. "We waited a long time for the chance to show our innocence. I hope now that we will finally get an investigation into who really committed the bombing. I think the government owes us an apology. They have owed us an apology for 12 years."

Remarkably, the Oakland City Council passed a resolution declaring "that the City of Oakland shall designate May 24 as Judi Bari Day and celebrate and honor the work of Judi Bari ...and that the City shall encourage its schools, civic institutions and citizens to memorialize Judi Bari's work through art, media, festivals, school assignments and other creative means."

On May 24, 2003, the city of Oakland, which had once tried to prosecute Bari for the terrorist bombing that critically injured her, held a ceremony in her honor at the site of the crime on its thirteenth anniversary.

The Assassination of Leroy Jackson

Three years after the attempt on Bari's life, Leroy Jackson, a 47-year-old Navajo activist fighting for reduced logging of the Chuska Mountain forests on the nation's largest Indian reservation—a vast tract that includes sections of Arizona, New Mexico, and Utah—was planning to inform federal officials of corruption inside the tribal logging company, the Navajo Forests Products Industry (NFPI).

As leader of the crusade by Dine (Navajo) Citizens Against Ruining our Environment (Dine CARE), Jackson negotiated with the NFPI in an effort to pressure the tribal company to conduct its logging in a way that was reasonable, sustainable, and in compliance with federal environmental standards. After negotiations broke down, he sought a legal solution. He was reported missing on October 1, 1993; eight days later, New Mexico police found him dead inside his Dodge van. His suspicious death, occurring shortly before he was to testify in Washington, has inspired comparisons to the death of Karen Silkwood under similar circumstances.

Even though Jackson's sudden demise was preceded by numerous threats on his life, it was ruled "accidental death due to methadone overdose." In *The War Against the Greens*, investigative reporter David Helvarg noted their justification for this conclusion: "An adverse reaction to the drug can cause bleeding from the nose and mouth, which is what the police concluded caused Leroy's blood to pool below his head."

Yet people who knew Leroy Jackson pointed out that the fitness-oriented activist could not have died of a narcotics overdose. Jackson was a long-distance runner who did not smoke, drink, or use drugs. Rather, the obvious hazard to Jackson's health was that, as Helvarg reports, he "had received a number of death threats and had been hung in effigy by angry loggers at a 1992 pro-logging rally. Jimmy Bitsuie, a board member of the Navajo Forest Products Industry (NFPI), the tribal-owned company Leroy was fighting, warned a reporter that 'somebody's going to get hurt' if logging was cut back because of Leroy's activities. And at a public meeting in Window Rock, Arizona, on September 28, a few days before Leroy disappeared, new threats of violence were raised by angry out-of-work loggers." And, as Helvarg notes, there was already a history of violence and unsolved deaths under the corrupt Navajo reservation government.

The FBI declined to investigate this suspicious death, even after a request from Rep. Bill Richardson (D-NM).

Robert Cracknell described having "a strong impression of a

suspect—a large male, in his mid-forties, heavy build, whose weight would be in excess of 20 stone [280 pounds], and heavily tattooed, either balk or shaven head. This man could well have been a bodyguard, employed to keep troublemakers away for creating too many waves."

"Now, though [Jackson] was involved in this particular investigation, it's possible he also stumbled upon something else—which would give extra weight to his evidence. I believe that something else may well have something to do with illegal workers."

The next part of his reading illustrated the frequently symbolic nature of the insights a psychic receives, and the difficulty of interpreting such information. "I now come to some psychic impressions I jotted down very quickly—and I have to place them in some kind of order."

"My first impression is that of an eagle. Initially I associated this with the tattooed suspect, that the tattoo may well have been an eagle. It may also be some kind of bar—a drinking place with Eagle in the name, or maybe Eagle Rock (if such a place exists)."

Cracknell also wondered about the significance of the name "Jackson," possibly referring to something other than Leroy Jackson, for he described the name coming to him a few seconds before he looked at the case. He suggested the possibility of a local landmark with the name "Jackson" that is significant to this case.

"But I believe that Jackson did in fact stumble upon some form of illegal labor and subsequently opened up a whole can of worms—hence his unfortunate demise," he concluded.

"Mr. Jackson was murdered to silence him," Nancy Myer stated. "He did not take any kind of drugs because he feared them. He saw too many friends lost to drugs. There is no way he would voluntarily have taken them."

"I also get the impression that he took quite a beating the night he died. The head injury alone he sustained that night would have killed him."

Betty Muench's reading showed the spirit of Leroy Jackson still focused on the earth, still devoted to the ecological concerns that occupied him while on the physical plane:

"There is this great white light within which forms a pattern much as the sky would over an area which has been cleared. There is this which will show that Leroy will still roam those places which will seem to bring the earth and the sky together."

"There will be this which will suggest that he is well aware of his condition and he continues to work this cause. Those with great causes will not often be able to move on within, once they will go within, but that in this instance it is as if Leroy simply wants to keep informed of what is occurring and he will see that there is this which will not stop because of his death. There is this which he is seeing and feels certain of then. There will be with this one Leroy the knowing of the need for him to go within and that he must then give up this cause but it is as if he seeks someone else; to stir this in someone else; to stir this in someone who would then seek to continue his fight."

"There will be this which will say that there will be many elements involved in his demise. There will be this which will have been told to a certain group that he will have been someone who could be heard and listened to and that then this will have changed their well-being. This will have been those who worked in the logging and who felt that this was a threat to their well-being. Actually they did not benefit as much from this logging as those who will have been at the head of the tribal company, and that these will have been the ones to plant the seeds which will have instigated the killing, and that then when this did occur it will have been as if everyone will have looked the other way." This description of the circumstances is supported in Helvarg's detailing of the tribal logging interests' culture of intimidation and terror.

"Where there is this greed then and where the federal government [in this case, the tribal authority] will back up this greed, then there is this kind of violence. There will have been in the meeting [with federal overseers] that which indeed would have changed the conditions in this operation and that then many would have indeed had to change their way of doing things. This would have been inevitable. There will have been then in the planting of the seeds of fear in those at the bottom rung of this ladder that which accomplished what needed to be done."

"There will have been in this then not all of the workers involved. It was not known by many, but there will be two very large men who will have overtaken Leroy and they will have taken him out of a situation by luring him with information. He will have gone with them willingly but that then he did not come back with them."

"There will be two very large men who stay close to each other even now because they have to keep an eye on each other. Others will suspect but no one actually inquires of them. They are wary of each other now and this is the weak link in all this for anyone who would want to seek further into the untimely death of a man who would have been successful in his quest. In that then he would have been complete and he would have finished what he came to do in this life and he could have left anytime after that with peace. Right now he roams the earth plane and he will know that he should not, but seeks still ... someone to take up his cause ... not to bring justice to his death but to justify his life."

There is deep poignancy in Jackson's continued focus on the earth, following the Native American tradition of revering nature as a sacred manifestation of the Creator. Seeing New Mexico's huge, ancient Ponderosa pines disappearing at a rapid rate was disturbing enough; even worse was the threat to holy sites that were the Navajos' open-air equivalent of churches. In his testimony before the Committee on the American Indian Freedom of Religion Act shortly before his death, Jackson told the U.S. Congress, "Many traditional peoples are being discriminated against and exploited right on their own native lands, simply because their ways are not 'progressive' or centered around Anglo notions of economic development."

So this was largely a cultural and religious issue for Jackson, yet his approach was not that of an extremist or fundamentalist. Like Judi Bari, he was not opposed to all logging, but simply favored logging practices that were prudent, reasonable, and sustainable rather than reckless and rapacious.

"This was a killing which was not ordered," Muench observed, "but also not brought to justice because the murder served the interests of the powerful. There is no end seemingly to what people might do when they perceive their well-being is being threatened."

Similarly, Bertie Catchings saw Jackson's death as the act of ordinary workers who were provoked by exploitation of their fears to take deadly action against an activist who "was a troublemaker."

"I have the feeling that they persuaded someone on the Navajo reservation to take care of Jackson. They explained it in such a way that they were going to lose all this money if Jackson kept on causing trouble. And so I believe it was a single-handed deal done by someone on the reservation."

"It was not something that was voted on or decided," Catchings added. "It was just a single person, and that person that did it … felt like he was being a big hero."

The first thing medium Janet Cyford picked up from Leroy Jackson is a "great love of these [American Indian] people from this man. He had such an empathy for them."

"He's showing me … that he didn't die where they left him; he was moved there. And there were marks on his body that would have proved that it wasn't methadone intoxication. He's showing me being taken, his almost lifeless body in a car, being dumped at this place." She pointed out that it is difficult to tell where he first was "what we would call dead, what medical people would say was dead," because of "my experience of the consciousness still being so close that it's watching what's going on. Marks on his body, around the neck, bruises, roughed up in some way."

"Would this have been in very open countryside? He's showing me that it is, and that the car that they had him in—and there were two other men in the car—two in front, and one sitting at the side of him; he was in the back of the car. He was injected with something that was much stronger than methadone … I'm looking at the countryside. The car comes out of almost a lane onto the highway … it's uninhabited. It seems as if there's farmland or some growth around there, it's green, and the car comes out from this lane and turns onto the highway, only five or six miles before."

"These people had met in a restaurant-bar type of thing the night before," echoing Cracknell's psychic impression that a bar was a site central to Jackson's murder. "They knew who he was, although he thought at the time he was just making conversation … these were people from this logging company, but there was a cover-up where the police were concerned about the state of his body at that time. He was *very* fit. He put up a fight with them."

"His body was in far worse a state than to have said it was just methadone intoxication," Cyford pointed out. "He was in a mess. His clothing was disheveled and dirty. When this was said that it was methadone intoxication, it was like, well, this is a bum, you know." As in the Kurt Cobain case, a drug-overdose conclusion seems to make it easier to dismiss the person, and thus the case, as less deserving of the authorities' time and attention.

As heartbreaking as this story is, Leroy Jackson's noble efforts were not in vain. In her article "The Dilemma of Indian Forestry" that appeared in the Summer 1994 *Earth Island Journal*, Native American environmentalist Winona LaDuke observed, "It is a tribute to Jackson's life that since his death Dine CARE has accomplished much of what he was trying to achieve. The Navajo tribal council has decided to conduct an audit of NFPI and has agreed to an EIS [environmental impact statement] on its logging plan — a first for an Indian reservation."

Chapter 6:
The Markle Massacre

"There is no agony like bearing an untold story inside of you."
—Maya Angelou

The unspeakable scene discovered by Little Rock police shortly before dawn on Monday, November 16, 1987, seemed straight out of fiction, southern gothic literature to be exact. On the ground floor lay the body of 45-year-old economist John Markle, the only son of Mercedes McCambridge, the legendary actress who had supplied the voice of the devil in *The Exorcist*. Markle had been killed by two shots to the head, from a .38-caliber gun and a .45, allegedly self-inflicted. Beside him lay a rubber Halloween mask of an old man he was alleged to have been wearing while committing the atrocities; a videocassette of *A Nightmare on Elm Street* sat in the VCR nearby. In bed on the top floor of the house, John's wife Christine, 45, lay dead of a gunshot to the head. Daughters Amy, 13, and Suzanne, 9, were found shot to death in bed on the middle floor.

What really happened during that night's raging thunderstorms? Did this easygoing, gentle husband and father suddenly turn homicidal and suicidal in reaction to his removal from his job on the full-moon Friday the thirteenth three days earlier? Would a man seized by a fit of violent insanity really put down the gun and use a second one, then stop again and use a third? And isn't it extremely odd, perhaps virtually unprecedented, for a man to shoot himself in the head with two guns?

The Official Story

The killings were ruled a murder-suicide by Medical Examiner Fahmy Malak. But as we will see, any ruling by the doctor who served as Arkansas' chief coroner during the 1980s deserves to be viewed with caution and suspicion.

Markle, a futures trader with a Ph.D. in economics, served as a vice president for the investment banking firm Stephens, Incorporated, the largest brokerage outside of Wall Street. He was said to be on medical leave since October 7, and was officially removed from his job on November 13, three days before the killings. His eight-year career at Stephens followed a successful seven years at Salomon Brothers in New York.

One week after the massacre, an Associated Press story stated that, according to Stephens, Inc., Markle had been fired "over a secret account he controlled ... The *Arkansas Democrat* reported today that Markle set up the account for his mother and worked out a scheme so that Stephens would absorb losses from investments he made for her." But can we accept the report by the *Arkansas Democrat* as the true story? As with Dr. Malak, grave questions have been raised as to its credibility.

"When the investments made gains, Miss McCambridge's account would be credited," the newspaper reported, citing unidentified sources.

As for Markle's side of the story, it died with him. Was there more to this case than the media told us?

Markle as Victim

Psychic detective Nancy Myer examined the basic facts of the case and a photograph of Markle, and noted, "This is one of the cruelest of cases. An entire family destroyed because of greed."

Myer saw the deaths as related to Markle's removal from the brokerage firm three days earlier, but with him as whistleblower rather than wrongdoer. "Just before he was fired, Markle discovered that someone in his company was doing something highly unethical and illegal. When he was fired he made the mistake of stating that he was going to report what he knew to the authorities. He also took documents that proved he was telling the truth. Unfortunately he did not give himself any backup way to protect himself from them. He was too naïve."

"What he discovered is a criminal act. What he did not realize was the terrible lengths the people involved would go to."

Describing what she saw, Myer explained, "I always visualize the case like a movie with a soundtrack that is terrible in quality. I saw two assailants and one lookout/driver outside. They gained entry with a key. That was interesting but not unprecedented with professionals. They certainly seemed professional in the planning and preparation for the killings and the dispatch with which they carried out the murders. They had no conscience or humanity. It was just a 'job' to them."

Bertie Catchings tuned in to this mystery and, like Nancy Myer, concluded that Markle and his family were murdered because he caused certain colleagues to feel threatened by his complaints about alleged financial wrongdoing; she even used the same word Myer used to characterize Markle's behavior — "naïve."

"I believe that John Markle was basically an honest person, and a little bit naïve in his dealings with people," Catchings observed. "Sometimes you have to be 45 years or older to really understand that people that sometimes present themselves as honorable people in good standing in the community are not necessarily ethical or honest. And my feelings that came to me at this time, looking at his picture, are that he was somewhat naïve about some of the people that were controlling this corporation where he worked, and that he saw some things there that weren't on the up and up, and he was questioning these things, and he brought it to the attention of at least one of the killers."

"And so it was all turned around as though he was the bad person who caused these things to go wrong," she continued. "Actually he was working and representing other people who were not so scrupulous, and what is so terrifying here is that someone who was doing the things in this brokerage firm that were not on the up and up, was somebody very close to himself and/or his family — it could have been ... someone that he very much trusted, probably someone he'd known a long time, and he was more or less put in a set of circumstances to take the heat for whatever went wrong, and by being let go from that firm without explaining who was really the cause of the unethical dealings at that corporation, he expected maybe to have some compensation for his embarrassment—I don't think he really had a choice; he had to take the heat—because he was so locked in, that all fingers were pointing to him as the scapegoat ..."

Catchings said Markle was "probably a very brilliant man and knew how to do his work well and do it honestly, but then when it came to doing some things that were not honest, then the people couldn't take that chance of the truth being known, and so he was hushed up, and therefore anything that might later be discovered that was in error would all depend on John Markle. Therefore he became a great scapegoat, and to try to say it was suicide and murder ... the killers thought that would be a clever thing ..."

"So actually, there seems to be, in that particular corporation at that time, a group of people that were connected, and one of the assassins might actually have been paid," Catchings continued. "Actually, of the three people that were involved, there was one who was less personally involved with the activities that took place at the corporation, but was there to make sure that there wasn't any mistake, and also because one of the killers was a little squeamish about this ..."

Medium Betty Muench's automatic-writing spirit group also found that the Markle family was murdered because of a business-related conflict. The tragedy was due in part to two misunderstandings—an unfounded, disproportionate fear of the threat Markle actually posed, and an exaggerated response by people who mistook some angry words for an order to kill.

The reading noted *"that there was something unusual being asked of John and that there will have been this intention to move away ... to move out of a situation in which at the time of his death, was only a proposition but one in which he will have seemed very important. It will be that there will have been then this which will have been secretive and it was thought that he will have the intention*

132

not only to move away but to talk about what was being asked of him."

However, this perception of his intention might have been mistaken or exaggerated, a misunderstanding to which Markle contributed by speaking too openly. *"In that then, without any documentation one way or another, John will have put himself in danger. There will have been this which will have occurred seemingly casual and without demand but that this was not the sense in another person with whom John was in conversation. In John simply trying to analyze this out loud, it was misinterpreted and it will be then the cause of these deaths. It was not even a serious enough a transgression or breach of business etiquette to cause this and that this will have been done out of a kind of anger and temporary rage, it will have been spoken as an aside that this man should be wiped out and that he should not leave anything of himself behind, this will have been the seeming thought spoken out loud by another who will have been taken very seriously by followers and by those who could not discern an order from a thought or a wish."*

This fervent wish for an inconvenient man to disappear, allegedly spoken by someone in authority at some unspecified level of command, echoes the story of Henry II wishing to be rid of Becket, (a theme that comes up again in the next chapter). *"There will be in this then the demise of a whole family out of a series of asides, that will not have had to do with anything but business which was not totally legal or so John thought."*

The Muench reading described the killers as *"three people, well-dressed, posing as something they were not ..."* Although they were not ordered to kill, yet did so because they *"could not discern an order from a thought or wish,"* they nevertheless ended up benefiting from the removal of John Markle.

"It will be that there will be in this situation where they are, this which seems like business as usual, but that each one will know something of the other and they live very close to the edge all the time. There is this sense of two men and a woman and that they will seem to have an alliance that keeps others fearful of them."

This reading also indicates that the people who took an offhand comment as a green light to kill a family hired others to do the horrible deed. According to this scenario, there are individuals at three levels, then—(1) a person who expressed a wish to be rid of a perceived threat posed by Markle, (2) subordinates who acted to turn the wish into reality, and (3) killers rewarded in some way by these subordinates.

In this reading, Markle was described as now realizing what he did not understand at the time—that he was perceived as a formidable presence, *"that he will have been taking up much room in this situation and that others will have felt overpowered by him but that he will not have known that there was this feeling about him and his decisions ... and he did not know this would place his family in danger."*

The self-image described here seems consistent with what is known about Markle. Although he held a prominent position, by all accounts he did not perceive himself or conduct himself as a bigshot. In demeanor and appearance, this hard-working, highly successful executive came across as mild, casual, and perhaps a bit eccentric, far from the stereotypical ambitious 1980s yuppie.

Regarding the business deal Markle allegedly spoke about, resulting in such horrendous tragedy, the Muench reading observed that *"John indeed will have known many details in this proposition, but that he did not see it as a workable concept and that he was however not intending to expose something that was only in the stages of forming. Much of this crime will have been committed out of fears of others and that there was no real basis of these fears. In ... the callous manner of these deaths, there can only be now this which can bring justice out of a kind of fear of each other and of others who will have known of how this was carried out ... a misunderstanding and the loss of lives needlessly. The three exist still and speak of themselves in glowing terms but they all fear each other ..."*

An Indirect Business Connection?

A spirit communication by medium Janet Cyford matches the above readings on the most important point, finding John Markle to be a murder victim rather than a murderer, but finds the workplace

134

connection to be indirect and the crime not to be premeditated homicide. An enemy from work, wanting to cause Markle trouble, suggested to a couple of hoodlums that John had a lot of money in his house. As in the Muench reading, a nasty hint by someone angry at Markle was taken to an unimagined extreme.

Tuning in to the spirit of John Markle, Cyford stated, "This man was quite an outstanding man in the community, and ... had attended something sometime before that was like a fundraising event ... There was a young man in the crowd that first saw John at this time," and this man saw Markle as a rich, successful target to rob, as Markle had supposedly just received a generous severance package.

"The two guys that shot him, that I saw, it all seems that they'd had some word dropped in their ear, within their earshot ... something being leaked that this man had been given a 'good handshake' ... it's an English expression, like a golden handshake, a good amount of money." And they were further told "that he had in his home the money that he was given."

Did the instigating person or persons suggest the thugs kill Markle, too? I asked.

"No, they didn't say kill him, too. *They* [the two thugs] took it that far. It was *carefully* dropped in the right hearing by somebody who wanted trouble for him. And I think it went far further than they'd envisioned it going. But it was almost like, 'If you kill them, that's fine.'"

"They went and demanded to find where the money was. They hadn't got money in the house, so they were threatening that they'd shoot the wife and the two daughters till he came up with the money. They knew that he'd got the money. Of course he hadn't got it in cash. But they were too stupid to realize that. So they shot the daughters and the wife and finally him ... and it couldn't be traced to anybody else; if they had been asked 'who told you to do this,' they'd just overheard that he had a lot of money in the house."

Regarding Markle's conflict in his former workplace, Cyford noted, "There's some argument as to why that firing went on ... but that is not related to the death of this man. Very definite no ...

the people responsible for this [multiple murder] thought there was money involved, that he had money there."

At the fundraising event, according to this reading, "there was a young man. Dark looks—dark eyes, quite round in the face, this man is related to this killing. This man is in prison now, but he's not in prison for this. Now, there's two of them—although it says three guns—there were two people that took part in this, and the two that took part in it were related, cousins, something like that. They'd gone to his home and there really doesn't seem to be any motive for this other than they think they're going to find some money there."

"There's a very low IQ in the guy that sets this up, although he looks quite presentable ... When this was going on, this John thought it had got something to do with his financial connections to his business ..." (Could this thought of John's at the murder scene—a general impression that it was business-related—have been what was picked up by the other psychics and interpreted as a more direct business connection?)

"... but it wasn't that he thought that the people that had fired him had sent these gunmen."

"You know how ... sometimes, they'll follow a bank president home or a bank manager home, tie his wife up, take him to the bank, and that sort of thing. It was that sort of thing. It was that sort of mentality—when he refused, and these two guns, this one man holds two different guns and shoots him in the head" after his wife and daughters were shot. "I think there was quite a lot of stuff that was stolen from the house, but he thought he was going to get more ... but there wasn't, and this was where they'd got angry, and they take him downstairs ... they were trying to make him go somewhere where he could get money for them, and he refused. I get the impression of him being not quite six feet, but quite burly. If there hadn't been guns, he could've taken care of himself ..."

"But as for [the Markle family] being at peace, nobody's left in this sort of state. The children would've been—immediately there would've been people there in spirit for them," Cyford emphasized. And even though John Markle, unlike the rest of his family, carried uniquely heavy burdens at the time of his sudden death, he joined them in experiencing peace and healing upon crossing over. "You know, this business about people being 'earthbound,' there's such a lot of rubbish talked about that sort of thing ... If this man had been trying for years to clear his name, then you could say that he was still very much tied up with this, but I think he's moved on."

"Quite honestly, when he found that his children and wife were killed, he didn't want to live; he was not going to give in to them."

In the official story, however, Markle himself is presented as the villain. It is quite possible that certain individuals, perhaps completely innocent of his murder but eager to hide financial wrongdoing that might be revealed in an investigation of the work-related conflict that ended in Markle's dismissal, put out stories of alleged improprieties by Markle to encourage the murder-suicide conclusion. With the assistance of the establishment-friendly local newspaper and an obedient coroner, Markle's enemies in the corporation at the top of the Arkansas oligarchy could see to it that the official version of reality painted him as a crook and mass murderer, thus avoiding investigation into the firm's affairs that could uncover something they might be trying to hide—nothing horrible, but perhaps unethical or illegal financial practices. Yet, as in White House employees' removal of potentially harmful documents from Vincent Foster's office, this kind of "guilty" behavior can look like something a lot worse to some observers. Did some of this book's psychics, like some in the general public, tune in to this attention-diverting "cover-up" behavior by some in the company and, adding it to the already suspicious aspects of the murder scene, read too much into the workplace connection?

Janet Cyford indicated that perhaps this finger-pointing behavior by some in the company blaming Markle backfired in just this way. "I think they suggested that this killing was related to his firing, which would have put suspicion on them." This could almost be described as an example of appropriate karma if they disseminated, without proof, a story portraying an innocent man as a multiple murderer.

"Going back to this firing in the brokerage firm," she continued, "there was something he was trying to set up that they didn't like ...

He presented something to them almost as a fait accompli and they didn't like it, they didn't like the plan. There's three other people that are in that firm—it's very strange why they should have said that [about Markle killing his family and himself over a business controversy] because it put a spotlight on them."

"I think that there's been a story put out to possibly stop people looking more deeply into their affairs," Cyford pointed out. However, "he's saying quite emphatically it was not people sent from that place."

"This wasn't a contract killing or anything like that ... These two men went there thinking that they were going to clean up that night, and it may well be that they thought he'd been paid off to leave that firm, and that there was money there."

As Cyford tuned in to the part of the story that concerns Arkansas law enforcement in the wake of the massacre, seeing it through John's eyes, she spoke with an understandable tone of bafflement, pointing out that "this was packed up and put away ... as though the authorities couldn't come to a reasonable conclusion about it ... it was as if the police couldn't get any further with it, and nobody bothered after that. Nobody bothered at all."

A Minority Report

In spite of differences in the above readings, they agree on the key point at the heart of this mystery, concurring that, contrary to the official story, John Markle was a victim of a multiple murder, not the perpetrator; and that the killings stemmed, directly or indirectly, from some business-related resentment towards him. However, the verdict is not unanimous. Psychic detective Bob Cracknell provided the dissenting opinion in this case, responding that his "immediate reaction ... is that this was in fact suicide."

This is an appropriate moment to remember that even when we are dealing with some of the world's most skilled psychic detectives, there are bound to be instances of disagreement. The 80-percent accuracy rate Cracknell achieved when tested at Oxford was rightly hailed as phenomenal—yet even an 80-percent accuracy rate leaves plenty of room for error.

Psychics play a more exalted and spectacular role only in the realm of fiction—and even in fiction, a realistic portrayal is likely to show them ultimately as fallible human beings. As Dr. Iris Hineman, the character in the film *Minority Report* who created the crime-preventing Pre-Cog program, wryly observed, "The Pre-Cogs are never wrong ... but occasionally they do disagree."

Cracknell conceded that "the strongest argument against [the suicide conclusion] would appear to be that he was shot twice in the head," a central aspect of the crime that he said calls for more investigation that should look into whether "either of the two shots caused instant death. Also, is it not possible that there was an involuntary pulling of the trigger, immediately after the first shot entered the head? Is it not conceivable that the shock of the first bullet hitting the head could have caused an involuntary jerking of the hand holding the gun, and therefore causing the trigger to activate? This is something that I feel definitely needs to be clarified."

As for how a supposedly gentle family man could commit such atrocities, Cracknell said, "It is not a unique situation, where seemingly normal behavior belies an inner torment and struggle. There are too many recorded cases of seemingly normal people going crazy."

Indeed, although the very thought of fathers and mothers slaughtering their own children strikes us as horrifically unimaginable, this sort of crime occurs more often than most people realize. Some of these cases have received more publicity— Houston mother Andrea Yates, Chicago nurse Marilyn Lemak, Ukrainian immigrant Nikolay Soltys—yet the statistics show these better-known cases to be the tip of a sizable iceberg. In 2002, there were 450 instances of parents killing their own children in the US. And the youngest, most helpless children are the most likely to be victims.

In "Why Parents Kill," an article that appeared in *Slate* magazine on March 12, 2002, Dahlia Lithwick reported, "Children under the age of 5 in the United States are more likely to be killed by their parents than anyone else. Contrary to popular mythology, they are rarely killed by a sex-crazed stranger. FBI crime statistics show that in 1999 parents were responsible for 57 percent of these murders, with family friends and acquaintances accounting for another 30 percent and other family members accounting for 8 percent."

Citing research on the characteristics of fathers who kill, Lithwick observes, "Most frequently—like [Adair] Garcia or Soltys—they kill because they feel they have lost control over their finances, or their families, or the relationship, or out of revenge for a perceived slight or infidelity." As we will see, despair over finances was alleged to be a motive that drove Markle over the edge. Lithwick also notes, "According to a recent article by Elizabeth Fernandez in the *San Francisco Chronicle*, studies further reveal that fathers are far more likely to commit suicide after killing their children." Again, Markle fits the profile, according to the official story.

Exploring the possible connection of Markle's firing to drastic acts of violence on his part, Cracknell wondered, "Could those circumstances be that he had been, perhaps unwillingly, drawn into a financial scam? And when it was uncovered, he was apparently left 'holding the baby.' Was he about to spill the beans but realized that his involvement was so great that criminal charges would finally be brought against him, involving shame and the ignominy of being in prison?"

"That he killed his family is, I feel, undoubted. Did he then shoot himself but fail in his attempt to end his life? And did another person present administer the coup de grace?"

Assisted suicide is a rare enough phenomenon; here we are presented with the prospect of assisted suicide-murder. It seems to defy belief—yet the same can be said for every other explanation of this senseless massacre. And it is worth remembering that although Cracknell's psychic reading of this case is the minority view here, history is filled with countless examples of minority opinions that proved correct.

Perhaps two scenarios were both simultaneously true: Markle was involved in illegality, and so were others; he feared public disgrace and felt desperate and suicidal, while they feared his revealing what he knew, and pondered ways to shut him up. Perhaps Cracknell tuned in to suicidal thoughts that occupied the mind of Markle, while the other psychics picked up on a plan being formulated by or one or more of his enemies who wished to be rid of him. If so, whose intentions were carried to fruition?

Puzzling Evidence

Let's look at the "official" story. A United Press International story the day after the killings, headlined "No Reason Known for Apparent Murder-Suicide of McCambridge's Son, Family," reports that Markle had left a suicide note that "said he had killed his wife and his daughters and was going to kill himself," according to Sgt. Phill Wilson. But it did not say *why* he killed his loved ones. A suicide note can of course be compelled by the real killers, as most observers believe happened to investigative reporter Danny Casolaro (Chapter 1). A short, perfunctory note, just enough to officially "take responsibility" for the act, naturally raises suspicions. "Wilson said police had no motive for the slayings or suicide," the article continues, "but there were unconfirmed reports that Markle had serious financial trouble related to his job ..."

Investigators said Markle called a friend about 2:30 A.M., told him he had an emergency and asked the friend to come over.

"The unidentified friend came over and found the house unlocked but could get no response from anyone in the house. He flagged down a police car, and officers went in and found the victims."

This account leaves us with more questions than answers. Exactly when and why did he call his unidentified friend? Why didn't he call police instead?

Two days after this report, Stephens, Inc. began giving its side of the story, announcing, "On October 6, Stephens, Incorporated learned of a previously undisclosed account controlled by Markle with an out-of-state brokerage firm," and had placed Markle, who had suffered previous heart trouble, on leave until the matter could be investigated.

The next day, the *Arkansas Democrat* said Markle had mixed his mother's money and the company's in the out-of-state account, posting investment gains to his mother's account and losses to Stephens'.

None of the psychic detectives' examinations of this case found him to have been stealing. In Janet Cyford's spirit communication, he admits to nothing worse than transactions that could arguably qualify as insider trading, but nothing that harmed the investment firm.

But even if it is true that Markle was cheating his company, is there any evidence to indicate that such a scandal drove him over the edge? The information we have on his final days and hours seems to prove otherwise. If he were truly distraught and unhinged to the point of being suicidal and homicidal, why did he behave like such a normal, loving dad, telling Amy that final evening, according to a friend she spoke to on the phone, that he would take her and the friend skateboarding on the weekend? This, along with everything said about him by friends and neighbors, does not square with what Pulaski county coroner Steve Nawojczyk told the media: "It was an act of macabre benevolence. He wanted to spare the girls the publicity."

In most states, presumably, a coroner would confine himself to physical examination and not pronounce judgment on the mental state and actions of a complete stranger. Was his baseless public declaration of Markle's motive his own bold opinion, or was he repeating the party line of the Arkansas establishment to bolster a verdict decided upon without any meaningful investigation?

An article on the tragedy by Mary T. Schmich of the *Chicago Tribune* described John Markle as a dedicated husband and father who, despite his financial genius and prestigious position, was easygoing, family-oriented, and seemingly not the type to over-react to any setback he might suffer in the workplace.

"Markle was considered a brilliant, witty and slightly eccentric family man," Schmich noted. "Though his wife and daughters were involved in many community activities, friends called them a private family ..." A friend "recalled that he used to take his kids and their friends to rock concerts and sit happily through the fracas reading a book."

As Schmich reported at the time, "Many who knew Markle say that he was so intent on providing his children with happy childhoods because his own was so unhappy," going back to age five when his parents divorced. The more we view this tragedy in light of these facts and simple logic, the more unthinkable it becomes that this gentle man could have been a killer. Yet, as Bob Cracknell's reading and the statistics on child-killers remind us, human behavior sometimes inexplicably defies logic altogether.

Paper Trail

The family conflict would be made public with the release of an angry 13-page letter Markle purportedly wrote to his mother, in which he complained that nothing he had ever done seemed good enough for her. Over McCambridge's objections, the letter and other writings, including a diary, were made public five months after the killings.

If the writings are genuine—and forgery cannot be ruled out on the part of an audaciously corrupt Arkansas system that has committed more spectacular outrages—they point to an alleged desire by Markle to commit suicide. For instance, when complaining about some of his mother's actions, he writes, "I wish you'd never done a lot of things you did. Night mother." McCambridge had starred in a Little Rock production of the play 'night, Mother, as a woman whose daughter kills herself.

The diary entry allegedly written by John on October 27, 1987, is the most damning piece of evidence against him: "None of these people deserve me. I have put all of their futures in jeopardy. My relationship with my mother has been destroyed. I fear I have placed my family at considerable financial risk, i.e., I am broke and they my children have no inheritance left because of my action. Christine says I have put the family last and I have. There really is only one choice now."

Yet these words are dramatically contradicted by his actions. If he was truly depressed, like so many millions of people struggling with personal crises that seem overwhelming, his actions at the time show him to have been dealing with it in a healthy, positive, and creative way. He was busy updating his resume in the days before his death and discussing a move to Australia—perhaps simply to get away from a horrible work situation (whether brought about by his own wrongdoing or his company's), or perhaps to give his girls a better life, or maybe both. Seeking a simpler, safer, saner environment for his family appears to have been a motivation for his earlier move from Wall Street's Salomon Brothers to Stephens in Little Rock. In 1987, as earlier, the evidence shows him to have been driven by what would be best for Suzanne and Amy, and it is virtually impossible to imagine him raising a hand to harm either of them.

The diary's dramatic declaration that "there really is only one choice now" because "I am broke and they my children have no inheritance left because of my action" makes little sense in light of the facts. The message from John that came through in Janet Cyford's reading—that he could easily have started over elsewhere—is amply supported by what we know about him. He was widely recognized as a superstar of the financial world who could write his own ticket. Even hidden away in Arkansas, he was prominent enough to have been interviewed in 1987 by *Forbes* magazine (sadly, the interview would end up in the December issue under the title, "Epitaph for a Trader"). And his proven willingness to trade money and prestige for simpler, healthier living conditions no doubt broadened his already numerous options.

Janet Cyford's spirit communication showed him to be considering "being a financial consultant," an idea he had discussed with his wife according to this reading. "He'd had enough of working in that way with that company, that even if it meant that they'd have to have a smaller house, and start again, but he could still keep a roof over their heads. They'd talked together about ways that they could start life in a different way to keep everything going ... There was something he was saying about the daughter going to college—and I stopped and looked at [older daughter Suzanne's] age. She wouldn't have been college age, but he may well have been preparing for that sort of thing."

The worst scenario Markle could have faced if guilty would

have been spending time in prison, a not-unheard-of consequence for overly ambitious traders bending the rules to make a killing in the financial world at that time. Yet these white-collar criminals generally weathered the storm, paying their debt and sometimes emerging from the ordeal with different values and a healthier perspective. And it is a safe bet that such people's children did not starve to death while the family's breadwinner was serving time. Furthermore, couldn't John's wife Christine have supported the family if necessary? For numerous reasons, the idea that Markle was driven to kill himself—not to mention his family—as a reaction to financial distress simply does not hold up logically.

So the diary seems to contradict much of what we know of Markle's life in November 1987. The 13-page letter to his mother also has its suspicion-provoking peculiarities, such as when he reminds her of an incident on the set of *Johnny Guitar* when she "and Joan Crawford were both drinking and fighting like hell" and "Sterling Hayden physically separating you after Joan had thrown a gin bottle at you."

While Markle may very well have written this, it sounds more like someone else's creation of what a distraught, angry John would write to his movie-star mom, using facts gleaned from a Hollywood biography or old gossip columns, and conveniently including a written record of John's intention to commit a desperate violent act. Was this ancient movie-set rowdiness really such a memorable and important family issue that he put aside his increasingly overwhelming work-related and family-related burdens to fixate on it?

On the other hand, the extreme sentiments expressed in the letter might not be as unusual as we would like to believe. Conflict and resentment seem to occur with unusual frequency and intensity for the children of celebrities, producing a high rate of alcoholism, drug abuse, and suicide. Markle's letter might indeed have been real—and not terribly unusual in the kind of distress it revealed— including the *'night, Mother* suicide reference, a comment which, if written by John, was probably intended to do nothing more than provoke guilt on the part of Ms. McCambridge.

Cyford's reading found his depression to have been caused by others' wrongdoing, "more a frustration of being in amongst that corruption, being blocked at just about every turn … The thoughts that I'm getting from him …" She paused, then noted, "and you know, Ed, something else just came to mind—I wonder if he'd tell me the truth now."

I asked if it is unusual for someone in spirit not to tell the truth, remembering Betty Muench's comment from the Jon Emr case that it would be exceedingly unusual for someone on the other side to try to continue perpetuating a fraud. Cyford replied that "I've never come across that before," yet at the same time has never come across a case quite like this one before. Her communications with John found the letter to his mother to have been real, "a type of therapy," but found the existence of the diary doubtful. "I see an appointment book, but I don't see a diary at all. Do you know whether this so-called diary had appointments in it? My impression of him is that he kept what things he wanted to know in his head. He's quite an astute man, that, you know, whatever you write can be used against you, so it's like he's trying to find in his mind, 'What on earth could be construed as a diary?'"

The diary, if real, is more devastating than the purported letter, for it shows us a self-avowed criminal becoming increasingly distraught as he hints of plans to do something horrible to put himself and perhaps his family out of their misery. But this alleged journal should also raise a warning flag, recalling all the times alleged lone-nut assassins in high-profile cases were said to have kept a diary that conveniently recorded their guilt. What percentage of grown men keep such journals in the first place? Diary-keeping is usually a habit of young teenage girls, and even then, very few. And where would John Markle have found the time? By all accounts he devoted himself obsessively to his trading operation, working late into the evening. The few precious remaining hours appear to have been devoted to activities with his family.

Is the possibility of forgery too farfetched to consider? Not in the Arkansas system that, as we will see, was not above faking autopsy results.

The fabrication of written evidence by powerful authorities might not be as rare as most of us think, according to skeptical observers such as essayist-novelist Gore Vidal, who, in a 1976 essay for the *New York Review of Books*, questioned the origins of the diary purportedly written by the man who shot Alabama Governor George Wallace.

Vidal pointed out that "[Arthur] Bremer's diary is a fascinating work—of art? From what we know of the twenty-two-year-old author he did not have a literary turn of mind (among his effects were comic books, some porno). He was a television baby, and a dull one. Politics had no interest for him. Yet suddenly—for reasons he never gives us—he decides to kill the President and starts to keep a diary on April 4, 1972 ..."

"On his arrival in New York, he tells us that he forgot his guns which the captain then turned over to him, causing the diarist to remark 'Irony abounds.' A phrase one doubts that the actual Arthur Bremer would have used ..."

After noting the Bremer diary's highbrow references to *Moby Dick, A Clockwork Orange, War and Peace*, and "the Scrolls in those caves," which clash so jarringly with the author's suspiciously poor spelling of simple words, Vidal concludes that "we are dealing with a true author. One who writes, 'Like a novelist who knows not how his book will end—I have written this journal—what a shocking surprise that my inner character shall steal the climax and destroy the author and save the anti-hero from assasination!' Only one misspelling in that purple patch. But 'as I said befor, I Am A Hamlet.' It is not irony that abounds so much in these pages as professional writing."

Similarly, the diary detailing John Markle's descent into criminal insanity seems a bit too perfect, a bit too conveniently grotesque, like the "Freddy Krueger" Halloween mask he allegedly wore to commit his atrocities in imitation of the *A Nightmare on Elm Street* video that sat in the nearby VCR—in a word, overkill, like the literal overkill of the two guns with which he reportedly shot himself in the head. Is it unthinkable that the diary was something created to demonize and frame him so that investigators would not delve into the financial dealings of the rich and powerful with whom he had clashed?

A Corrupt System Exposed

Numerous investigators of 1980s Arkansas have described the state as an oligarchy lorded over by a handful of financial giants who allegedly controlled the politicians, the judicial system, and newspapers. To get a clear understanding of the system that ruled the Markle tragedy a murder-suicide, it is vitally important to observe the machine in action in similar cases. A typical feature of a corrupt system is an easily controlled coroner who can be relied upon to make rulings convenient to the state's controllers. The quick official conclusion that Markle had used a total of three guns to kill his wife, daughters, and then himself—with two simultaneous shots to his head—was not the first such credibility-straining ruling.

Three months earlier, Medical Examiner Fahmy Malak had made what would be exposed as perhaps the most notorious of his numerous controversial decisions, in the case of the deaths of Kevin Ives and Don Henry, teenage friends who were found run over by a freight train in Alexander, about 25 miles southwest of Little Rock. Dr. Malak ruled that the boys had smoked an excessive amount of marijuana and gone to sleep on the tracks, side by side, failing to be awakened by the loud engine or blaring horns as the engineer strained to bring the train to a stop.

Kevin's mother Linda Ives, refusing to believe the ruling of accidental death, decided to challenge the system and eventually got results—a grand jury investigation and a second forensic opinion on cause of death. As reported in 1992 by Brian Ross on NBC's *Dateline*, "... to the astonishment of experts who later conducted a second autopsy, Dr. Malak failed to notice clear evidence of beating marks and a stab wound. But Dr. Malak never admitted making a mistake." Don Henry had been stabbed and Kevin Ives struck on the head with a rifle butt. The grand jury ruled that the boys had been murdered.

Some of the doctor's other conclusions would be humorous if they had occurred in fiction instead of real life. In 1988 he found that Raymond P. Allbright, shot five times in the chest, had committed suicide. In a 1989 case, Malak falsely accused a deputy county coroner of killing a patient by removing life support without consulting the family; Malak had misinterpreted a medical symbol on the brain-dead patient's chart, taking *"after* family consultation" to mean *"without* family consultation." When the body of James Milam was found decapitated, clearly the work of a sharp knife, Dr. Malak ruled that Milam had died of an ulcer and that his dog had bitten off and eaten the entire head and then thrown up. The doctor swore that the victim's chewed-up brain and skull were found in the regurgitated matter. Any doubt that the state's chief medical examiner was making up a fairy tale was removed when the head was later found.

Governor Clinton shrugged off complaints, and two months after the railroad killings proposed a pay raise of 41.5 percent for Malak, prompting Linda Ives and other angry, grief-stricken citizens victimized by the doctor's rulings to form an organization called Victims of Malak's Incredible Testimony (VOMIT) to press for the coroner's removal.

Too Late for Justice

The effects of the questionable justice system that enabled and supported Malak's decisions, to the detriment of ordinary folks like Linda Ives, would eventually strike close to home for Clinton in the massacre of the Markle family, whose youngest member, Amy, was a playmate of seven-year-old Chelsea Clinton. Chelsea and mother Hillary attended the memorial service along with approximately 600 other people, including Mercedes McCambridge, who, the Associated Press reported, "fell to her knees and put her face to a patch of clover under which the ashes of her son and his family had been placed in a church cemetery."

Now, as if losing her only son and his family were not horrible enough, Ms. McCambridge could only stand by helplessly as John Markle officially joined the ranks of Richard Speck, Charles Manson, Ted Bundy, and other mass murderers in the public mind. The psychic detectives and mediums who examined this mystery, though not unanimous, call the official conclusion into question. And so does an honest examination of the disturbing peculiarities of this case and others in the strange world of 1980s Arkansas.

CHAPTER 7:
THE MURDER OF MARTIN LUTHER KING, JR. AND MYSTERIOUS RELATED DEATHS

"Indeed, the major activity of the prophets was interference, remonstrating about wrongs inflicted on other people, meddling in affairs which were seemingly neither their concern nor their responsibility." —Rabbi Abraham Joshua Heschel, King's friend and civil rights colleague

April 4, 1967:
New York City—A year to the day before his assassination, Dr. Martin Luther King, Jr. delivers a passionate speech against the US government's war in Vietnam. Later in the year, he will propose the most radical vision of his career—a nonviolent "Poor People's Campaign" planned for the spring of 1968.

April 4, 1968:
Memphis—Dr. King is shot to death by a sniper. A rifle found on the sidewalk bears the fingerprints of James Earl Ray, a criminal drifter who has rented a room in the boarding house across the street from King's motel. King had been under surveillance by federal agencies and by the Memphis Police Department, which withdraws security an hour before the shooting and also fails to issue an all-points bulletin or an order blocking exit routes out of the city, allowing the killer or killers to escape.

151

December 8, 1999:
Memphis—A jury finds that there was a conspiracy in the murder of Dr. King.

June 10, 2000:
Washington, DC—The Justice Department, concluding a limited reinvestigation of the King assassination, announces that there was no conspiracy and recommends that there be no further investigation.

James Earl Ray: Fall Guy?

The reading by medium Betty Muench shows the spirit of Martin Luther King, Jr. to be doing well—actually, much better than well—in the higher realm where he is so fully in his element, growing in energy and power as a sort of spiritual magnet attracting the prayers and wishes of others. More on this later …

I asked about the role of James Earl Ray, the small-time crook who pled guilty on March 10, 1969, and withdrew his guilty plea three days later, saying he had been threatened and coerced. Ray spent the next 30 years fighting for a new trial; one of his attorneys, former King associate William Pepper, insisted after years of investigation that Ray was an innocent patsy, as did King's family. The bullet that killed King was never matched to Ray's rifle; and although Ray's fingerprints were found on his rifle found lying on the sidewalk outside the boarding house, his fingerprints were not found in the room from which he allegedly shot King.

In a reading done by Muench when Ray was still alive, her spirit guides stated, *"There will be those who will be found out and it will be brought out and that then this is the situation around the confessed killer Ray. This one will have been used and this one will have only learned by maturing, and that he will have set justice back by admitting to this crime. He will have sold his soul to the devil and in that he is now seeking a savior. There is this which can be saved and that a trial will show that there is enough doubt that there can be further investigation. This will be difficult to find evidence at this time as certain people will have been able to dispose of evidence including certain (other) people who could have made a difference in this investigation."*

It is difficult to know for sure how many people who could have helped bring us the truth have been *"disposed of."* A cabdriver remembered only as "Paul" who witnessed the assassination told what he knew to police and died violently that same night; reporter William Sartor, on the trail of an alleged mob connection to the assassination, died the night before he was to interview a source; and the two judges who appeared to promise Ray his best shot at getting a trial, in 1969 and 1974, both died suddenly in their chambers while reviewing his case—mysteries we will explore later in this chapter.

But surprisingly, according to Muench's reading, the assassination which apparently had to be covered up with additional murders was itself a kind of "accident." *"Since King was always under surveillance there was this possibility of misinterpretation in the killing of King. This was done in a way that will have caught everyone off guard and so then those authorities could have acted surprised as they were indeed surprised. They at this time will be so convinced of their innocence that they will be very credible in their own defense. Indeed there were government influences in all this but they lose the meaning of covert and overt and time will have erased any true involvement."*

Muench later commented, "This reading of the killing suggests that there was so much surveillance of him that certain commands were misinterpreted and that indeed then this was covered up, not only to hide the real killer, but to hide the incompetence of certain people in local and federal government."

This would seem to indicate that some highly placed individual gave a pointed yet unspecific order, something like "Stop King before the march on Washington—do whatever it takes" "or "Get rid of this threat"—a modern-day replay of King Henry II's lament about Thomas Becket, a declaration taken by subordinates as a green light to do anything to neutralize King.

For the spirit of Dr. King, investigation into his death is not a vital concern for him now. *"There is for King now this energy which he is more and more wrapped up in and his interest would seem to be to carry on his work as he intended, rather than to go back into his murder and create a trial that will be both time consuming and fruitless as to the real truth."*

The message channeled through Betty Muench—essentially, "Don't waste your time investigating my assassination"—might seem a bit surprising, especially coming from a man whose own family and admirers have made the search for the truth such a high priority. Yet trance medium Philip Solomon independently received the same message from the spirit of King, who emphasized that *"it's not really important what happened on that day any more, it just happened and that was it. I don't hold any grudge against anyone ... In your world many in my family now believe things were not as certain people suggested they were and I am touched to think even all these years on people care for me, love me, and even that my family are still striving to find the truth, but it is best that it is let go. Let it lie, in the words that my own father always used ..."*

In Solomon's reading, King said Ray did not kill him, but did not elaborate (probably because Solomon was the last of three mediums to make this spirit contact, and that ground had already been covered). The Muench reading, drawing on a variety of energies in addition to that of King, goes into more detail: *"Indeed now Ray was a willing patsy but that he will have information that should be known and if a trial is the only way for this to be known then it no longer has much to do with the death of King but more to do with the involvement of Ray and others who will have acted out of fears, one feeding into the other, and that there will have been then the use of them all ... the use of the ignorance ... which is all Ray is truly guilty of ... if a trial does not come about then King would still be satisfied that his energy, his name, goes on and that it grows in power ..."*

The term "willing patsy" sounds like an oxymoron; it would seem to mean a willing participant who was convinced it would be in his best interest to plead guilty, a minor player who lacked knowledge of the total picture and never realized he would be hung out to dry. Evidence indicates he clearly knew more than he was willing to say and feared retribution if he were to talk.

Bertie Catchings concurred that Ray's main role was to be the fall guy. "I think he was just a scapegoat, and he is an innocent person," she said. She saw Ray as having received some kind of favor, probably involving money, from an organized crime group involved in King's murder, and owed them a favor in return. "And I don't think James Earl Ray was aware of the code or what was involved" when they needed a favor in return.

"And so it was presented to him—'Look, you need to help us out here,' and he said, 'Oh, I can't do that. I wouldn't be able to do it ... I'd get caught doing it' ... and so he reneged and refused." Then the mob "decided, 'Well, this is better, because we can fix it so someone else will do the assassination, and Ray can take the blame.'"

According to Bertie Catchings, he was also being pressured into taking the blame after refusing to take part in the killing. "He was approached again," Catchings said, "and told, 'since you're so squeamish in particular about shooting anybody ... we did your work for you, but you must take the blame for it.'"

Ray "was so frightened he did not know what to do. He knew that to cross these people would be a death sentence, so he allowed himself at that moment to confess and say that he did this, because he was scared to death."

"For him to explain the truth of the matter would be a little bit complicated," she added, "and maybe he thought he would tell part of the truth and clear himself, or maybe he was going to tell the whole truth. But he did not kill King."

Similarly, in a reading that combined information from the spirit of King with the input of her own spirit guides, medium Janet Cyford noted, "I don't think [Ray] did it. I think there was some conspiracy ... and there was some promise made to him that the authorities didn't keep." In a part of the reading that strongly echoed Catchings' psychic insight, she stated that Ray was involved with the conspirators "and he knew what was going on, but he was promised that if he took responsibility for it, that he'd only do so much time ..."

Robert Cracknell observed that "... whoever pulled the trigger and shot Dr. Martin Luther King had been primed and was being used. He was given a loaded gun and told to pull the trigger." On the issue of whether Ray was involved, Cracknell stated, "Everything screams at me psychically that *yes he was*, and the only question of miscarriage of justice against him is that the authorities were able to close the case with a conviction, knowing full well that there were many others involved ... As far as Ray was concerned, to be paid for shooting somebody—especially a black person—would not have affected his conscience at all, but he didn't have the wherewithal to plan it himself."

In the same vein, Nancy Myer saw King's death as "due to a conspiracy that James Earl Ray was a part of. It has always surprised me that he survived as long as he did with the information that he had. That probably occurred because he had no credibility and because his knowledge only went so far up the line." Myer noted that in the original plot, Ray "was to have been one of the shooters as far as he knew. Actually he was set up."

The consensus of these psychics that Ray was being manipulated by powerful conspirators is supported by the research of Dr. Philip H. Melanson, author of *The Martin Luther King Assassination: New Revelations on the Conspiracy and Cover-up, 1968-1991*. Melanson explores the curious and revealing fact that Ray, who was in the habit of using the names of people he knew as aliases, suddenly began using the names of four men from the Toronto area after his escape from prison in 1967, although he had never been to Toronto. Three of the four men bore a close physical resemblance to Ray. Melanson notes that the man whose name became Ray's primary alias, Eric S. Galt, "also had two scars—one on the palm of his right hand, another on his forehead (just barely to the right of his nose). So did James Earl Ray." Ray came to resemble Galt even more closely when he, like Galt, had plastic surgery to change the shape of his nose—a highly unusual way for a small-time crook to change his appearance.

Melanson makes a compelling case that the US intelligence community—which had access to Canadian government files on defense-contractor employee Galt and the other aliases, and which viewed the antiwar King through its own distorted lens as a national security threat—was directing the actions of Ray. Revealingly, the earliest wanted posters referred to Ray as Eric S. Galt, despite his having used one of his other aliases at the Memphis rooming house—further evidence that Ray was a pawn unwittingly playing out his role according to a pre-written script.

Ray insisted he was told what to do by a handler named Raoul, who, Melanson writes, "directed his every incriminating move in connection with the assassination: the rifle purchase (Raoul allegedly told Ray that the rifle was a demo model to show gunrunning clients); the rental of a room near the Lorraine Motel (to negotiate a gunrunning deal); the purchase of binoculars in Memphis."

Blaming Ray and then having him escape—or having him silenced—would be the logical strategy for the people who were using him, and the evidence indicates that this was indeed the plan. Ray escaped to Canada (where he waited for a month in his boarding-house room and departed shortly after a man was seen delivering an envelope apparently containing cash and/or a plane ticket), then England, Portugal, and England again, where, two months after the manhunt for "Galt" began, he was arrested before he could reach his final destination of Angola. Melanson theorizes that "the plan would seem to have been to implicate the real Eric S. Galt just long enough to allow Ray to escape to Angola, where he could be comfortably disposed of," although that part of the plot did not work out as planned for the conspirators.

Although Ray spent decades insisting he was framed, he turned curiously evasive and quiet whenever questioned by assassination researchers about aliases and other specific details that might shine a spotlight on the conspirators who manipulated him. This is understandable. If he had shared the story of his involvement with the plotters, he would have made himself appear guilty—or perhaps reveal genuine evidence of his involvement in the murder scheme—while at the same time risking retaliation for talking. Clearly, his strategy was to reveal just enough to clear himself—

and no more. Melanson and assassination investigator Harold Weisberg, who also interviewed Ray, both concluded that Ray was holding back the truth about his involvement with the perpetrators, a view that is echoed in the insights of the psychic detectives who examined this case.

Viewing the tragedy from a broader perspective, Myer stated, "Martin Luther King was looming as a political power of some magnitude. There was great fear in the minds of some Southern power mongers that he might even dare to run for president. He certainly was going to influence politics and jobs in the South." She said two powerful organizations in the South were involved in the assassination.

Catchings expressed a similar opinion. "He was just getting too powerful in the machine's eyes," she emphasized. "Martin Luther King was moving pretty fast—if he could have stayed alive, say another 20 years, he could possibly have been president. That would not have been out of the question." Indeed, even in 1968, there was a Draft-King-for-President movement.

Similarly, Cracknell pointed out, "Quite definitely, Martin Luther King was an embarrassment, and I feel that it was politically expedient that he should be eradicated" as "a very sensitive political 'hot potato.'" And although "sufficient evidence could have been established to discredit him as a man of human failings (possibly something like a small sexual indiscretion) ... he had achieved such a position in the eyes of millions of American people that it was obvious something like that would not condemn him in the eyes of his followers. Neither would it stop him."

Death in the Judges' Chambers

James Earl Ray entered a guilty plea on March 10, 1969, on the advice of his attorney Percy Foreman, but withdrew the plea three days later, claiming he had been coerced. For the rest of his life, Ray fought a losing battle to get a trial; he and his subsequent lawyers felt the system was rigged to prevent any legal proceeding in which the real story might come out.

However, according to Ray, during those 30 years there were

two occasions when he held out hope of getting a fair hearing.

His first chance came later that same month. Ray mailed a formal petition requesting a new trial to Judge Preston Battle on March 26, 1969, citing an alleged violation of a court order by Foreman. Battle returned to work from a vacation on March 31, and that afternoon asked assistant prosecutor James Beasley who Ray intended to have represent him in a new trial; this message was relayed through a prison official, and Ray provided the new lawyer's name. Beasley went to inform Judge Battle and found him dead, supposedly of cardiac arrest, slumped over Ray's papers. As Ray later noted, "I can't help but think Judge Battle's indirect query to me about representation indicated he was giving serious consideration to my petition."

The other occasion when Ray was optimistic about his chances for a trial was on a 1976 appeal to the US Court of Appeals in Memphis, where the three-judge panel included Judge William E. Miller, who had a reputation for fairness and independence, and had made a ruling favorable to Ray two years earlier. Oral arguments were heard February 3, 1976. On April 12, after the three judges voted in the chambers but before publication of the decision, Judge Miller died in his chambers, allegedly of cardiac arrest, while studying the Ray case. In May, the appeals court ruled unanimously against a trial.

Bertie Catchings saw foul play in the death of Judge Battle, noting, "I believe that he felt like there was something that just didn't fit right, all along in this case, and he may have mentioned that casually to a few people, and it all got back to the source of this gang, this group of people ..." A powerful southern organized crime boss (discussed in greater detail later) "was trying to send a message to anyone involved, that 'this is what's gonna happen to anybody who tries to cross me in this matter ...'"

"And when Judge Miller died the same way, messages were sent to those other two [judges on the US Court of Appeals panel] that were going to vote—'this is what can happen, and this is what will happen to you, and you'd better not say anything about it' ... and they were frightened, they were made believers, and they agreed between themselves there was no need to take a chance, to risk their own lives. And so, again, the powerful machinery got to these people, and that's why [Ray] didn't have a chance from the start."

Betty Muench's reading on the two judges started by describing how Ray fit into the picture, finding that "*the energy involved in this situation with Ray will be across all lines. There will be local, state, and federal involvements. There will be this then which will not seem possible to pin down to any one simple conspiracy. There will be this which seems intended … that there will be this confusion of the lines when the lines of power become intertwined … there is this which is out of order; no order=chaos. There is in this situation then the chaos which seems to lend to the protection of those who would be truly at the center of this crime.*"

"*There will be this which will show that Ray was in the wrong place at the wrong time and that he will have been a petty player in the local scene and will have had a loud mouth at times which will have made him a perfect candidate, a prey in a sense. There will be this which will have many today believing there was something other going on, but they could not have sorted this out in a courtroom any better.*"

Regarding Judge Miller, who died in 1974, the reading states: "*There will have been with William Miller this which will have had him so anxious about all this that he will have been in personal fear. He will have been overcome by this and it was intended that it be so. He will at this time seem to be punishing himself for having had the fear to begin with.*" But what person being threatened with dire consequences would not feel fear? Dr. King himself was said to have been afraid, knowing what probably awaited him.

Judge Battle, who died while reviewing Ray's case in 1969, put up a brave front, but to no avail. "*There will have been a strong resistance by Battle, and Miller will be suffering personal torture because of his fear and thus blames himself for a cowardice that is not true. There will be in this chaos this which will not have permitted law and order and that then both these judges will have been in an impossible situation.*"

In addition, the spirit guides note that some kind of blackmail was used against Miller and Battle, just as was done with King. *"There will be this which will seem to have assisted this process of the fear and it will be that both will have had certain things in their own lives which will have been threatened to be exposed should they pursue this and appear in front of a court on this trial. There will be this which will suggest that with Miller it will have been something on a state level; and with battle it will have been something with the federal level. There will have been threats of exposure about them and they were not prepared to carry this out."*

"Miller will have assisted his own demise by his own fear and Battle will have assisted his own demise by being too confrontive. Both will have been put upon in ways that will go beyond the description of conspiracy. They will have been challenged and both within themselves took their own way out of it. Miller died of fear instilled in him. Battle died of frustration and anger instilled in him."

Beaten down by the threats and intimidation, their spirits were crushed and their physical bodies soon followed. Nancy Myer saw the same thing—death brought on by the pressure of intimidation, noting that, "Although the deaths of Judge Battle and Judge Miller are fascinating in light of the conspiracy situation, I do not believe they were murdered. I get the feeling that the stress of threats they both received and their internal struggle to decide what was the right thing to do caused the strain on their hearts that led to their deaths."

"When you wade into conspiracy waters," Myer continued, "it's easy to see tentacles of possible links throughout the whole system. Then the natural odd consequences of life can take on a strange tone when they may not be truly connected."

Robert Cracknell also warned not to be too quick to see conspiracy. "Both died from heart attacks before they could deliver their judgments. There was nothing necessarily unusual about that, but was it a coincidence that both men died of a heart attack, when both were about to make a judgment regarding the alleged killer? I think we are satisfying the whim of a hungry public who, though well aware of a conspiracy, are only too eager to gorge themselves on an extra course of supposition!"

161

"I am sure many people directly involved, or on the periphery, in the case of Martin Luther King have died, but not necessarily because of their involvement," he noted.

If these two judges died of "the stress of threats they both received," in Nancy Myer's words, this indeed would not be classified as murder. Yet the result was the same as if they had been murdered and, ironically, compared with the torment of being intimidated and hounded to death, a quick bullet might have been more merciful.

The issue of possible related killings is vitally important yet has been barely noted over the years. When a cover-up is carried out with ruthless efficiency over many years, the original crime obviously had to be committed by powerful individuals or groups, not by a sick loner languishing behind bars. The question of whether the two judges who met identical untimely deaths under the same extraordinary pressures were actually assassinated leads to disagreement, even among psychics seeing the same scenario, with the "*Rashomon* factor" creating subjective disagreement over whether sudden death under "the stress of threats they received" is or is not a form of homicide. Yet there were at least two other important individuals closely connected to the King case who some researchers suspect to have been brutally silenced.

Murder of a Witness?

Like Dr. King himself, a quiet young cabdriver remembered only as Paul was murdered in Memphis on the evening of April 4, 1968. Ray's lawyer William Pepper investigated and was unable to find Paul's last name with any certainty, but found witnesses who, after three decades of silent fear, finally recounted Paul's account of the assassination and the price he might have paid for speaking the truth.

According to fellow taxi driver Louie Ward, who broke his silence after 26 years, Paul had driven his Yellow Cab taxi to the Lorraine Motel to pick up a passenger. While loading luggage, Paul saw King get shot, and immediately called his dispatcher. As reported in Pepper's *Orders to Kill*, Paul told Ward "that he saw a man come down over the wall empty-handed, run north on Mulberry Street, and get into a black and white MPD traffic police car …"

Bertie Catchings noted that "there were people there that Paul saw and could describe—and had described—and so he had to be killed … and it had to look like an accident … It seems that sometimes when people commit murder, they try to do it in a way that would seem [like] something connected with a person's trade …"

In this tragic case, in which a man "was trying to do the right thing, there was a pipeline from the police department that went right straight back to the people that killed Dr. King," she explained. And the silencing of this cabdriver "had to be done quickly, so they could focus on James Earl Ray, and let him take the fall."

According to Nancy Myer's psychic vision of the case, "Once those who killed Martin Luther King learned of Paul's existence, they hunted him down and silenced him. The same conspirators who are responsible for the murder of Dr. King killed this man Paul." A hit man was "assigned to murder Paul. He and a friend tracked him down, captured him, and killed him, and then threw him out on the highway to obscure what they had done to him."

Betty Muench's reading on the death of Paul supports the conclusion that there was involvement by some Memphis police in a plot to silence his testimony. *"There is this energy of Paul and it is as if he will still be fuming over this which will have been done to him and that he will have been someone who will have been innocent as to what was occurring. He will have been someone who was indeed in the wrong place at the wrong time …"*

"It is as if Paul is keeping close to the energy of this one King in order that he will be able to lend his knowledge to the overview of this crime and to assist to unfold this truth for all to see and know. Paul in life was not a political person and did not tend to be involved in any such pattern and he was not capable to deal with those involved. In that then there will have been his mistake of trying to tell anyone and everyone of his knowledge. He was indeed removed so that he could not speak out any further. He was identified to those in the hats [more on this later] and that then he will have been under their

control at the time of this death … one more death would make no difference to them … the Memphis Police Department will have much involvement as well as certain governmental agencies."

Research reveals that the Memphis Police Department (MPD) and Hoover's FBI clearly shared close ties and overlapping functions. Frank Holloman, who headed both the Memphis Police and Fire Departments, had been an FBI agent for a quarter century, including service as agent in charge of the Atlanta office, which took the lead in the war on King.

Is it a mere coincidence that on the morning of April 5, 1968, the Memphis Public Works Department carried out a police order to cut down the bushes next to the fire station, following the eyewitness testimony of King's chauffeur Solomon Jones, *New York Times* reporter Earl Caldwell, and the Reverend James Orange that they saw smoke rise from behind the bushes when King was shot? Is it a meaningless detail that two black firefighters at the fire station across the street from the Lorraine Motel were transferred elsewhere the day before the assassination, or that for the first time, black detectives were not included in the security detail the city provided King?

Moreover, why did the MPD fail to follow its usual procedures of issuing an all-points bulletin and closing off exit routes out of the city? Unpleasant as it might be to recall, racist criminality so permeated the Southern law enforcement and judicial systems at that time that killers of black people routinely escaped punishment. And while police participation in murder and cover-up sounds unthinkable today, King's murder occurred less than 4 years after the police-assisted murders of three civil rights workers in nearby Neshoba County, Mississippi. Seen in the perspective of the times, it is hardly inconceivable that history could repeat itself in this way.

In addition, the CIA's Office of Security, which also had targeted King, had significant connections with the FBI and with local police departments. Several of its officials were former FBI agents, and CIA resources were shared with local authorities that helped the agency in its war on dissenters. Hoover worked closely with Major General William Yarborough, Assistant Chief of Staff for Intelligence, sharing daily intelligence on the antiwar threat in general and King in particular. In short, the FBI, CIA, Memphis Police Department, and eventually military intelligence would in effect be operating as one entity by the spring of 1968, and stopping King was their number-one priority.

Regarding the significance of the hats mentioned earlier: *"There is an image of a hat which will be like that worn by military men or police or even cab drivers ... ,"* Muench's reading on Paul states. *"There will have been many of these kinds of hats around ... he did not seem to recognize that this was unusual but that there will have been these hats around at the scene of this murder of Dr. King and that there will have been these without insignia. There will have been in all those hats that which will not have had any identification and that then, it escaped any significance to Paul. There will have been in this then some way in order to identify those involved to identify each other and to make away before they would be asked to identify themselves. There is in the use of this ruse that which will suggest that these hats will have been used in this plot because there will have been so many ways to use such hats and that then there will have been this which could also easily be found in any uniform shop. There will be this then which will suggest that the Memphis Police Department will have known who to interrogate at the scene and who to avoid."* Muench said the image of the hat appeared to be like that of a security guard or a milkman.

"There will have been some with those hats who were there and knew much about the plot but that they will have worn the hat and then been passed over. In that this will have been known by the Memphis police then the conclusion is that they too were involved in this plot. There will be one by the name of 'Jarris' who will have been much a part of this story in this time."

The Mob Connection

Who is the key player in this story whose name sounds like "Jarris"? Could "Jarris actually be "Harris?" Memphis police officer Caro Harris was a member of the security detail assigned to King. He and other officers were seen around the motel on April 4 around 5

P.M., but disappeared after 5:30, in what appears to have been the stripping away of the civil rights leader's security.

But the name that came through from the realm of spirit sounding something like "Jarris" is most likely "Jowers." Loyd Jowers, owner of Jim's Grill across from the Lorraine Motel, broke his silence during the 1990s, claiming to have played a role in the assassination. According to the chronology constructed by assassination researcher William Pepper, "On the weekend of March 15 James was instructed by Raul [Ray's alleged handler] to leave Los Angeles and drive to New Orleans where he would receive further instructions. At this time Memphis produce man Frank Liberto asked Loyd Jowers to repay a 'big' favor. Jowers, who had been alerted earlier by another mutual acquaintance, was told by Liberto that the brush area behind his Jim's Grill was to be used as a sniper's lair for the assassination of Dr. King, who would at some time in the next three to four weeks be staying at the Lorraine Motel ... A gun would be provided."

"Jowers was told that the police would not be there," Pepper notes. "A patsy was also going to be provided and Jowers would be handsomely paid. Liberto explained that the money came out of New Orleans."

The New Orleans connection was Mafia boss Carlos Marcello, who, according to Pepper's research, accepted a contract to kill King. Pepper cites the deathbed confession of gangster Myron Billet, who said he "attended a meeting in the small town of Apalachin, New York, a favorite mob meeting place ... three government agents (from the CIA and FBI) offered one million dollars to Carlo Gambino and Sam Giancana to arrange for the killing of Dr. King. The offer was not accepted. The agents indicated that it would be placed elsewhere." It was eventually handed over to the fiercely racist Marcello.

Bertie Catchings seemed to be describing Marcello and his organization, whether she realized it or not, in her psychic vision of the King assassination, seeing a bigoted crime boss as the central figure. She described "a group of organized crime people ... Not all organized crime people would be this vindictive ... but in this particular organization it was one who particularly did not like the black people to be anything at all—just keep them as low as you possibly could ... and this man had quite a lot of power."

Based on what she called his "terrible vendetta" against African-Americans, this organized crime kingpin felt that "Martin Luther King, Jr. needed to be shot down and made an example of, hopefully to discourage other black people from pushing onward ... It just became an obsession with this man and his few close people connected with him ... In my vision, I'm hearing him say these words—'The only good nigger is a dead nigger'—he was just that vicious."

This prominent crime figure and his associates had killed other people in various disputes, Catchings emphasized, so it was not that big a step to target King, who "was absolutely getting too prominent ... But of course we know that by killing King they would only add more energy to helping the black people to forge ahead and gain more support and more sympathy from the whites ..."

The alliance of alleged lawless elements of the U.S. government with organized crime during the 1960s has been well-documented. Mafiosi assassins had been hired by the CIA to target Fidel Castro, Rafael Trujillo, and Patrice Lumumba. And FBI Director Hoover's mob ties have also been detailed at great length. As James Dickerson points out in *Dixie's Dirty Secret*, "Hoover and Marcello had at least two things in common: both maintained a friendship with New York mobster Frank Costello—and both were unrepentant racists." A column by Norman Solomon and Jeff Cohen further illuminates this disturbing alliance, describing the case of Dick Gregory: "In 1968, the activist/comedian publicly denounced the Mafia for importing heroin into the inner city. Did the FBI welcome the anti-drug, anti-mob message? No. Head G-man J. Edgar Hoover responded by proposing that the bureau try to provoke the mob to retaliate against Gregory as part of an FBI 'counter intelligence operation' to 'neutralize' the comedian. Hoover wrote: 'Alert La Cosa Nostra (LCN) to Gregory's attack on LCN.'"

King's emergence in 1967 as a powerful antiwar leader gave organized crime an additional reason for wanting him gone. His campaign to re-channel the nation's treasure to the home front "made him unpopular not only with the government but with the Memphis cartel and the Dixie Mafia, both of which, according to sources, were making enormous profits off the war," writes Dickerson.

Did a Reporter Get Too Close?

Journalist William Sartor, a stringer for *Time* magazine, pursued the Mafia link to King's murder and died suddenly in Waco, Texas in 1971, the night before he was to interview a significant witness. His death was ruled a methaqualone overdose.

As with the case of the two judges who collapsed and died while reviewing Ray's case, Robert Cracknell urged caution about seeing conspiracy in Sartor's death, although he did not flatly rule it out, calling the death "suspicious."

Nancy Myer tuned in to this mystery and observed, "Mr. Sartor had been contacted by an individual who claimed direct knowledge of the conspirators in the King assassination. He gave Sartor facts that made sense, and Sartor wanted to pursue the information further with this witness. They agreed to meet."

"Sartor was on the way to meet with this witness when he was murdered."

"The killers never knew who was talking to Sartor because he gave a false name, and Sartor refused to give them any identifying information as to who it was," Myer explained. "Sartor knew they were going to kill him anyway so he did not reveal anything that would have compromised the safety of the witness."

"Sartor tried to convince the killers that he didn't know anything and that he really regarded this as a wild goose chase. They took no chances and killed him anyway, knowing that the fact that they were there would give Sartor all he needed to blow the lid off the case."

Bertie Catchings pointed out that "the organization that was behind this was powerful enough that they could misfile or hide medical records, and just fix it so that they wouldn't be able to figure out what happened to this man."

"Again, a highly organized group of racist people were able to have in their hire enough people in the right places to cover up all of their misdeeds ..." Catchings described the killer as a paid assassin who "was not necessarily involved with a racist organization."

An automatic-writing spirit contact by Betty Muench disclosed that *"there will be in this murder of Sartor that which will have [had] him taken out by those who would be able to perform without any detection as they will have worked under certain auspices and approval."*

According to this reading, a woman was used to distract Sartor. *"... he will have let his guard down and he will have shared some time and some light entertainment with someone who will have been placed there just for him ... to keep tabs on him and to keep him under guard for a time. There will have been in that little slip of his guard that which will have been his demise and he will have felt that he was responsible and has no outlet to vent his guilt in that. He will have taken a chance that night of his death. There will be others who will have shared some time with him who do not seem to enter into the recorded account of his actions at that time."*

The reading noted that *"he would have been killed in some other way if this [use of the woman to lure him to his death] did not work."*

And there is said to have been another woman in this story, an unfortunate victim in a dangerous place at the wrong time. *"There will be this which will not seem to be on record but that there is a female involved who is no longer alive, one who also took a chance and lost. [She is] known to the witness as well [the witness Sartor was going to interview.]"* One wonders how many other victims might have similarly been lost to history.

But much of the crucial information Sartor was seeking on organized crime's role has come out bit by bit over the years. In the 1992 book *Double Cross*, Sam Giancana's brother Chuck recalls him boasting that the Mafia killed King. Jules "Ricco" Kimbel, a US government covert operative and organized crime figure who appears to have been in Canada the same time as Ray, was interviewed two decades after the assassination and described obtaining aliases for Ray in Canada, his role setting up Ray as a patsy, and the involvement of Sal and Frank Liberto in King's murder. Frank Liberto, Marcello's representative in Memphis, admitted his part in the assassination shortly before his death in 1978, just as Billet and Jowers confessed their roles late in life.

And Liberto's admission echoes the earlier statement by black grocery store owner John McFerren, who said that one hour before King was shot, he overheard Liberto yelling into the phone, "Get him on the balcony, you can pick up the money from my brother in New Orleans, don't call me here again." It was McFerren's story which led Sartor to pursue the Liberto-Marcello connection. After sharing his information, McFerren was "threatened, burgled, beaten up, and shot at," report John Edginton and John Sergeant, producers of the BBC Television documentary *Who Killed Martin Luther King?*, in an article for *Covert Action* in 1990.

"There are other Memphis locals, particularly in the vicinity of the Lorraine Motel and Jim's Grill, who are still afraid to talk or who have suddenly changed their original stories," Edginton and Sergeant noted at the time. "At least one of them is still visited from time to time by a man reminding him to stay silent ... Finally there was the known presence in Memphis on the day of the assassination as well as a week after, of a notorious anti-Castro mercenary and CIA contract employee. Years later, when questioned about why he was in Memphis on the day of the assassination, he admitted 'it was my business to be there.'"

Jowers, seemingly cited in the Muench reading as central to the assassination, allegedly received a large cash payment hidden at the bottom of a bag of produce delivered by one of Liberto's companies. According to William Pepper's account, Jowers was visited twice by the mysterious Raoul to be instructed on his role in the planned assassination; after the fatal shot rang out at 6:01 P.M. on April 4, Jowers picked up the rifle that had been dropped by the shooter, ran back into Jim's Grill, and broke down and hid the weapon.

On December 8, 1999, a Memphis jury found Jowers guilty of conspiracy in the murder of Martin Luther King, Jr.

The War on Dr. King

The Muench reading's mention of federal agencies collaborating with the Memphis Police Department to destroy Dr. King might sound farfetched, but is supported by the record of FBI assistance of local authorities' operations aimed at intimidating black citizens.

Perhaps the most notorious example was the entwining of Hoover's agency with Mississippi's Sovereignty Commission, the KGB-like agency that spied on, harassed, and defamed anyone who opposed white supremacy. Their achievements on behalf of Missisippi taxpayers included committing break-ins, spying on 300 Jewish teenagers assembled for a B'nai B'rith convention on the Gulf Coast, and compiling dossiers on blacks, white liberals, and even Lorne Green, Michael Landon, and Dan Blocker after the three *Bonanza* stars canceled out of a scheduled appearance in Jackson because the event was to be segregated. High-ranking officials of the commission included former FBI agents. On at least one occasion, Commission director Erle Johnston even consulted with the FBI to get their blessing before delivering a speech. When Johnston stepped down in 1968, his replacement as director of the state's white-supremacist secret police was longtime FBI official Webb Burke, who formerly headed Hoover's FBI Academy.

The Sovereignty Commission's activities, begun during the 1950s, would later be replicated by the FBI's COINTELPRO (counterintelligence program), which a Senate committee would eventually conclude was a "vigilante operation aimed squarely at preventing exercise of First Amendment rights of speech and association."

In addition, both organizations devoted considerable efforts to influencing and manipulating the media; young Dr. King, the target of more COINTELPRO harassment than any other individual, decided to stay at the motel that would become his death site after the FBI disseminated an editorial to friendly media sources who obediently printed what Hoover told them, attacking King for staying at a fancy white-owned hotel during an earlier trip to Memphis. They suggested an alternative: "the fine Hotel Lorraine." The lure worked, as the pressure placed on King through the power of the press resulted in a switch to the black-owned Lorraine. And an instruction to the Lorraine from an alleged Southern Christian Leadership Conference advance man, which everyone in King's party emphatically denied making, changed King's room assignment from the inner courtyard to the balcony facing the street.

In *The Last Crusade*, an account of Dr. King's final days in Memphis, author Gerald McKnight details the intimate involvement of the FBI in Memphis' local affairs. "To counter the SCLC-sponsored spring mobilization," he notes, "Hoover directed his agents to make certain that all channels of information-sharing with liaison sources, particularly local police, state police intelligence units, and regional military intelligence groups, were operational ... Initially, the mid-winter 'wild cat' strike of 1,000 blacks drew only scant national attention. From the outset of the strike, however, the FBI characterized Local 1733's 'work stoppage' as a racial matter with potential national security implications ..."

"From this point on," reports McKnight, "all administrative memoranda from Memphis to FBI headquarters in Washington were routed to William C. Sullivan, head of the Domestic Intelligence Division, and Cartha D. DeLoach, the FBI's senior liaison executive officer with the Johnson White House and Capitol Hill. Moreover, having classified the strike as a security-related matter fraught with possible racial unrest, the bureau saw the need to alert military intelligence and keep it posted on events as they unfolded in Memphis." All of this high-alert federal activity was for what McKnight reminds us was in reality "a local labor dispute," but to Hoover another occasion to target King and "militant" Memphis blacks who were challenging the established order.

The struggle for black equality had always been inherently "subversive" to Hoover, who had mercilessly hounded the African-American leader Marcus Garvey during the 1920s, years before Martin Luther King, Jr. was born. The FBI chief's war on black America was an ongoing obsession that lasted a half-century, and he had always stepped up his surveillance efforts during wartime, claiming that dissatisfied black people would be tempted to join the enemy.

In probing the circumstances surrounding King's assassination, it is also vitally important to recall the extent of Army domestic surveillance at the time. When the Army began its own secret operation to spy on dissenting Americans in the late 1960s, they targeted not only antiwar activists but the civil rights movement as well. As noted earlier, as of April 4, 1967, King clearly became an object of surveillance on both counts.

Showdown with LBJ

To King and millions of Americans, the planned Poor People's Campaign was a logical response to an emergency that demanded a desperate, last-ditch effort; to the prideful President Johnson, however, it might have looked like a recipe for extortion and personal humiliation. LBJ no doubt felt threatened by King as early as October 1967, when the civil rights leader said at a press conference that if the government would not shut down the war, the government itself would have to be shut down by the people. A month later, King began plans for his campaign against economic injustice

Like most of the psychics who examined this mystery, the spirit guides channeled by Betty Muench described the assassination as having occurred in the context of the clash between King and the ruling establishment. This reading goes into chilling detail:

"There will be this which was not, of course, spoken of from high up but that there will have been this which implied and realized that there was a need to change certain of the attempts to create problems for the government ... especially internal problems which suggested civil unrest. There will have been this in Johnson that will have wanted an untainted administration but that he was already too far and too deeply involved in certain actions, that if they came to the fore then he would be seen for the politician that he was. There was this which will have been for his own personal image that he will not have wanted this demonstration to continue. There will have been in that then this which will suggest that he will have spoken to the people that he knew could move the word and obtain the desired result. In that then he is as guilty of the death of King as anyone would be."

In other words, the fateful decree could be summed up as, "Will someone rid me of this meddlesome minister?"

This possibility might strike some people as outlandish, yet there appears to be support for it in the historical record. As William Pepper reports in *Orders to Kill*, "On January 10 President Johnson ordered army Chief of Staff Harold Johnson to 'use every resource' to diffuse the civil disturbances planned and projected by Dr. King for the spring. Some of those in the loop have confirmed that there was no longer any doubt that at the highest levels it was understood that the gloves were off—no holds were barred in the effort to stop Dr. King's 'invasion' of the capitol." (Ironically, the elimination of King caused the opposite of the desired effect. Riots broke out in 29 states, leaving 39 dead and 2,500 injured.)

When King's son Dexter was asked on the ABC News show *Turning Point*, "Do you believe that Lyndon Johnson was part of the plot to kill your father?" he replied, "I do." In their syndicated column, Jack Germond and Jules Witcover expressed the logical immediate reaction many of us would have to Dexter King's reply: "This answer came in the face of strong collaboration between King and President Johnson in the civil rights movement ..."

Yet is it not also true that our strongest fury is reserved not for our usual enemies, but for members of our own team who we feel have betrayed us? One need only look at the fate of some of King's fellow peacemakers to see this principle in action: Mahatma Gandhi assassinated by an Indian Hindu, Anwar Sadat murdered by Egyptian Muslims, Yitzhak Rabin shot to death by an Israeli Orthodox Jew. Similarly, Malcolm X was killed by members of the Black Muslim sect from which he had broken away.

Johnson's complex personality contained vast reserves of contradictory qualities. He could be magnanimous, probably doing more than any other U.S. president ever did to ensure the health, comfort, and equal opportunity of the working man and the poor. Going against his own grain as a politician and as a Southerner to enact civil rights legislation in visionary defiance of the only political and social system he had ever known, Johnson accurately predicted that, as a result, his Democratic Party would lose the

South for a generation.

Yet the other side of his personality was marked by stubborn, egotistical pride, and a raw ruthlessness that by some accounts knew no bounds. He clearly took King's antiwar activism as an act of monumental ingratitude (as did moderate black civil rights leaders who attacked King for his stand), and King's subsequent threat to bring the Nation's Capital to a standstill in the spring of 1968 might have been seen by the president as a personal affront and the final straw.

Looking at the available evidence, it is hardly unreasonable to suspect that high-level orders to "do whatever it takes" to stop King might have resulted in his assassination by someone further down the chain of command, considering that covert operatives of the executive branch of the US government who labeled King a threat to national security were in the habit of assassinating "troublemaker" leaders overseas during the 1960s; and considering that Hoover's FBI had tried to blackmail King into suicide as early as 1964, when much less was at stake.

Messages from Dr. King

Medium Janet Cyford's reading points to a surprising piece of the story not found in history books—and, intriguingly, this unexpected information that came through in her communications with the spirit world appears to be independently corroborated in a portion of Robert Cracknell's psychic vision of the case, as we will see.

Although Cyford has communicated with "the other side" for virtually her entire life, she was understandably a bit awestruck when the visual image and voice of the legendary Dr. King came through to her. She recalled another time she had seen King in astral form, at a lecture given by King biographer Taylor Branch. As she watched the author speak, she had a strange thought. "Another part of my mind began to wonder how tall Martin Luther King was ... as I looked back at Taylor Branch, [King] stood beside him, and he's quite a short man—you know, Taylor Branch stood about maybe six feet, but Martin Luther King came up to his shoulder." Later I would look at photographs of King leading protest marches and notice that, compared with many of the men who surrounded him, he could almost be described as short and pudgy; or perhaps more accurately, "not as tall as expected" for a man engraved in most people's minds as one of history's towering figures.

Cyford recalled "that he was so interested that this white guy was taking such an interest in the man's life—and I think when someone does a series of books like that, although they might not believe that they're contacting that consciousness, a lot of the information does come through from the person they're writing about. It becomes a mind-to-mind journey."

"The day leading up to this man's passing ... I'm looking at food. I don't know whether there'd been a large lunch, whether they had already eaten, or whether it was something that was planned after this gathering ... I get the feeling from him as he gets nearer to me that he likes his food, you know, that there could have been a weight problem with him."

Food and a weight problem might appear to be rather mundane and therefore meaningless details at first glance, yet, as I had learned earlier from another medium's reading on a different case, a person's final thoughts, no matter how trivial, can make a powerful imprint that carries over to the other side. King's final words and thoughts were indeed largely about food, and some of the last words he heard were about his weight. Just before King and his colleagues stepped outside, he joked with his Memphis Reverend Samuel "Billy" Kyles that "I don't want to go to your house for cold food," recalling a dinner of cold ham and Kool-Aid at another preacher's house. Kyles kidded King that he was getting fat. Out on the balcony, King told Jesse Jackson, "I want you to go to dinner with us this evening," and asked Jackson not to wear blue jeans to dinner—possibly the last words he ever spoke.

"There'd been some changes about where they would stay or where they would eat, and it seems as if they were told at the last moment," Cyford noted. "In fact, there were other parts of the family that had to be got in touch with to redirect them." Possibly this refers to King's brother A.D., who had arrived in Memphis late the previous night. The brothers spoke about a sermon Martin was to deliver on Sunday. A.D., a preacher himself, would end up delivering it on Martin's behalf. That sermon remains as obscure as "I Have a Dream" is famous, yet is arguably as important since it reflected the civil rights champion at the height of his evolution. It was entitled, "Why America May Go to Hell."

"Has he a daughter?" Cyford asked. "He's giving me a picture of the youngest daughter who—she looked about 14, but he was saying something about her coming of age ... you know, he was a very wonderful family man because these important turning points in his children's lives were always celebrated ... He didn't feel very well that night. There was some gastric trouble, and now he looks back on that with almost a sense of unease as well. It was affecting, you know, fear changes the gastric juices and things like that. He wouldn't have thought of it as fear at that time, but obviously has had time to look back at that."

King indeed was sick—as well as apprehensive—the night before he died. Having arrived in Memphis amid reports of death threats, his flight having been delayed because of a bomb scare, he was understandably fearful. The detrimental effect of his apprehensive emotions on his health, conveyed so vividly through Janet Cyford in this spirit contact, is echoed in the recollections of King's top aide Ralph Abernathy in *And the Walls Came Tumbling Down*: "Another manifestation of his fear was the illness that would sometimes overtake him when he was about to face danger ... the best example was Selma, where for a number of days he was so sick with 'a stomach virus' that he was unable to function as leader of the movement and had to delegate responsibilities to me and to others."

"This was no mere attack of nervous stomach," Abernathy recalled. "He ran fever and was racked by chills, alternating with heavy sweats. No one could have doubted that what he suffered from was a genuine illness. This happened not once but a number of times during the years between 1954 and 1968. Sometimes he was even hospitalized."

In the middle of describing King's illness, something else suddenly caught Cyford's attention, and in a hushed tone of surprise and awe, she asked, "Do you know anything about Mahatma Gandhi? Because he's standing here. He's with him."

"Now I'm wondering if I knew about him or not," she continued. "I think I know he would often talk about nonviolent resistance and things like that, but *the man Mahatma Gandhi is standing with him*, and he, Martin Luther King, is not much taller than Mahatma Gandhi, as he shows me the vision of the two of them."

Intriguingly, medium Philip Solomon's communications with King also found him describing spending much of his time on the other side with Gandhi. While King has often been associated with the nonviolent liberator of India whose work he studied at Crozer Theological Seminary, he could have just as easily shown up with any of a number of other individuals with whom he shared a special connection—perhaps his father, who shared his name and his calling as a preacher; his mother, whose powerful bond with him went beyond the usual when she, too, was assassinated; or, if someone more famous, perhaps another black civil rights leader or one of the slain Kennedys, who, when push came to shove, became his valuable allies, and whose martyrdom will link them forever with King in the public mind. Yet in the readings by both mediums, it is Gandhi alone who shows up, seemingly accompanying King as a combination of friend, teacher, and elder brother.

"So we're coming back again to that night," Cyford continued, "to feeling very weary, very apprehensive that I would throw up or I would need the bathroom, or something was not right with him ... They're [her spirit guides] also saying that he was recovering from some bronchial—I don't know whether it had been a cold, but it was a cough, that sort of thing."

This message echoes Andrew Young's recollection that King "had one of those colds that came on when he was depressed" on the night of April 3.

"So he was not feeling up to par. He didn't feel like making a speech ... He also didn't know what exactly he was going to say— there were thoughts in his mind, and I think this man worked a great deal in an inspirational way and not from notes ..."

As described in this spirit contact, the ailing civil rights leader, who planned to stay in the motel and get some rest, changed his mind and came to speak after Abernathy called and told him the audience was clamoring to hear him. Fierce thunderstorms and a tornado tore through Memphis, eerily reflecting the turbulence within the city, the nation, and Dr. King himself at that highly charged and foreboding moment in time. As Janet Cyford indicated during her reading, he spoke totally without notes as he delivered one of the most powerful and moving speeches of his life.

"We do know at some unrevealed conscious level of ourselves the pattern before us," Cyford observed, perhaps partly explaining his apprehension the night of April 3. People who saw his speech that night found it to be one of his most inspirational orations, but had one complaint: Dr. King seemed to be morbidly predicting his own death.

"... We've got some difficult days ahead," King told the crowd at the Mason Temple. "But it really doesn't matter with me now, because I've been to the mountaintop. And I don't mind. Like anybody, I would like to live a long life. Longevity has its place. But I'm not concerned about that now. I just want to do God's will. And He's allowed me to go up to the mountain, and I've looked over, and I've seen the promised land. I may not get there with you...."

"He had a very important conversation with one of his sons," Cyford said, "and I don't know whether this had been the day before or that afternoon, but I'm looking at the son ... it was an ongoing conversation, that parts of it had been by telephone. The son had said to him, 'You don't sound well' or 'How are you?' or 'You don't sound like yourself' or something like that."

"And this is comical, he had shoes that were not comfortable ... I wonder if that's symbolic—it could've been both ways ... didn't like the role that he was in at that moment." Dr. King probably had never been more uncomfortable in his metaphorical shoes than he was during his final months. In addition to the recently stepped-up persecution of him by government agencies, he was under attack from moderates and the mainstream press, who condemned his antiwar efforts and plans for a massive Poor People's March as radical and counterproductive; and derided by young black militants as a

179

foolish Uncle Tom whose nonviolent strategy was outdated.

"Do you know when his father died? ... If it wasn't the father, it would have been his grandfather—it was someone that had been very instrumental in keeping him on the straight and narrow in his younger years ... he felt those that had gone on before him around him."

"When he passed over?" I asked.

"No, before. I'm still in the hotel room. And it had gone on during that day, he's coming up with things that had gone on during that day, that he'd been thinking of his father, but the father, or the grandfather, kept walking into his mind, things that they'd said to him down the years, which means to me—and he understands this—that they were gathering to be there with him ..."

"He wants you to know that in retrospect as he looks back, every speech that he made, he would come out of the crowd thinking, 'Well, it didn't happen that time.' This man knew he was gonna go in this way, and he always thought it would be when he was talking to the people, whereas it didn't happen like that ... So each time he had finished a public appearance, it was, 'well it's not this time' ... He never thought he'd make it into his fifties." Perhaps King was haunted in particular by the assassination of Malcolm X, who was beginning a speech when he was struck down in a hail of gunfire in front of his wife and children.

"Now I'm under an awning—I'm him, under an awning ... it really is a sharing of energy—it's like a dark blue ... almost like his last memory ... he's saying it's the exit, which might be like the back part of some hotel."

"A car was coming to the back to pick him up. I've always wondered whether that guy who was accused of shooting him ... I don't think he did it, I think there was some conspiracy. There was some promise made to him that the authorities didn't keep ... He was involved with [the conspirators] and he knew what was going on, but he was promised that if he took the responsibility for it, that he'd only do so much time." This description of the part played by James Earl Ray is virtually identical to that of other psychics who did readings on this case.

When this remarkable sharing of the final 24 hours of King's life finally reached the horrible moment of his assassination, what came through was astonishing and perplexing.

"There's this awful sadness that comes over him, that belongs to Martin. This sounds very ridiculous, but it's almost like—he's likening it to Judas. Someone that was close and ... wanted him to do something, and when he wouldn't do something ... and this person was very, very loosely wrapped." King knew this young man, who appears to have been the son of someone he knew, "and tried to help him at some point."

"He tried to look at the reasons for it. There was someone in his association—I don't mean in his organization—that came into his orbit, if you like, and got angry with him about the way something was going. And the son of that man took it upon himself to do away with him ... it brings it back again to Judas. If you think about the story of Judas, Judas got in touch with the authorities to force Jesus of Nazareth to show his hand. There's a similarity here; Judas wanted him to do things in a different way. Judas thought he [Jesus]'d got such power that he could strike could strike masses of people dead if he wanted to. Judas was not too tightly wrapped, and when he found that [Jesus] didn't use the power in that way, to protect himself or protect his people, there was a lot of disagreement with somebody else that said, you know, this is the time that we could become powerful, we could rule, and he held that source of trouble down, that that wasn't his way, changes have to be made in a nonviolent way."

After this reading by Janet Cyford, it was a bit eerie to read Coretta King's description of her husband's final meeting in her book *My Life With Martin Luther King, Jr.*: "He went around the room and told each person what they needed to do; he criticized them one by one. It was like the way the Last Supper is described, when Christ told Judas that he would betray Him and then spoke to Peter and the others. Martin said that he wanted anyone in the organization who turned to violence to be fired, and then pointed out who was getting out of line. The meeting got very emotional, and he got upset and left ..."

Janet Cyford's reading found a conflict over tactics to have been brewing within King's organization. "There was a faction amongst his followers, if you like, that wanted greater action," she noted during the reading. "And the son of one of them—it wasn't as if he was told to do it or anything like that—it was just that he got caught up in—you know, some people get caught up in what other people are saying and off they go and take the action themselves."

But how does this piece of the puzzle fit in with the rest of the evidence? I did not receive much information in answer to this question through this spirit contact, other than a statement that the high-level cover-up came in later. Everyone's perspective is unique, and understandably, from Dr. King's perspective, this deadly betrayal appears to have been the heart of the story, perhaps making the rest of the story pale in significance for him.

When I had no further questions and was ready to move on to another case, Janet Cyford said no, not yet, the spirit of Dr. King had more to say and she was not ready to let him go. "I'd like to continue just, say, for another fifteen minutes with him," she said, "because it's important."

Cyford described Dr. King's concern for his widow Coretta. "He's asking me to pray for her ... I feel very concerned about her ..." The concern appeared to involve ulcers, either actual ulcers or the potential for ulcers if she allowed stress to affect her health. "It seems as if she's very aware of him," Cyford added, "that she dreams of him and things like that."

Shifting the focus to his children's lives, Cyford observed, "His eyes fill with tears over this. You know ... they wonder what their father or grandfather would have thought about these things if he were still alive ... and he tries to let me know that he *does* know about them. He *does* attend the weddings and the funerals and the christenings and the continuation of the family."

"He knows that I would look for verification, verifiable evidence that it's him, and things that he would give me would not be in *my* mind, because when you've got a very public figure like this, I always question if I heard [the information] somewhere."

Another Psychic Sees a Judas

Examining this reading that proved so amazingly accurate in bringing forth specific details, what are we to make of the message that a young black man played a role in Dr. King's death? Like most experienced mediums, Cyford learned a long time ago not to modify, interpret, or attempt to "make sense of" what comes through, no matter how nonsensical or impossible the message or image appears. And she bluntly described this message as she received it: This young Judas killed Martin Luther King, Jr.

Yet we have also seen that, even in the most lucid spirit contacts, it is difficult to separate the real from the symbolic. Cyford wondered, for example, whether the message about King's uncomfortable shoes was meant literally or as a psychological metaphor. Could the telepathic message that "this man killed me" be meant in a broader or symbolic sense, akin to saying that so-and-so "stabbed me in the back"?

If this traitor was indeed close to King's inner circle, the authorities who were spying on King and his associates stood an excellent chance of being aware of him and his tendencies. The depiction of this unstable young man as a glory-seeking loudmouth further supports the possibility that King's powerful enemies could have learned of his leanings and capitalized on his disruptive and destructive potential. One of Hoover's preferred methods of destroying civil rights leaders was to exploit internal differences and grudges learned about through the FBI's usual surveillance as well as its "racial informant" program—tactics alleged to have played a role in the assassination of Malcolm X by Black Muslims three years earlier.

Treachery and evil certainly know no color boundaries. King had been stabbed and nearly killed by a black woman at a book signing in Harlem, and his mother would be shot to death by a black man (both being cases of sick individuals projecting their own deranged delusions onto the famous, rather than acts of conspiracy, according to a reading by medium Betty Muench). So it is not unthinkable that an African-American could have been somehow involved in the assassination. After all, as mentioned earlier, recent history reveals a definite pattern of people "killing their own" in the murders of King's fellow peacemakers Gandhi, Sadat, and Rabin, each widely perceived as a visionary leader reviled by hardliners as a sellout.

Can this reading be reconciled with the others that found a conspiracy in which James Earl Ray was a pawn? Robert Cracknell—who had no knowledge of any of the other readings, nor was he asked about the possibility of a traitor among the people surrounding King—tuned in to this mystery and found both treachery from within and conspiracy from without. Cracknell perceived that King had become " a very sensitive political 'hot potato'" and that "it was politically expedient that he should be eradicated" by powerful interests, yet also noted, "I have the strongest feeling that the assassination was planned, initially, from within the camp of Martin Luther King and that there must have been some collusion between them, government agencies, [and] FBI ..."

This finding of a Judas, which came through so powerfully from two psychics, might strike some people as unsettling, outrageous, and even offensive. Yet in examining this mystery, a sensible starting point is to humbly admit how little we know after all these years about this case.

As in the Cyford reading, the internal dissension perceived by Cracknell took the form of passionate criticism of King for allegedly failing to wield power in a more aggressive, worldly way. As Cracknell described it, the conflict was not necessarily about violence versus nonviolence, but rather an argument over whether to respond in kind to the type of hardball tactics that were being used against King and his colleagues. More specifically, he noted, King was being pressured to answer blackmail with blackmail, "to the point where he would be told, 'War is dirty. We can win this war ... you must publicly state the information we are giving you, so that these people can be seen for what they are.'"

There surely was enormous potential for this type of pressure being brought to bear on King when one recalls that he had taken on battles on a variety of fronts and had reached out to join forces with numerous individuals and organizations that shared some of his goals but not necessarily his high-minded tactics. For example, he had built alliances with labor unions such as the Teamsters, which allegedly had connections to people in organized crime, who allegedly had compromising information on Hoover's personal life. The powerful sources of the "helpful" information, as Cracknell saw it, were primarily concerned with serving their own self-interest, and "were perfectly happy to use him to further their own political ambitions and ends by feeding him information and pressuring him ..."

Yet it would have been thoroughly out of character for King, who would never fight violence with violence, to respond to blackmail with blackmail. By taking the high road, he had already achieved undreamed-of success in his battle for justice; to suddenly start playing a dirty type of political hardball would not only be morally questionable but ultimately impractical. "As a man with a highly developed conscience, I consider it doubtful that he would have used similar damaging evidence of misdemeanors or wrongdoing against the opposition," Cracknell observed.

As mentioned earlier, emotions were so running so high during the final meeting of King and his colleagues that he got upset and walked out. If this was the psychological state of the civil rights crusade's most seasoned veterans, who had maintained their equanimity through years of killings, beatings, and threats, what might we expect from an impulsive, unstable young man, allegedly the son of someone in King's orbit, whose anger—perhaps ignited by militant elements trying to influence King, and easily capitalized on by the government agents spying on King's organization as part of a campaign to destroy him—might have exploded in a horrible act of treachery?

"I May Not Get There with You"

The consensus of the combined psychic readings matches the findings of assassination researchers who have presented extensive evidence of a high-level conspiracy. In December 1963, shortly after the killing of President Kennedy, Hoover's FBI declared its intention of "neutralizing King as an effective Negro leader." A

1964 FBI memo discussed the urgent need for "the removal of King from the national scene."

The Bureau's tactics included extensive surveillance, a defamation campaign, and disruption of King's efforts through dirty tricks, planting of informants, and blackmail of King to pressure him into committing suicide. In addition, as reporter Jeff Cohen wrote in *The Rebel* on November 22, 1983, Hoover "used anonymous phone calls and 'poison pen' letters to create dissension among King's staff and associates in the Southern Christian Leadership Conference"—an aspect of the government's war on King that might be connected with the finding of a Judas in two of the psychic readings.

Yet, by 1968, the already overwhelming pressures on King took on a whole new dimension. As the Church Committee found during the 1970s, FBI agents were told in March 1968 to neutralize King, lest he become a "messiah" who could "unify and electrify the militant Black Nationalist movement." In addition, his opposition to the Vietnam War during his final year subjected him to Army surveillance as a perceived national security threat, as did his plans to bring his Poor People's Campaign to Washington in the spring.

In an eye-opening investigative report for the *Memphis Commercial Appeal* on March 21, 1993, Stephen Tompkins wrote that the Army's intelligence branch "spied on the family of Dr. Martin Luther King, Jr. for three generations," often targeting black ministers such as King's father. "The spying was born of a conviction by top Army intelligence officers that black Americans were ripe for subversion—first by agents of the German Kaiser, then by Communists, later by the Japanese and eventually by those opposed to the Vietnam War. At first, the Army used a reporting network of private citizens that included church members, black businessmen ... and black educators ... It later employed cadres of infiltrators, wiretaps, and aerial photography by U-2 spy planes."

"As the civil rights movement merged with anti-war protests in the late 1960s, some Army units began supplying sniper rifles and other weapons of war to civilian police departments," Tompkins reported. "Army Intelligence began planning for what some officers believed would soon be armed rebellion." As King planned a massive march on Washington, "the Army's intelligence system was keenly focused on King and desperately searching for a way to stop him … the review of thousands of government documents and interviews with people involved in the spying revealed that by early 1968 Army Intelligence regarded King as a major threat to national security."

William Pepper also found extensive evidence of the military and intelligence communities' determination to neutralize King. In a surprising development, Pepper obtained a "remote viewing" of the assassination by David Morehouse, a prominent government-trained psychic spy. According to Morehouse, King was murdered by low-level intelligence operatives, "a sniper team that came out of assassination school. They were always deployed in areas where riots were taking place or expected to take place. They had a hit list, a sequential hit list of people they were to take out … they had an egress route out of the area; or a 'potted plant'—people that would pick them up." They were instructed that King and other like him were "enemies of the State."

Morehouse said Pepper planned to argue "that the US government has used this as an intelligence collection tool for 20 years … He will say, 'Look, a military remote viewer has brought this information back, and it was collected using military technology.'"

The initial prevailing suspicion on April 4, 1968 was that King was struck down by a segregationist individual or group. That was not unreasonable as a first hunch—white-supremacist terrorists had indeed committed numerous murders during that decade—yet is unlikely in light of all that we know today. In the scenario presented by several dedicated researchers—and supported by the combined insights of prominent psychic detectives—the killing of Dr. King looks less like the segregationists' murders of American civil rights leaders such as Medgar Evers, and more like an eerie repetition of the assassination of Congo's President Patrice Lumumba seven years earlier.

Like King, Lumumba was unjustly targeted as a threat to U.S. national security. In a storyline similar to what has been uncovered in the King case, the CIA hired Mafiosi—in this case, from Europe—as well as Belgian mercenaries to brutally eliminate Lumumba. And—in a plot that mirrored the high-level efforts to destroy King through the planting of black informants and the stoking of some African-Americans' resentments against him— the U.S. government enlisted the aid of Lumumba's jealous rivals whom he had defeated in the election, offering huge bribes to gain their treacherous cooperation.

The intelligence community's preferred methods of silencing dissidents during the 1960s were revealed in horrifying detail in a leaked memo that was included in a report released by the Senate Intelligence Committee report released on April 26, 1976: "Show them as scurrilous and depraved. Call attention to their habits and living conditions, explore every possible embarrassment. Send in women and sex, break up marriages. Have members arrested on marijuana charges. Investigate personal conflicts or animosities between them. Send articles to the newspapers showing their depravity. Use narcotics and free sex to entrap. Use misinformation to confuse and disrupt. Get records of their bank accounts. Obtain specimens of handwriting. Provoke target groups into rivalries that may result in death."

That's right: "... that may result in death."

And the dissenters who were the subject of this particular policy memorandum were not even genuine political leaders but merely leftist counterculture figures, particularly antiwar rock musicians. If rock stars were considered national security threats who had to be destroyed (and one now might wonder how many of their scandals and untimely deaths were really their own doing), a leader of the stature of Dr. King was not likely to last very long.

Dr. King's premonition of his death in his final speech was no mere morbid coincidence. He knew he was targeted for destruction and that his antipoverty and antiwar efforts were likely to fail. Struggling with growing doubts about the usefulness of nonviolent action, and plagued by the deep depression that overtook him during his final weeks, he nevertheless saw no alternative but to continue to play his role the best he could. His solution for America's ills in

1968 was still rooted in the same spirit of love and understanding he had expressed 10 years earlier when he refused to press charges against the woman who stabbed him in the chest and nearly killed him (leaving him with permanent scar tissue in the shape of a cross over his heart after the knife's removal). "Don't do anything to her," he said. "Don't prosecute her; get her healed."

"What would Martin Luther King, Jr. say about [fill in the blank]?" is a frequently asked question, second only to "What would Jesus do?" As astonishing and improbable as it might sound to some of us, Dr. King's opinions on today's issues did come through in this chapter's spirit contacts.

Although best remembered for the desegregation battles above all else, King passionately insisted in his first major speech at the Lincoln Memorial, during the Prayer Pilgrimage of 1957, that "this must be followed by a positive program of action" that included "the right to vote" and "economic uplift for Negroes and poor white men." *Significantly, these are the same two issues he addressed here through mediums, without being asked.*

In the same way that Dr. King's spirit continues to watch over his family, his concern also extends to ever-broader circles of his wider family—black Americans, Americans in general, and the rest of humanity. During Janet Cyford's reading, conducted on December 8, 2000, she received the message that he was deeply troubled over that week's allegations of intimidation and disenfranchisement of black voters in Florida.

Intriguingly, the second issue King emphasized in his 1957 Prayer Pilgrimage speech—"economic uplift for Negroes and poor white men"—also came through from spirit, in the contact by medium Philip Solomon. When Solomon asked a question about the fight against racial discrimination, the spirit of Dr. King quickly changed the subject to poverty:

"It made me feel wonderful, but wonderful to see my people uniting to help themselves [in the fight for integration], more than any esteem it would bring for me. But I always believed, Philip, that the cause of all the difficulties, especially in America, was poverty, and not just the poor black people but for poor whites too, and other

groups as well, even the Native American Indians, the Red Men, were mostly poor and only lived on reservations that probably at some time in history had belonged to them. I always believed it was important for African Americans to be people who understood the pain of others too and would strive for equality and fairness for all. This didn't always make me as popular as you might imagine with all African American people, Philip! Many believed that the racial injustice that they suffered as a black race should be my prime impetus for change, but as I have already said to you I always believed that poverty in some circumstances can breed injustice and cruelty just as much as racism can."

Solomon also conveyed a reassuring message from Dr. King about his life on the other side:

"It is a wonderful place, Philip, where almost anything can be achieved if you wish it to be so. I spend much of my time preaching and still try to bring an influence of spiritual goodness towards your world ... Although I deeply miss my family and still dearly love them all and often think of them and try to assist them from my role in the Spirit World, I am happy to be where I am in this world and to be making my own personal progress, I hope ultimately towards progression that is satisfactory to my Lord and no-one else. I told you Philip I was not the angel that many people believed but a mere mortal man who tried very hard to open himself to God and to try to help others to have a better and fairer life. I asked for no retribution against others when I was sent to the Spirit World and I ask for no tears to be spilled. I am happy in this wonderful world that has been provided for me. Do not concern yourselves with me but strive in your own world to find equality and fairness for all. That is part of your progression."

Medium Betty Muench also found King's work to be continuing, perceiving his energy on the other side as "moving and churning all the time. This to me suggests that Dr. King is not getting much respite from his work and that it has carried over into his spirit life. There is much better guardianship on that side and he is safe in that at least." Dr. King "... is pleased that his name goes on and that seems to help him build power within."

His current exalted state was described by Muench's spirit guides at the beginning of the reading: "... *this one will be coming in very close and that this will hold seemingly greater power than ever. This one will be King and that this one will have more and more power. He will have gathered forces on the spirit side and he will be guided in this however so that this does not go out of control. There will be much force on the side of King and he will seem to gather energy from others who will have been wronged in all matter of ways. There will be this which seeks him within and he does not know time-as-such to think through his life as King. He will be seemingly bombarded with those who seek his guidance within. There will be this then which would suggest that the killing of Dr. King would not silence him and that he will gather power in ways that will have been much easier now than in the body. The tangible body can only do so much but now in this form, he can gather all manner of force and he can continue to influence the earth plane. There will be those [who killed him] who will not have understood this about spirit ...*"

Just as it would be a mistake to ignore the broader picture of the assassination that has come to light—the high-level persecution of King, extensive evidence of a plot and frame-up, Mafiosi deathbed confessions, possible cover-up murders, and so on—it would also be a mistake to ignore the reassuring reality revealed to us from these contacts with the world of spirit, namely, that "death" is an illusion, and that one's soul, one's identity, and one's life mission never really come to an end. The vibrant continuation of King's life and work on the other side brings to mind the words of one of his towering predecessors, the anti-slavery activist Sojourner Truth: "I am not going to die, I'm going home like a shooting star."

Chapter 8:
Through the Looking Glass—
The Bizarre Disappearances of
William Colby and John Paisley

"... and [Joseph's brothers] drew and lifted up Joseph out of the pit, and sold Joseph to the Ishmaelites for twenty shekels of silver. And they brought Joseph into Egypt ... And they took Joseph's coat, and killed a he-goat, and dipped the coat in the blood; and they sent the coat of many colors, and they brought it to their father; and said: 'This we have found. Know now whether it is thy son's coat or not.' And he knew it, and said: 'It is my son's coat; an evil beast hath devoured him; Joseph is without doubt torn in pieces ...'"—Genesis 37:28

Did William Colby die accidentally or was he murdered?

This question, it turns out, might contain a huge erroneous assumption, for when I read medium Betty Muench's channeled answer to my question about "the circumstances of his death," I was informed that the former CIA chief who seemingly died while boating on April 28, 1996 is not yet in the spirit world.

Two months after receiving what Muench called "the most bizarre answer I have gotten yet," I spoke with renowned psychic detective Greta Alexander. Although she was swamped with a heavy workload and not particularly eager to participate in a book project that deals primarily with homicides, she shared her psychic insights regarding the Colby case. "He's still alive," she stated with absolute conviction, echoing the Muench reading's assertion that Colby had been abducted. In fact, all the readings by psychics and mediums found a kidnapping, not an accident or a murder on the day he disappeared, though the story grows murky after that initial crime. But why was he abducted? "He knew too much, hon," said Alexander, who has worked on numerous missing-person cases.

But how could this particular scenario even be possible? Wasn't it reported that Colby's body was recovered on May 6, 1996? The answer to this enigma might be found, oddly enough, by going back two decades and exploring a nearly identical disappearance—and a stunning development in that earlier case that may cast doubt on "official stories" in general, and may well be the key to unlocking the Colby mystery.

Southern Maryland Boat-Accident Mystery 1: September 1978

John A. Paisley, a high-ranking CIA intelligence analyst, went sailing on the southern Maryland Chesapeake Bay on September 24, 1978 on his boat Brillig, named after a nonsense word from "Jabberwocky" in Lewis Carroll's *Through the Looking Glass*. His boat was later discovered unoccupied about 15 miles from the site where Colby's empty boat would one day be found.

In October, a body was found; it had a gunshot wound in the head, markings around the throat indicating foul play, and 38 pounds of diver's weights around the torso. Curiously, the boat had no blood or brain tissue, ruling it out as the site of the shooting. The bullet wound was above the left ear, although Paisley was right-handed. Most startling of all was an inconvenient detail pointed out by Paisley's wife Maryann: the corpse was five-foot-seven-inches, yet her husband was five-foot-eleven. *Through the Looking Glass* was indeed a fitting theme for the case of the missing CIA official.

The authorities essentially pretended they did not hear Maryann's protest, and focused their investigation only on whether this was a case of murder or suicide. Suicide was the official ruling. An FBI report in 1979 found "no credible evidence" of any possibility other than that Paisley had killed himself. A 1980 *Washington Post* article noted that FBI and Senate Intelligence Committee investigations "accept what these probers feel is the most plausible view: that the Russian-speaking Paisley, who had been estranged from his wife and was undergoing psychiatric treatment, committed suicide by shooting himself in the head and falling into the bay after weighing himself down with two diver belts ..."

Even accepting for the sake of argument that the body was Paisley's, there are compelling reasons to doubt the suicide conclusion. According to Maryland police, the bullet recovered from the corpse's head was "slightly heavier than would normally come from [Paisley's] type of gun." In addition, Paisley's close friend Betty R. Myers pointed out that he had sold his 9-mm automatic pistol during the summer. And Maryann Paisley's attorney Bernard Fensterwald noted, "Jumping off a boat with gun in hand, pulling the trigger while in the water, is, to be charitable about the matter, a weird way to commit suicide."

Paisley's son Edward said he believed his father had been murdered, after hearing from Dr. George Weems, coroner of Calvert County, and marina owner Harry Lee Langley. Both had viewed the body when it was found, and Weems said the markings on the corpse's neck showed that it had "been squeezed or had a rope around it." But Weems' superior, Dr. Russell C. Fisher, angrily denounced Weems' conclusion, attributing the neck marks to decomposition.

Maryann said she believed John had been killed after a struggle, because "a table (aboard the Brillig) had been pulled away from the wall. Several screws had been pulled loose, and it was tilted at an angle which would have made it impossible to use." Also, a partly eaten meal found on board suggested he had been interrupted on the boat during lunch. Even though this circumstantial evidence on the boat led her to a conclusion of murder, she did not believe the body presented as that of her husband was indeed his. Maryann pointed to discrepancies between the corpse and John Paisley's body: differences in hair color, waist size, weight, and, most remarkable of all, height: five-foot-seven versus John's five-foot-eleven.

Was he abducted and killed? Abducted and kept alive? Psychic detective Bertie Catchings stated that "Paisley was kidnapped and taken away for questioning ... and a cadaver was chosen from a man who had a similar appearance to John Paisley ... Paisley would not have been able to put up that much of a struggle." He "was picked up by another boat and taken away ..."

Catchings examined the pictures I provided of Paisley and of the corpse, and pointed out that "the other body in this picture was a cadaver ... someone that had been killed—for whatever reason; I don't know if there was a particular reason to kill him, except that they wanted this investigation to be stopped ... The actual bone structure does not seem to be the same as John Paisley."

She found that "John Paisley was questioned quite extensively and he did live for quite a while ... he was taken to another country, and in time he did die, but not right away, because he was of great use."

Medium Janet Cyford tuned in to this case and stated, "I have an impression of this man sitting naked to the waist, his arms tied around his back, very emaciated ... I think he's in spirit. I think he died some five or six years after this."

"This body was not his not at all, but someone lost their life ... to be put in his place."

"He was taken for what he knew," she said. "I don't know who took him. I don't think he was taken very far away from the Chesapeake Bay."

"Would there be any places that were prisons, that were wartime places that were not used anymore?" Cyford asked. "Because it's somewhere along that coastline there, where he was kept. I don't know who did this, I'm not being shown, but there's a lot of nastiness around him."

"He never told them, he couldn't tell them what they wanted to know ... but you know, I hate to say this, but it was people in this country who did it."

"It was something about those years, '62 to '64, that he'd been involved in there, but I don't think it was anything to do with the Soviet stuff ... It seems senseless ... it was heavyhanded."

Cyford's point about "not being shown" who kidnapped Paisley once again illustrates a key principle of mediumship. "I've been taught from spirit that there are spiritual laws that will not allow them to tell you, 'This man did it, or that man did it' … I've had people come to me, I had somebody this week whose son had been shot, and she really would have liked me to have said, 'This is the guy that did it,' but there's a natural barrier that goes up. And when I've asked [spirit guides] why that is, it's that it's against spirit law. They must be given a chance to own up to that rather than having someone in spirit pointing to them."

For reasons perhaps known only to God, the Paisley and the Colby mysteries were the haziest, most indecipherable cases of all, in contrast with cases such as that of Vincent Foster, Ron Brown, and Martin Luther King, Jr., in which a fairly coherent narrative could be constructed from the combined insights of the psychics, viewed alongside the known facts.

Nancy Myer saw Paisley dying an accidental death while sailing, maintaining that people are seeing intrigue that isn't really there because of Paisley's work in the intelligence field. Robert Cracknell, on the other hand, saw a disappearance in which Paisley himself might have been complicit. "My immediate reaction to this case is that Paisley did not die in 1978," he noted. "There's a feeling of definite collusion with others for him to disappear, and the reasons for his disappearance would be to set up a new life. His destination could well be a South American country. Bearing in mind his previous employment and connections, this would not be too difficult."

"Possibly his first safe port of call would be to follow the coastline and enter into Mexico," Cracknell pointed out. "From there he would have had ample opportunity to make arrangements for traveling further down into South America. The obvious question is why did he feel the need to disappear and start a new life?"

"I do not necessarily feel that this had anything to do with his previous employment, though with his being employed in such an organization there is a tendency to connect any mystery with that shadowy world within which he once worked. I feel, however, that this was not sinister."

Cracknell added that "I get the strong impression of a name—the name of Enrique, or Enriques. I cannot be more specific as to whether this is a Christian name or surname. I believe this Enrique has some connection with Brazil, where subject may have traveled from Mexico ..."

"I believe, however, that it is possible Paisley is now dead—having died from natural causes ... People do disappear for many reasons, and I strongly feel that this was simply a deliberate disappearing act on his part in order to start a new life."

A reading by Betty Muench in 1997 found him alive at that time, an aging man living and working in peculiar circumstances after being abducted. "*There is this which will seem to be moving over the head of this one John. There will be in this then the sense that he will be in a situation which will have him paying close attention to something overhead ... watching a liftoff of some kind. There is this energy of Paisley being involved and then not in some other realm (not dead).*"

This spirit contact noted, "*There is this which will have the sense of being involved in a work that is all-consuming to him and that while his life as Paisley is not the same as it was, he is still acting out ... thus then living. There will be this energy which will suggest that this man is dedicated to work and that this then is what keeps him going and that the demands then on him are great.*"

"*It is as if he is sequestered in a situation in which there is this work being done and [of] which then he is a part and he will have been a part of this plan all along. There will be this which will suggest that while he will regret much of what came about around his so-called demise, that he will have been someone who will have had the best interests of his country in mind and that he is still convinced that this is what he is involved in at this time. There are secret works which will suggest that those who will be undercover will have an important part in these works.*"

Why was he kidnapped in the first place? It appears that, as an intelligence analyst, he insisted on adhering to the cold, hard facts in his evaluation of Soviet strength rather than bend his findings to fit the desired policy-mandated conclusions, according to this reading:

"It is not that he was about to reveal anything. He was not in agreement with the coming changes that were already being set up around the relationship between the U.S. and the Soviet. There will be this which he will have felt was a threat and that he would have stood in the way (so others thought) of the play for the Soviet to simply lay down and quit; and in that then he did not believe that they would do this. This was a plan that had been in the making for a very, very long time and in this time, he still cannot realize that this is so and he is being treated in a manner as if to placate him and his beliefs ..."

It has been reported that during the 1970s, CIA analysts such as Paisley were pressured to inflate their assessments of Soviet military and economic power (a controversy that naturally brings to mind the reported complaints by CIA and MI6 analysts that they felt pressured to alter their findings to support the invasion of Iraq). This policy of inflating figures did not sit well with the fact-oriented Paisley, whom Bertie Catchings described as "one of the good guys that wouldn't have thought twice about telling the truth."

In the book *Widows*, an account of the efforts of CIA wives to uncover the truth about husbands lost in espionage mysteries, authors William R. Corson, Susan B. Trento, and Joseph J. Trento write, "For a generation the CIA had been regarded as an 'independent' source of unbiased intelligence information." But all that changed beginning in the Nixon Administration.

The authors note that "Paisley found that as the military exaggerated their estimates of Soviet strength to garner more budget money from the administration and Congress, acrimony over the estimates increased. Defense contractors and right-wing groups began to make a political issue of the CIA's 'low-balling' of Soviet spending. Conservatives saw the CIA as a liberal bastion. To make matters worse, military intelligence received orders requiring them to develop estimates to support the new administration's defense policy, regardless of what the facts showed. Beginning with Kissinger, the Office of Strategic Research received serious pressure to 'adjust' findings to suit political expediency."

Paisley had been second in command at the Office of Strategic Research. Although he officially retired in 1974, he continued working as a consultant—with top-secret information about Soviet military capabilities—until the time of his disappearance.

Further describing his circumstances, which are difficult to comprehend, Muench's spirit guides state: "*There will be this which he has bought into and that is the security aspect of the U.S. This is being presented to him as the major reason for his sacrifice, in that he will have known much about the Soviet operation. He did not think that this could be changed but that the plans were in the offing even then. In this time then he is in a situation which is well-guarded and he is not a prisoner but he is agreed to this self-imprisonment for reasons that are made to sound very important to him. In this then he is in a psychological condition that has to be understood before one can judge his agreements.*"

"*At this time John will be watching an experiment which is seen by other eyes … there will be this which will seem to be done in a remote place that is not within the borders of the U.S. and that there will be this which occurs in a place from which there is much activity which while observed by certain eyes is not observed by the world news gatherers. It is totally not within their purview.*"

"*In that then there is this one who is slight of build and who then is seemingly very old, but who makes a contribution still and that then there is this one who will simply depart [die] and no one will know about it … no one will mourn him as he has already been mourned, and there will come this then which will be waiting for him on the other side …*"

My questions for Muench included an inquiry about whether the perpetrators of his disappearance were American or Russian, and the above channeling seems to point to Americans. Yet this is not quite the case, according to the spooky conclusion of the reading: "*The ones who will have seemingly instigated this with John will be those of a certain group who will have not been within the power of the U.S. government but others who will have called upon him for a service. Those others will not have been simply American or Russian. There is this which is a greater power and is of many cultures and people from all manner of race ... very powerful connection here."*

If this reading is accurate, the Paisley disappearance leads into clandestine areas that are murky, disturbing, and bewildering. However, this case might provide enlightenment in another area, in helping unlock the secrets of the eerily similar disappearance of Paisley's one-time boss 18 years later.

Southern Maryland Boat Accident Mystery 2: April 1996

William Colby vanished on Sunday, April 28, 1996. Although the 76-year-old former CIA director's empty, capsized canoe was found in the waters near his southern Maryland retreat, Colby's wife Sally firmly believed he was still alive. When she called him from Houston around 7 P.M. the previous evening, he told her that his only plans were to eat dinner and go to sleep after a day of working on his boat. The next day, alerted by worried neighbors, police found a scene that was inexplicable: the always-orderly spymaster had left a plateful of clam shells and a half-finished glass of wine sitting out, had left his computer, radio, and house lights on, and the house unlocked.

People who knew the fastidious Colby found it extremely unlikely he would have left the house in such a condition, and equally unlikely that he would have gone canoeing in turbulent weather at night, failing to wear a lifejacket for the first time in his life.

Bertie Catchings laughed at the official scenario. "That is just so ludicrous, you just couldn't imagine anybody with any intelligence believing that he did it that way ... Most people are creatures of habit. Even the most uneducated people have habits that they do—they get up at a certain time, they use a certain cup or fix their coffee a certain way, or they lock up their house or they carry their lifejacket. And this man [according to the official story] did a number of things that were not creatures of habit; if he'd just done one thing [differently], there might be an explanation."

Did he, then, meet a terrible fate that was no accident? If so, it would hardly be the only suspicious case of its kind. It is a tragic and curious reality that directors of the CIA—even ex-directors—seem more likely than the average person to suffer peculiar misfortunes. When William Casey was about to testify regarding the Iran-contra scandal, he coincidentally had a seizure that necessitated the removal of the part of the brain that controls speech. In early 2000, former CIA director Stansfield Turner survived a plane crash in Costa Rica that killed his wife and four other people and injured 13. A report on *WorldNetDaily.com* quoted an intelligence source who claimed "it wasn't an accident," although no definite conclusion can be drawn from the testimony of a single anonymous source.

Circumstantial evidence pointing to possible foul play prompted speculations as to who might have wanted Colby dead. There were surely countless Vietnamese and antiwar individuals who hated him for his role during the Vietnam War as head of the notorious Operation Phoenix, which ruthlessly eliminated tens of thousands of South Vietnamese civilians who were known or suspected to be "Vietcong sympathizers."

In addition, it was no secret that many CIA loyalists hated him for revealing secrets to Congress in 1975, feeling the agency was betrayed and damaged by his candid disclosures of excesses such as the bizarre CIA plots to assassinate Fidel Castro. (Some knowledgeable observers, though, say Colby was more crafty than candid at that time, strategically sharing selected evidence of wrongdoing which, however foolish or outrageous, was nevertheless legal and drew attention away from more grievous illegal transgressions.) Colby had also made enemies when he fired the controversial head of counter-intelligence, James Jesus Angleton, in 1974.

In addition, Colby's name comes up in the saga of the Nugan Hand Bank, an Australia-based institution that was allegedly set up primarily for the purpose of CIA drug-money laundering. Shortly after the bank's criminal and fraudulent activities were exposed in the press, Michael Hand, one of the bank's founders, fled and went undercover, and partner Francis Nugan was found shot to death. In Nugan's possession was William Colby's business card with an appointment date on it. Although it took place during the early 1980s, might the Nugan Hand scandal—or a related matter—have had repercussions more than a decade later because of the billions of dollars allegedly involved?

Yet, as described earlier, "Who killed William Colby?" might not be the correct question after all. None of the psychic readings found him to have been murdered on April 28, 1996, and some found him to be still alive much later. But how could this be possible? After all, eight days after Colby's disappearance, a corpse was recovered from the water near his home, and it was reported that Sally Shelton-Colby identified it as her husband's body. However, all may not be as it appears, and as we shall see, one psychic's reading—if it is true—contains an explanation for this seeming discrepancy.

Robert Cracknell stated, "I feel strongly that Colby is dead; that he was abducted and later killed."

"It could have begun by an opportunist burglary involving two men—one black and one white. They may well have set out to rob the house. Colby, however, being somewhat tenacious and aggressive, could well have resisted—causing the burglars to take the necessary steps of abduction and murder."

"I feel strongly, also, that this case has yet to be closed," he concluded. "In fact I feel quite positive that it will be solved."

Bertie Catchings seemed to find it more difficult to focus clearly on the Colby mystery than on the other cases she examined. "Colby, I believe, was kept alive for a while ... and then he was disposed of," she stated, echoing Cracknell's insight into the case. On the question of motive, however, Catchings said that Colby, like Paisley, appeared to have been kidnapped and eventually eliminated because of knowledge he had of espionage-related corruption. "I think that a 'machine' believed that this CIA director had too much information ... and so they wanted him killed."

"... Since he'd already started admitting that some of the things he did were wrong [revelations of CIA secrets during the 1970s], he could say more things and he could name names ... because he was there. And if he said these things, they would be believed."

Kidnapping followed by death is also the scenario in Nancy Myer's psychic reading, which unfolds in detail:

On April 28, 1996, Mr. Colby received a phone call from a former colleague. He asked to stop by to discuss an urgent matter. Mr. Colby trusted this man and invited him over.

When the man arrived he had three other men with him. They moved like military men ...

Colby did not know the other three, and was initially nervous. His colleague assured him there was no problem.

A discussion ensued about Colby's files on an old case. Now Colby got nervous and he wanted them to leave. He denied that he had any documents connected to this case. He told them he was tired and asked them to leave.

The tallest of the men approached Colby and threatened him. Colby was irate. As he started to react the three young men restrained him and forced him out the door and into a large black car.

There was a fourth man in the car with the motor still on.

Colby was taken to a secluded location where he was questioned exhaustively. While being interrogated Mr. Colby suffered a massive heart attack and died.

A separate crew of men cleaned up the evidence at the house. This was a professionally executed action. They had not intended to kill him. He was only supposed to be frightened into silence about his knowledge of a crime that a high government official was connected to.

Like the other psychic detectives and mediums, Nancy Myer found that Colby was taken against his will; he was not an accident victim, nor was he deliberately silenced. As is usually the case, Myer saw this scene unfold like a movie. Is it possible to reconcile this scenario with the insights of psychics who saw Colby remaining alive? Did the "movie" stop a little too soon—is it possible he collapsed under the strain, as the vision shows, but did not actually die on that occasion?

Greta Alexander, a psychic detective consulted by police on numerous missing-person cases, also saw Colby as having been kidnapped. Alexander, however, saw him as still alive, as did the spirit guides channeled by Betty Muench two months earlier, as well as the sources contacted in spirit in Janet Cyford's reading.

"I have an impression of a man sort of in his early eighties," Cyford said. "I have a gentleman here [in spirit] that's saying this is his son. He is talking about some financial difficulties that surrounded his son, and I think his son's still alive, which would be [Colby]."

"There's another boat around this boat. I think this was set up in some way, not so much for this man to disappear, but for him to meet somebody ... The boat didn't turn over while he was in it—he got into another boat, and somebody turned that boat over afterwards."

"He would be in his eighties now ... and there's a great deal of confusion in his mind; I don't know whether this man had the beginning of Alzheimer's or whether he's drugged now, or something like that, but he's in a very poor, fragile state of mind and everything else."

As in Robert Cracknell's reading, this spirit contact finds a motive involving money. "There were some financial dealings. I don't think *he* was in financial trouble, but somebody else connected to him was ... There's something wrong about this computer on and the dinner half-eaten, as if that was set up like that. He'd made the arrangements after he'd talked to his wife, to talk to somebody ... Now, I don't know where he is."

Cyford then received an impression from spirit about "the south."

"Was he in the south when he disappeared?"

"He was in southern Maryland," I replied. I asked if there is any information regarding motive.

"To shut him up about the other person's financial difficulties," Cyford replied.

"He's in South America somewhere," she added, after receiving further clarity on the vague "south" reference that came through earlier. "But I don't think he's long for this earth—I think he's very weak and very fragile, and will soon be in spirit."

"There was some sort of scuffle with this as well, with this man getting very angry about being pulled into this. I don't think that this was a kidnapping in the sense that they came and got him from the house—it was set up to look like that afterwards. He went willingly, and then when he started to blow the whistle or make noise about it ... I think he was injured in some way, an injury to his head in some way."

"He's not being ill-treated," she noted, nor is he incarcerated. Such measures are hardly necessary on the part of captors holding a physically and mentally frail old man.

Greta Alexander also perceived Colby being taken south of the border, as well as traveling through a Scandinavian country. Most astonishing of all, as we will see, medium Betty Muench's spirit group found him at the other end of the world. If Colby indeed was kidnapped and kept alive, his location might have changed numerous times.

In Betty Muench's reading, Colby's energy came through partly in symbols, with a stunning revelation:

"There is this energy which will seem within to search and search for William. But that there is not action, not movement. There is then a line drawing of an eye and it will be looking to the east. There will be this which will suggest that there is this one William who is not indeed on spirit side and that there is this which will suggest that he lives."

After this bombshell, the narrative got curiouser and curiouser: "There is this also which will seem to have the sense of him being hidden away in some situation in which there is a front in which there is this activity which is of a low nature. There is this which is like a house of drug use but that this is in the far east and that there is this which will seem to have him seemingly indulging in this but that in reality he is not."

"There is this which will show a man seemingly sitting with his elbows on his knees and talking. There is this one who seems very much in charge of something. There will be this which suggests that there is at the root of this some activity which will seem to require his personal attention. While this one is coherent and working, there is a sense that he is being there without his full consent. There is this which has been pressed upon him and that he does not fear death as

205

much as captivity. There is this which will suggest that the captivity is not of some foreign power but his own government keeping him in a situation until some other event can occur. While this will not seem to make sense to others who will think of him as deceased and who mourn him, there is this which will come forth in a given time which will show that he will have been put into this situation and that while he can never return to tell the truth, he can think and he can send mental messages and he will do this often in his seemingly isolated state. In that state it is easy for him to develop abilities that he will not have known existed for him and in so doing he gains a certain personal power which contents him."

With Colby not being found in the spirit world, Muench believed that the level of clarity and detail picked up by her spirit guides was largely attributable to Colby's own powerful mental focus, which might go as far as to include what might be called psychic powers. She noted that "he has certain ability in this and uses it often." Perhaps the lifelong mental discipline required of a master spy gave him a considerable head start in this area.

In this reading that Muench called "the most bizarre answer I have gotten yet," the story grew even more eerie: *"There is this one who has a strange duty which he accepts now but that he does not agree with how this is being carried out. This would seem to have to do with the Far East and thus this would be China and that he will hide within the very activity which will have kept China from advancing for so long. There will be this which will be his front and that he will not like the view of the front of his own home now."* As it was described earlier in the reading, the front appeared to be what used to be called an opium den.

How could Colby end up in such a place if he indeed is being held by rogue American operatives?

At least one possibility comes to mind. Four decades ago, the CIA did indeed maintain a foothold on China's border, overseeing commando raids from Nepal by exiled Tibetans into their occupied homeland.

Although the freedom-fighting campaign failed to restore sovereignty to the young Dalai Lama and his countrymen, it did benefit the United States in the form of unexpected intelligence windfalls. In the August 16, 1999 *Newsweek*, reporter Melinda Liu describes the documents captured in a guerrilla raid: "Among the captured 'working papers' were Beijing's plans to move many more troops into Tibet, and documents that provided the first concrete evidence of the Sino-Soviet rift ... The Tibetans provided human intelligence and other important 'insights into China's ... early efforts to develop a nuclear weapons capability,' a former US operative told *Newsweek*."

So even though the ill-fated Tibetan campaign—and the CIA-run camps on China's border—were officially closed down in the mid-1960s, it is conceivable that, following such success in intelligence-gathering, the agency might have continued at least a limited clandestine presence there. Among other uses, such an outpost in the middle of nowhere might be the perfect cover for "relocating" someone who needs to be hidden away, near China or even within China close to the mountain-wilderness border.

Yet this scenario appears to stretch credibility. "It was very clear when it said China," Betty Muench noted, adding, however, that "it is so hard to imagine such a story line." The reading concluded poignantly:

"*He will know that he must abide by the working rules that exist for him. He would think clearly but he would not work well in isolation for long. He will be joined by another who will not become missing, but who will be seemingly lost in another way, in another place, but will ultimately end up with William. There is much energy around this and it will be very important but that he cannot be found or returned to his own life. He serves hesitantly and still in the body of Colby.*"

What kind of secret might Colby have revealed had he not been allegedly kidnapped and dragged off to a bizarre exile? A follow-up reading on the question of why Colby was kidnapped takes us on another roller-coaster ride through the looking-glass (just when we thought things couldn't get any stranger), this time into an apparent top-secret facility:

"*There is this on Colby, this which begins with a mound of green pulsating light ... there is this which would seem to be out of the science-fiction realm ... this which is round and moves and is like a caterpillar but that is not animal. There is this which will suggest that there is something happening which will hold many secrets and that Colby will have had access to much of this. There was this sense that he wanted to expose this to the public view and that this will be the root of the seeming dismissal of him in this fashion ... that he would be exiled and that then he would not be able to play any part in the expose."*

The penchant for candor on Colby's part described here is believable, having been amply demonstrated when he revealed deep CIA secrets to Congress during the 1970s. Yet the description of the secret facility he allegedly witnessed sounds outlandish, as the spirit guides themselves note:

"There will be this which will not be known by very many people and that it would indeed sound bizarre to most people, but that he will have seen it and known that it was real and that he could not share this with anyone. There will be this which has been confirmed that he did not share with his wife ..."

Although Colby was hardly being held in chains, according to this scenario he knew better than to try to escape, and tried to make the best of his situation at the time of this reading: *"... while he is supposedly not a prisoner, he will not be able to leave his present situation. He cannot have contact with the outside world and in that then there is this distance and remoteness which will seem to give him a purpose and keep him busy so that he does not try to leave and in the process get himself really killed. There is this which will show that this will have been thought to be the better avenue to take in the event he is needed at a later time for forms of consultation and identification."*

The guides then described what Colby saw in the secret location. *"This expose of this object that he will have been witness to will have been something that many fear ... and that this will be something that all the world will want to know about ultimately but only in the due time as dictated by certain underground governments within 'our' present government ... the present government of this country and not just the administration, but all administrations."*

"This remoteness, this feeling of living in hills and far away, is only to keep him from forms of communication. There is no seeming covert energy felt here. There is no purpose that exceeds what is seen. He plays out a role there in some kind of leadership but that he indeed knows he is not free and he knows he is not the one doing the leading. This will have more to do with intergovernmental ploys, in which there is agreement to keep this information from any part of the world. When a certain few consider their opinions to be what must be done then there is no freedom within any system ... while this might seem to engage a cooperation between governments, it is still done with covert processes which need not be. What is seen by Colby will become known and there will be no other way ultimately."

It would be difficult to dream up a fictional story more spectacular. Did Colby see hard evidence of *X-Files*-type secrets, something which, if revealed, would perhaps be the biggest story of millennium? If the accounts describing "Area 51" and other secret installations are based in reality rather than myth, a crucial part of the story involves awesome technological marvels of God-knows-what origin, which could play a vital role in the birth of a new paradigm for mankind.

This startling portion of Muench's reading received equally startling corroboration from Dr. Michael Salla, author of *Exopolitics*, in his March 3, 2004 radio interview with George Noory on *Coast to Coast AM*. Describing William Colby's close friendship with John Lear, the Lockheed L-1011 captain who also flew missions for the CIA before coming forward with controversial revelations about alleged extraterrestrial contact, Dr. Salla claimed that Colby was most likely aware of the same astounding secrets.

If this is true, Colby might not be the only CIA director to have witnessed such wonders. One expert on the intelligence community, Dr. Richard Boylan, has suggested that CIA chief George Tenet learned of such projects during his visits to Los Alamos. Scientists working at the top-secret Los Alamos facility were sometimes flown to the mysterious Area 51 on Nevada's Nellis Air Force Base; and Dr. Boylan claims that Tenet "might have gained a glimpse into another world" when he visited Los Alamos, and "that what he had learned had both frightened and intrigued him."

If Colby indeed had knowledge he wished to share about an alleged extraterrestrial presence, then he could be described as having been ahead of his time—*but only by about 5 years*. On May 9, 2001, 20 retired officials from the Air Force, intelligence community, and Federal Aviation Administration held a press conference to call for congressional hearings on the UFO issue. They insisted that the government has been concealing evidence for more than a half-century, and promised that 400 reputable witnesses are ready to testify under oath (their organization's website is www.disclosureproject.org). Do the 400 witnesses—highly accomplished individuals influential in government, industry, and the military—have credible accounts to share, or did they all simultaneously lose their sanity and band together to destroy their hard-earned reputations by telling identical fairy tales? Either way, their remarkable organized effort is a huge story, yet it has been virtually ignored.

Frankly, it was difficult to decide whether to include this reading on what Colby allegedly saw, because so many of us have been conditioned to reject and even ridicule anything that is outside of a limited range of preconceptions. But my role here is to report honestly and accurately what came through in these readings. Is it conceivable that in the case of William Colby and his secrets, the truth might be radically unlike anything we would have imagined possible, lying outside our long-settled comfort zone and challenging our lifelong beliefs? A century ago, would we have believed it possible that men would walk on the moon, a polio cure would be found, and, more ominously, a garbage-can-sized bomb would destroy a whole city? Do we currently know everything there is to know, so that we will never be amazed again? Or might our future, like the future of the people who lived 100 years ago, hold breathtaking surprises?

The various psychic accounts of the Colby mystery veer down some surprising roads, and the truth seems to be obscured behind a thick haze. And yet, despite the differences in the readings, there is amazing unanimity on key points: (1) Colby did not die in a boating accident on April 28, 1996, as the official story says; (2) Colby was not murdered on April 28, 1996, as "conspiracy theories" tell us; and (3) Colby was kidnapped.

Of course, nothing came as a greater surprise than initially asking about "his death," only to be informed he was not dead, and to be told the same thing in two subsequent readings. Although the idea of faking a death is as ancient and familiar as the Biblical story of Joseph, any mention of such a possibility still holds the power to startle us. Such was the case when I discovered in late 2000 that Sherman Skolnick, a researcher who is widely regarded as a "conspiracist," had reported that some people "claim that was *not* [Colby's] body they buried."

However, in any discussion about an allegedly living, breathing Colby, one crucial, contradictory detail persists—Sally Shelton-Colby's reported identification of her husband's body. A possible answer to this question in Betty Muench's reading can be better understood if we first look back to John Paisley's nearly identical disappearance and examine the pattern. In the first performance of the "boat-accident illusion," in September 1978, the most unwelcome loose end was Maryann Paisley's protest that the recovered body was not that of her husband. One might logically assume that in the apparent duplication or imitation of the same trick in April 1996, the perpetrators would not allow a repeat of the same complication.

Muench's reading stated that Mrs. Colby was pressured to avoid looking further into this case. The kidnappers "created this diversion [in the boat-accident ploy] ... and she will have been right in thinking that this was not her husband." As noted earlier, Sally did not believe reports that William had drowned after allegedly going canoeing without a lifejacket at night in turbulent weather, leaving behind a partially eaten dinner, and leaving his computer on and the house unlocked. When she had spoken to him by phone at 7 P.M., the 76-year-old Colby had said his plans were to take a shower and go to sleep after a day of working on his boat. A full week after his disappearance, *The Daily Telegraph* reported, "His wife is convinced that he is alive ..."

According to this reading, the body produced was that of a man who had been murdered, perhaps obtained from a morgue, "*and ... it was not indeed William Colby.*"

Is this book presenting this astonishing scenario as the gospel truth? Not at all. It is simply one theory on an unusually murky case in which it is exceedingly difficult to pin down a coherent storyline. Yet, at the same time, it is certainly intriguing that each medium attempting to contact Colby on the other side failed to locate him, finding instead other beings in the spirit world who informed us that he was not there yet.

If ex-CIA chief William Colby indeed languished for years in a peculiar exile imprisonment because he knew too much, perhaps he occasionally thought back to his glory days and reflected ruefully on the sacred words engraved in the CIA headquarters lobby: "Ye shall know the truth, and the truth shall make you free."

Epilogue

In this examination of tragic mysteries that reveal human nature at its worst, a silver lining can be found, oddly enough, in the very nature of the work performed by psychic detectives, who remind us that we are much more than a body and five senses; and mediums, who bring us dramatic, comforting evidence that life and love go on eternally.

Plenty of so-called skeptics, of course, claim that it is impossible for anyone to be psychic or communicate with the departed. Yet, as someone who approaches every subject skeptically, I eventually found the evidence of psychic ability and spirit communication to be impressive and even overwhelming. Just as scientific testing of mediums at the University of Arizona found dramatic evidence of soul survival, sixth-sense insights and contacts with the spirit world in search of illumination of this book's mysteries brought through remarkable details time and again.

Yet perfect accuracy remains beyond the grasp of imperfect human beings. Even the best of psychics find it an ongoing challenge to make sense of the indistinct hints and symbols they receive. In addition, impressions that are vague to begin with must be filtered through the intuitive individual's long-accumulated attitudes, biases, and preconceptions. For a medium, other beings come into play, and thus even more subjectivity enters the equation. In many of the spirit communications featured in this book, messages were filtered first through the point of view of the person being contacted on the "other side," then through the understanding and beliefs of spirit guides helping to facilitate the contact, then through the attitudes of the medium, then mine, and finally yours. As in the children's game of "Gossip" or "Telephone," the oft-repeated message can sound radically different by the time it reaches the final hearer.

So we need to approach these messages with caution. After all, even concrete information perceived by our physical senses can be surprisingly unreliable. Justices of the US Supreme Court apply the same law to the same exact facts, yet often split 5-to-4 in their decision. Leading economists educated in the same universities examine the same data and divide sharply into bullish and bearish camps. And even when a message is painstakingly crafted so as not to be misinterpreted, and the media and public analyze every word with careful attention—such as when the Federal Reserve Chairman issues an opinion—confusion can still result. Look at how former chairman Alan Greenspan's comments of March 2, 2001, were headlined in the next day's papers: *New York Post*: "Greenspan Gives Bush's Tax Cut Seal of Approval." *New York Times*: "Greenspan Urges Caution on Tax Cuts."

If our physical world perceived through the senses is subject to such wildly varying interpretations, imagine how much more challenging it must be for a psychic or medium to make sense of fleeting and subtle pictures, sounds, and thoughts. Even when they describe virtually identical psychic visions—for instance, when Bertie Catchings and Nancy Myer found Ron Brown's death to have been caused by gunfire from men appearing to be camouflage-clad troops—the two psychic detectives interpreted the scene differently, with Myer perceiving combatants in the Yugoslavian civil war, and Catchings seeing the killers as terrorists disguised as military combatants. This kind of *Rashomon*-like subjectivity is an inescapable characteristic of human perception. "No one has a monopoly on the truth," medium Betty Muench emphasized after one of her readings. And even though her peers in the psychic field considered her one of the best mediums in the USA, she humbly noted that her spirit guides do make mistakes.

Describing the challenging process of mediumship, Janet Cyford likens it to using a typewriter floating on water. And communication might be as difficult for souls on the other side as it is for a medium making contact. As Cyford has explained, "Many potential mediums and the public at large believe transition into Spirit bestows natural abilities for contact with the earth plane upon their deceased loved one. Nothing is further from the truth. They strive to learn how to impinge evidence of themselves upon our dense vibration in the same way we strive to receive it."

In addition, individuals in spirit only show up when they feel like it, only discuss what they wish to discuss, and sometimes are still confused about the facts. Just as we do not automatically become holy angels when we die, neither do we become all-knowing geniuses.

And solving crimes generally is not a high priority for the souls contacted, a fact that might seem somewhat surprising at first. As Janet Cyford emphasizes, "I've never known someone in spirit to point a finger." As she describes it, they are obeying a fundamental universal law that allows the wrongdoers to exercise their free will to make amends on their own.

So while people in spirit are eager to address a number of important matters, they sometimes seem to treat the issue of who committed a particular crime almost as a subject that's inappropriate to discuss in polite company. Thus we are presented with the spirit of Colonel Shelton giving the same answer repeatedly about his wife's death—a mere vague reference to "a stray bullet." Similarly, when James van Praagh contacted the spirit of Nicole Simpson on the *Roseanne* show, the message that came through was "I am learning to forgive." (Roseanne bluntly replied, "Why didn't she say 'OJ killed me'"?) And when medium George Anderson contacted actor Robert Blake's murdered wife Bonny Lee Bakley on his April 2002 television special, the messages he brought through did not include details on the circumstances of Bakley's death. Although that may be what loved ones *want* to hear, Anderson explained to Bakley's sister and mother that "the souls, out of love know exactly what we *need* to hear."

From the higher, truer perspective of the realm in which they now reside, establishing the truth of exactly how they made the transition from this world to the infinitely better world is not of great importance to them, although this might be difficult for us to understand from our earthly viewpoint. Charles Shelton's main message to us—that he and his beloved wife are together now, and that's all that matters—appears to be typical. In a similar vein, Martin Luther King, Jr.'s message is primarily one of spiritual encouragement, and he bluntly tells us through one medium after another that exploring his murder—particularly, making an obsession of it—is not the way he wishes to see those who cared about him, especially his own family, spending their time on earth.

Perhaps this should not come as a surprise. Souls who have returned to the spirit realm have regained a clearer awareness of the truth that the great masters have always taught us to broaden our wisdom and ease our suffering—namely, that as the Hindu sages told us many millennia ago, this physical world is "maya"—illusion—or as Jesus put it, not our real home. Souls in Heaven, looking back on a life they perhaps now see as a kind of dream from which they've woken up, generally seem to have no great yearning for revenge, and often not even for justice or the establishment of truth for the historical record. After all, they realize, this earthly drama was in an ultimate sense less than real, and we leave behind all our material wealth while only taking with us what we've gained spiritually. Time and again the message from spirit is the same: life on earth is all about learning to love, and the details of the drama are not as important as they might seem.

Another central universal law brought up by some mediums is karma, which could be defined as Newton's third law as applied to human actions. Although this is widely assumed to be an Eastern belief, Jesus in fact emphasized this principle clearly and simply when he said, "As ye sow, so shall ye reap." Given this timeless reality, the wrongdoers in this book's mysteries not only do enormous harm to others but also ultimately to themselves.

Although the light shined on these cases reveals much that is disturbing, the sixth-sense perspective ultimately offers much that brings comfort, especially in the wake of the incomprehensible death toll of September 11, 2001 and subsequent wars, which is too staggering to comprehend, even though it pales alongside other mass slaughters of the last century.

Will we use the more reflective mood of these difficult days to our advantage, perhaps looking more deeply into the nature of reality to re-learn a basic truth that has been largely forgotten in our materialistic age—namely, that we are not our bodies but rather are indestructible souls making temporary use of physical bodies to assist God's work here? This is not to minimize even one iota the grief and anger being suffered by so many families, but simply to step back and observe reality through a wider-angle lens, so to speak, seeing essential—and ultimately reassuring—parts of the picture not perceived by the senses.

Unfortunately, however, in this society we are still conditioned to mock sixth-sense perception and especially the practice of "talking to the dead." Following the lead of the media, most of us ignore illuminating scientific investigations such as the testing of mediums by Dr. Gary Schwartz's team at the University of Arizona—research that appears to convincingly confirm that the spirit world is real, that death does not really exist, that bonds of love outlast physical death, and that the "other side" is in touch with us and is indeed a genuine source of valuable information.

Yet the media has disregarded the research. It almost seems as if they have no interest in studies of sixth-sense perception and soul survival unless the results are something they can laugh at.

Profound comfort can be found in the abundant and easily accessible evidence that is right in front of us. Why do most of us not even bother to look at it? Why should it be difficult to choose between the payoff of feeling smugly superior by mocking the unfamiliar, and the infinitely greater rewards to be gained by looking at the facts and making an increasingly enriching connection to higher realities and even to Divinity?

Skepticism and common sense are essential in this quest. If one wishes to explore the truth about such things as Heaven and immortality, one can examine the stunning newly available scientific evidence along with the teachings of such authorities on the subject as the great spiritual masters; or one can rely on the Committee for Scientific Investigation of Claims of the Paranormal (CSICOP)— well-known as the organization the popular media turns to for a "skeptical" view regarding a wide variety of metaphysical topics, but which does not appear to have maintained the fairness and objectivity required of true skeptics.

In the 2001 book *Skeptical Odysseys*, a collection of essays by CSICOP officials commemorating their 25th anniversary, the organization's creator and president Paul Kurtz writes, "Unfortunately, there are virtually no efforts to corroborate what [mediums] have said by any kind of independent tests ..." Incredibly, later in the same paragraph, he concludes, "Actually these so-called mediums are using familiar 'cold-reading' techniques, by which they artfully fish for information while giving the impression it comes from a mystical source. What is so apparent is that gullibility and nincompoopery overtake critical common sense and all safeguards are abandoned in the face of guile, deception, and self-deception."

After emphasizing the lack of "independent tests" (in an essay written before the University of Arizona findings were publicized), Kurtz announces a bold and sweeping final conclusion for us anyway. This is logic that comes straight from the Red Queen of *Alice in Wonderland*: verdict first, evidence later.

We have been down a similar road many times before. The extreme subjectivity and even arrogance of the scientific establishment and the media were vividly on display when they derided the magnificent achievements of the Wright Brothers, Thomas Edison, and other scientific giants as hoaxes.

As Richard Milton reminds us in his incisive and revealing book *Alternative Science* (titled *Forbidden Science* in its UK edition), "In January 1906, more than two years after the Wrights had first flown, *Scientific American* carried an article ridiculing the 'alleged' flights the Wrights claimed to have made. Without a trace of irony, the magazine gave as its main reason for not believing the Wrights the fact that the American press had failed to write anything about them." Milton points out that "despite scores of public demonstrations, affidavits from local dignitaries and photographs of themselves flying, the claims of Wilbur and Orville Wright were derided and dismissed as a hoax" not only by *Scientific American*, but also "the *New York Herald*, the US Army and most American scientists." He also describes how the public flocked to see Edison's electric lamps while scientists and engineers could not be bothered to witness what they called "a fraud," "a hoax," and "a completely idiotic idea."

Similarly, in *The Afterlife Experiments*, Dr. Gary Schwartz expresses his surprise "that some of the people who are most convinced that this entire subject is based on fraud were willing to criticize our work without ever looking at the data." What the critics do not want to see includes astonishing demonstrations by skilled mediums, such as Suzane Northrop "speaking virtually non-stop for over ten minutes, asking only five questions, yet producing more than 120 specific pieces of factual information with over 80 percent accuracy."

Perhaps the most amazing result of all was how well the mediums performed *when they could not see or speak to the individuals receiving the readings,* thus ruling out the possibility of any clever fake-mediumship tricks to elicit information.

Dr. Schwartz recounted how he met with seven of the most skilled mentalist magicians and cold-reading experts, and found none who would attempt to duplicate the mediums' performance under these same test conditions. In spite of their failure to seize this golden opportunity to demonstrate their claim that mediumship is a hoax that is indistinguishable from a mere magician's trick, some of the world's most brilliant and celebrated magicians—James Randi and Penn Jillette of Penn and Teller, in particular—remain among the most vocal detractors of spirit contact.

The compelling scientific evidence at this point—along with the so-far unanimous unwillingness of the "debunkers" to back up their claims in the laboratory—is indeed encouraging news for all who look at today's troubled world and, maintaining a skeptical yet open mind, wish for trustworthy evidence that we are infinitely more than mere flesh and blood, that our souls are immortal, and that Heaven exists.

Will it someday be commonly accepted that what we behold with our physical senses is actually a small and often deceptive part of the total picture? As this exploration of unsolved mysteries appears to indicate, there is more to know—and there are more ways of knowing—than most of us can imagine.

CPSIA information can be obtained at www.ICGtesting.com
Printed in the USA
LVOW10s1452280116

472285LV00023B/607/P